Y0-AGP-209

THE
ROCKET

Other Sports Books from Potomac Books, Inc.

Home Run: The Definitive History of Baseball's Ultimate Weapon
by David Vincent

Deadball Stars of the American League
by The Society for American Baseball Research and edited by David Jones

Burying the Black Sox: How Baseball's Cover-Up of the 1919 World Series Fix Almost Succeeded by Gene Carney

Forging Genius: The Making of Casey Stengel
by Steven Goldman

You Never Forget Your First: Ballplayers Recall Their Big League Debuts by Josh Lewin

Wrigley Field: The Unauthorized Biography by Stuart Shea

THE
ROCKET
Baseball Legend Roger Clemens

JOSEPH JANCZAK

Potomac Books, Inc.

Washington, D.C.

Library of Congress Cataloging-in-Publication Data

Janczak, Joseph
   The rocket : baseball legend Roger Clemens / Joseph Janczak.
       p. cm.
   Includes bibliographical references and index.
   ISBN 978-1-59797-088-4 (alk. paper)
   1. Clemens, Roger. 2. Baseball players—Biography. I. Title.
   GV865.C4384J36 2007
   796.357092—dc22
   [B]
                                        2007004053

Printed in the United States of America on acid-free paper that meets
the American National Standards Institute Z39-48 Standard.

Potomac Books, Inc.
22841 Quicksilver Drive
Dulles, Virginia 20166

First Edition

10 9 8 7 6 5 4 3 2 1

CONTENTS

PREFACE

Fans across the baseball world revere him for evoking the memory of many baseball greats such as Cy Young, Babe Ruth, and others. The media respects him for his candor and honesty. Fellow baseball players owe him a debt of gratitude; his strong character has raised the sport out from and above many scandals.

This book recounts the legacy of arguably one of the greatest pitchers in Major League Baseball (MLB), the legendary William Roger Clemens . . . the "Rocket." From his early years in high school and college baseball, to his MLB debut and his eventual seven Cy Young Awards, appearances in the World Series, his Most Valuable Player (MVP) Award, his election to 11 All-Star Games, and volumes of organizational awards, which, it is certain, has led his trophy room to be one of the largest in the sports world, we look into his legacy. This book is for the legions of baseball fans, including those who would otherwise no longer *be* baseball fans because of the many scandals and public relations gaffes that the sport has suffered during the last 20 years. He is the most recognized player both on and off the field. His career was no easy accomplishment for him. Not only was it necessary for him to attain on-field fame, but he also had and has a need to represent himself as a socially conscious gentleman and citizen off the field. His many charities and dutiful work toward ones in need would have led him to be a force in the public realm anyway. He is a philanthropist. But, undoubtedly, it took baseball's money to take him to a greater level.

Unlike many of today's fabricated and overhyped movie or pop stars who would not or could not be able to attain greatness if left to their own devices, the Rocket is 180 degrees the opposite. He didn't attain his status by sitting on his laurels or depending on hype. He earned it through good, old-fashioned hard work. He is able to garner the top dollar because his fans believe in him and, most important, he delivers on that belief.

This could also be looked upon as a book for the moms of the world. As they see Roger in a better light they will be inspired by his devotion to his family and how he serves as a role model to his sons and other young men. He's also a role model to other dads on the responsibilities of fatherhood. Because of his considerate nature he's even popular among the everyday staff and crew at the stadium. His intense desire to lend a helping hand follows along the lines of Sir Winston Churchill's quote, "The price of greatness is responsibility." Dedicated to everyone to the end, he's most comfortable in a pair of old jeans and boots, at home, rather than in the bling-bling of today's celebrity universe.

A seemingly endless procession of facts and quotes from the sports world and public figures fills this book about a man who, in many ways, has redefined or at least helped to redefine the way people view sports stars. Coaches, managers, agents, owners, fellow players, friends, family members, and fans tell a story that will be told generations from now. Even at the evening of his spectacular and long career, he has always been, and will always be, the ultimate performer—the Rocket.

INTRODUCTION

When I was a kid we all played baseball, just as most kids do. Most of the other kids had a problem pronouncing my name, so they called me Joe Jackson instead. Naturally the baseball nickname of "Shoeless" was soon tied to it, and I became a modern "Shoeless" Joe Jackson. Some of the kids would make comments that the original Shoeless would do it this or that way, so I began to read up and get familiar with the great so that I could do the same. This got me interested still more in the professional side of baseball, and then eventually I started to write about it all.

Shoeless Joe Jackson has come a long way.

There are only a handful of baseball greats who have changed baseball history, so to speak. Through the years people have made lists of who these greats are, but almost always the one who is undoubtedly on the list is Roger Clemens. I have kept up with him since his high school days and watched his progress with enormous interest. In Texas, high school sports get a large amount of press coverage. Roger would sometimes be mentioned in the news and this was especially true when he was drafted out of college and into the Boston Red Sox organization. The rest is history.

Houston has been very fortunate to have Roger Clemens as a resident. He has been an ambassador of our city to the rest of the nation and, in some ways, the world.

His baseball career has put our town into the spotlight even in the years that we are skipped over in the postseason. His charitable efforts have begun to shine as brightly as his career, and many decades from now his work off the field helping others will be remembered just as much as his work in baseball. He is one of the reasons that baseball has remained a favorite into the modern era while so many other sports' popularity is beginning to ebb away because of the competitive entertainment market.

I wrote this book not just as an author but also as a fan. It's important to document Roger Clemens's career from this viewpoint because there has been much written about his life and career by other forms of media. As a lifelong fan, virtually this entire book comes from personal memory and experience, with the facts then verified through various sources. With his amazingly long reign on the mound, the years past begin to get a bit fuzzy for everyone. It is also important for all authors, during their information-gathering process, to respect the privacy of the people about whom they are writing. In writing books or articles, some writers have resorted to hyping up negative charges in their works in order to garner attention or for their own advantage, or because they have nothing much better to say or research. Unless there is something really significantly drastic to write about, the negative should never be allowed to gain prominence over the positive. Sitting on the outside and throwing rocks are easier than having to perform the difficult tasks of researching information and getting to the truth. Unfortunately Roger Clemens has been the target for many of those negative barbs, but because of the great example he has set through the years he has quickly overcome them on his word. Sometimes it must be realized that pitching aces are just like everyone else—real people with real lives.

In the time that I have been interviewing and writing about baseball, I've met hundreds of major-league players. They've all been quite helpful to me in my quest to understand the behind-the-scenes work that is almost never shown on television and to give me an insight into what's going on in their domes. They're all very interesting and it's as if I have a couple of hundred new brothers. The first time I personally met a major-league baseball star was when Bo Hart and Jim Edmonds met up with me for questions at a Houston diner just before a game. They didn't seem to have some major-league mystique; they're great because they are like everyone else. It was as if I had known them forever. After that encounter it was a lot easier to relate to and interview other major-league players, who also turned out to be just like everyone else. My favorite memory is of being dragged into a St. Louis Cardinals victory pig pile in their clubhouse after a win. I was finally able to have fun in writing this book.

One might ask why Roger Clemens is important enough to have a book written solely about him. This book was written to answer that question. Fans want to have that one-on-one experience with a true major-league ace. During my research I knew ahead of time from my experience what a great guy the Rocket really is. But I was even more surprised by reactions when I asked individual players about their opinions of him, even opposing players. Universally, their eyes lit up as they spoke to me about Roger, and they immediately began to talk about how much the Rocket has done for them, their memories of him, or how they have modeled their career after the Rocket's. Everyone had positive things to say about him: what a great teammate he is or was in the past, how they followed his example, and so on. That in itself attests to his solidarity with his teammates.

As far as the people on the street, it's exactly the same. In Houston, and Texas, everyone is proud to have him as a "neighbor." They know how much he does for the city and area, as will be discussed in chapter 1, which covers his legacy. Everyone seems to be fans of the Rocket and for good reason; everyone has positive things to say about him.

It's hard to imagine that someone would have as much impact on a profession as he did when he first started out a quarter century ago. His longevity is, of course, a result of his intense workout schedule, which keeps him in shape and at the same time keeps him younger physically than he is chronologically. If only he could impress this upon the rest of society. Americans need to get off their couches or out of the food courts and do something physical as well as help others.

Roger Clemens is a baseball player whom the oldest of fans is proud to have lived to see and one whom the young will remember for the rest of their lives. And here, we have a career encapsulated into a book for readers to enjoy.

I would like to thank everyone in the Major League Baseball system who assisted in the gathering of information for this book. Everybody was so professional and friendly, from the household staff up to virtually every teams' media relations department, to the Major League Baseball Players Association for tracking down agents or players for me, to the commissioner's offices. So many agents of players were helpful in arranging interviews that resulted in needed insights and ideas. There were so many in the leagues that left me with memories I will always remember. I am so grateful to Major League Baseball for giving me the press credentials that enabled me to do my research. The Houston Astros' media relations department is tops in their field. Outside of the major leagues, virtually all major newspapers went to great lengths to help with information gathering, as did several colleges and universities. The University of Texas (UT), Rice University, Sam Houston State University, and Montgomery College of the Woodlands, Texas, patiently assisted with their resources while I researched.

The ultimate thanks should go to the baseball fan, for whom this book has been written. I hope that all enjoy the reading.

Chapter 1

THE LEGACY OF A LEGEND

It's obvious that Roger Clemens will *never* be allowed to retire from baseball. His fan base and public support will demand that he always be a part of the game for years to come. As father time creeps up, as it does with us all, the Rocket will eventually move from the pitcher's mound to another role in baseball, maybe in management or as baseball's representative in matters of the moment, but he will always be here for us.

His legacy, as you will see in this book, is Roger Clemens's intense dedication to his family, his team, and his fans. This dedication also overflows into a devotion to the social environment of his fellow citizen, especially children and the less fortunate in society. He has often said that he does it all for the benefit of the fan, and his actions both on and off the field prove that to be correct. His fans attend his games, and in some cases they have special needs. The Rocket works hard to fulfill these needs through charitable events.

Roger recently spoke to *Houston Intown Magazine* about how rewarding it is to do these things. "It's a lot of work and there are all sorts of complications running some of these events, such as our annual Roger-Giff Day of Golf for Kids Tournament, but when I see the people it's helping and learn firsthand about their stories it's well worth it. We've had a fabulous life and I think it's important to give something back."[1]

Roger Clemens leaves baseball a much better place than he found it, both on and off the field. The record of his career will be the stuff of legends for many years into the future. It is doubtful there will ever be anyone like the Rocket. As time goes by and fame subsides into time's dusty book of memories, his page will have less dust because of continued references made to him, much as in the case of Babe Ruth or Joe DiMaggio or Cy Young himself, all from a bygone era. Indeed, as one reads the baseball names from the past they are for the most part fuzzy until a great one appears here or there. It will be no different when future generations read about us when we ourselves are part of that history. One thing is for sure: the name of Roger Clemens will be one of the few that will stand out. They will read of a pitching ace with a stellar career.

In his 13 years with the Boston Red Sox, he brought the team to the brink of World Series wins. He achieved several bests in baseball, including twice attaining a 20-strikeout game (the only player ever to do so), an MVP, several Cy Youngs, best ERAs, and a strikeout level that clearly showed he was a rocket advancing to the stars. What set Roger Clemens apart is that he carried us with him to those stars and showed us that it wasn't just about him. His two seasons with the Toronto Blue Jays also bested a few of their records, and he undoubtedly could have done more for them had he not been traded to the New York Yankees so soon. With the Yankees, he experienced his first

World Series win. And for five seasons he was the ace on a team that for most of the history of baseball had been its flagship team. When he signed up with the Houston Astros so that he could be closer to home during his retirement, he was credited with bringing the team to its first National League Championship and to the brink of winning its first World Series. With the Astros he won his seventh Cy Young Award, still attaining unprecedented accomplishments well into his mid-40s. He leaves all this as his legacy in baseball. But what many people do not realize is that he leaves an even greater legacy off the field.

> *He leaves all this as his legacy in baseball. But what many people do not realize is that he leaves an even greater legacy off the field.*

His future fans will read about the teams that he once graced. When he left the Boston Red Sox in 1996 many of his fans were angry with him. However, the future fans of the Red Sox will look upon his presence there with an intense pride. The same can be said of fans of the New York Yankees, the Toronto Blue Jays, and the Houston Astros. The newsreels of today will themselves get old and grainy and yellow with age but not the Rocket's legacy. Just as today we are able to pick out and identify those greats from a past era, people will be able to point at the screen and recognize Roger Clemens many, many years from now. He did it on his own through his own abilities. Nobody handed his success to him.

Not only will future fans recognize Clemens in the future, they will learn of the example that he set for all of baseball, including his teammates, managers, owners, and the fans. The way he improved baseball with his unquestionably great example is truly inspiring. In his era there were steroids, strikes, fights, infidelities, dishonesty, cheating, and dishonor in pro sports. When the steroid scandal broke into the news he was one of the few greats who had set an example by not having used them. That example in itself more than likely saved many younger players, either in high school, college, or professional sports, from engaging in that activity. In addition, one book stated that Roger Clemens is the only known major-league baseball player who has always been faithful to his wife.[2] People who have known the Rocket know faithfulness and dependability to be his hallmarks.

Roger's wife, Debbie Clemens, told *Houston Woman Magazine*, "Roger doesn't bring his job home. When he's home, he's focused on his family. The biggest challenge is time together, and that is most important to us. We are like most families. We see movies with our kids, ride bikes to Toys R Us and go to HEB [a Texas-based grocery store chain] just like other families. People in Houston are so polite. When they see Roger and the rest of us with him, they wave or smile; but for the most part they respect our privacy."[3] Debbie clearly shows that the best luxury to have is to just be yourself. And now, after Roger's many years in the majors, she and Roger are used to being local celebrities wherever they go. She has been practical about the public attention shown to her and her family and carefully adjusts that attention in a way that avoids stress.

As soon as Roger made it into the major leagues back in 1984, he immediately reached out to help the less fortunate. At that time he was a young baseball star, and there was really no way he could consciously go forward without sharing a portion of his newfound wealth. He also shared all of his recent fame, lending his name to many worthy causes wherever his team was based and in his hometown of Houston. He did this quite naturally because as a child his family didn't always have a lot of money, but there was always an abundance of love and sharing. When he was at the Boston Red Sox he did a tremendous amount of good, along with some of his teammates, in helping literally hundreds of local charities in the Boston area, such as various group homes (which at one time were called "orphanages"), the Boys and Girls Clubs of America, and, most prominently, the Jimmy Fund Clinic at Boston's Dana-Farber Cancer Institute, which is the official charity of the Red Sox. The scientific breakthroughs at that hospital and the number of lives saved have truly been amazing. Roger never was one to get into the so-called bling-bling that has been associated with so many celebrities.

As the years progressed he became involved with more charities, as did his wife, Debbie, whom he originally met during his high school baseball days in the Houston area. Not long after they wed, they both began to work on charitable causes. In 1987 Roger and Debbie held the first annual Roger Clemens Charity Golf Tournament. It was a spectacular success. Roger and Debbie are avid golfers, and it was only natural to engage their love of the game as well as involve some of the celebrities whom they had met along the way to advance the cause of giving. Their tournament grew increasingly popular with the local citizenry and celebrities alike, and for several more years Debbie, with the dedicated help of her mom, Jan Wilde, and Debbie's brother Craig, put together the tournament with such detail and dedication that it grew into a recognized golf event nationally. Proceeds from the first year of the tournament benefited the Montgomery County Youth Services of Texas, which helps at-risk youngsters to realize their goals for life and to successfully tackle their challenges. The tournament was held from 1987 through 1991.

The Rocket's charitable causes are widely covered by the media and also listed on his website. His charitable works are as well known as his work in baseball. The Clemens's charitable endeavors were eventually solidified into the Roger Clemens Foundation in 1992 (www.rogerclemensonline.com). It was created to make sure that the funds that had been raised through those golf tournaments and events, such as silent auctions and donations, would be promptly and efficiently distributed to local charities. The goal of the Roger Clemens Foundation is to support the educational, physical, literary, scientific, and religious activities of area children who are in need. It emphasizes the needs of the underprivileged, special needs children, and at-risk children. From time to time the Roger Clemens Foundation hosts an open house so that area corporations, other businesses and leaders, and the public will become more aware of the work and activities of the charity. In 1992 the Cystic Fibrosis Foundation benefited from the first annual baseball camp program set up by Roger Clemens.

Roger and Debbie also worked to create the First Annual Roger Clemens–Doug Drabek National Celebrity Golf Tournament and Gala held in 1992. It was an even bigger success than what had been experienced in the past. Doug Drabek, a former major-league pitcher and about the same age as Roger and Debbie, had a career that closely paralleled the career of the Rocket. Drabek had also been drafted into the leagues in 1983, as had Roger, but Drabek finally made his major-league baseball debut in 1986 for the New York Yankees. Within a few months he had been traded to the Pittsburgh Pirates, where he quickly became famous. His ERA usually placed him in the top ten, and in 1990 with a 2.76 ERA and with 22 wins and only 6 losses, he won his first and only Cy Young Award in the National League. His achievement of 22 wins was the highest in the National League that year. He also helped take the Pirates as far as the National League Championship Series that same year. In 1992 he signed with the Houston Astros as a free agent. In one of his best seasons, 1994, he had a 12 and 6 record and a 2.84 ERA under his belt. Before the 1999 season began, he retired from the Astros and baseball for good. However, in the summer of 2006 his son Kyle was drafted into the minor leagues of the Philadelphia Phillies organization, after a great year of pitching as the star ace at The Woodlands High School in Montgomery County, Texas.

The first Roger Clemens–Doug Drabek National Celebrity Golf Tournament and Gala drew rave reviews. Proceeds went to the Sunshine Kids, the Limb Bank, the Homeless Youth Transitional Living Program, the Straight Way Program, the Wheel Chair Program, and the Youth Counseling Program.

Debbie and Roger also arranged a benefit called Christmas for Kids with the help of Neiman Marcus department stores in 1993. It helped the Arbor Pre-School, which aids children with special needs. In addition to that, the Second Annual Roger Clemens–Doug Drabek National Celebrity Golf Tournament and Gala was held, and the proceeds again benefited Montgomery County Youth Services. Roger's baseball camp, now attracting even more media attention, brought in donations for the Cystic Fibrosis Foundation. During each year the Rocket also attended many other charity events held by his teammates, who had charities of their own. In return, they would attend Roger's events so that there would be more media attention and even greater benefit for the charities.

The Boys and Girls Clubs, the Make-A-Wish Foundation, and the Arbor Pre-School benefited from the 1994

Roger Clemens National Celebrity Golf Tournament. The Boys and Girls Clubs help underprivileged children realize their full potential and become productive members of society. The Make-A-Wish Foundation gives hope to a child with a life-threatening illness through making one of his or her wishes come true, such as meeting an astronaut or a famous sports star or even simply riding in a fire truck. This was the year of the baseball strike, and even when the Rocket wasn't on the mound, he was still pitching for the cause of various charities in the Boston and Houston areas as well as nationally. The 1995 auction of donated items at the First Annual Champagne and Confections Silent Auction helped a Houston charity known as the Star of Hope Women and Family Center. The Houston area center helps women and their children, especially single moms, with a place to stay during times of financial or family crisis. In previous years, most homelessness was believed to be mainly a situation encountered by men, but as times changed and the culture along with its problems became more diverse, women and children started to face the same issues. The auction arranged by the Clemens family helped the center to succeed in its goals dramatically. To a greater extent, it helped to focus attention on the modern problems faced by women and their families who are going through a crisis.

Another charity widely known throughout baseball circles, the cookbook project, was expertly put together in 1996 under the direction of Debbie Clemens. Titled *A Confection Collection Christmas Cookbook,* the book was sold at various locations, and the proceeds benefited the Clemens's charities. Debbie Clemens follows a rigorous diet, and the recipes included in the book were ones that would fit into almost any lifestyle. That same year the Second Annual Champagne and Confections Silent Auction took place, benefiting more charities, including the Mission of Yahweh in Houston. The mission helps abused women and their children by giving them shelter, food, clothing, and, above all, hope. It helps to rehabilitate them so they can strive to become independent and productive members in society.

In the 1997 season Roger Clemens became a New York Yankees pitcher, and he worked with his new team to help various New York area charities and foundations. Fans who appreciated him on the field flocked to help out in the charities sponsored by the Yankees. In Houston, Roger and Debbie created a Spooky Halloween Festival and Silent Auction from items donated by various contributors. The people who attended wore costumes, and there was a contest for the best one, creating a fun atmosphere. Texas Children's Hospital and various other children's charities benefited from that Halloween auction. Texas Children's Hospital is truly a one-of-a-kind place for healing. Since the 1940s with the help of the great financier and benefactor Jesse H. Jones, it has been a leader in treating childhood illnesses. Most recently, a University of Texas baseball ace underwent a kidney transplant at the hospital. UT outfielder Carson Kainer had been diagnosed with a kidney disorder when he was only two years of age, and the family had been told that with time he would eventually have to receive a new kidney. Both Kainer and Clemens had attended the University of Texas as pitching aces.

The organizers at Rice University of the Battle of the Best Charity Softball Game, which was held the following spring, had put together donated items for a silent auction held at the same time as the game. Various major-league baseball players, including Clemens and many Houston Astros, who would eventually be his teammates, participated in the games that were held at Rice University's new state-of-the-art Reckling Baseball Park. Collections from the game helped many Houston area children's charities.

In 1999, the Harris County Sheriff's DARE (Drug Abuse Resistance Education) program, the Houston Hospice, the DePelchin Children's Center, Paws for a Cause, and the Spring Branch Education Foundation (SBEF) benefited from Morton's Legendary Evening, an event that honored Roger Clemens. Roger hosted the event, which raised funds for the charities.

The new century saw a continued dedication on the part of the Clemens family. The devastating attacks on September 11, 2001, saw the New York Yankees and the Rocket go into immediate action to help the families of the victims and of the fallen officers and firefighters. They signed commemorative items, such as jerseys, bats, baseballs, and the like for auctioned sales that benefited the families. In Houston, the Twin Towers Fund was helped out by the Baseball for America Auction in which the Clemens family donated memorabilia. The Texas Children's Cancer Center and the Texas Children's Hospital benefited from over $1 million collected by the sale of a cow as part of the Cow Parade Houston. The ceramic life-sized cow was decorated as a New York Yankee and dubbed the Rocket Man Cow. The cow had a mock pinstripe uniform and was autographed by the whole Yankees' team. The revenues were raised via an online auction of the cows. Roger also helped out at the Manhattan Ronald McDonald House of New York by bringing gifts and reading stories to the patients. One of their favorites was *Casey at the Bat*. He also attended children's days at such places as Planet Hollywood in New York and signed autographs for them.

In August 2003, Roger Clemens, his battery mate Jorge Posada, Jason Giambi, David Wells, Derek Jeter, and Bernie

Williams all teamed up for a benefit for Posada's Foundation. The foundation helps children who have craniosynostosis, a rare disorder characterized by premature closure of one or more fibrous joints between the bones of the skull before brain growth is complete, forcing the growing brain to create pressure on the skull. Posada's son suffered from the illness. The benefit helped families afford surgery that reduces the pressure on the skull of the growing child. It was held at the famous Copacabana club in New York City.[4]

Debbie Clemens also remained involved in charitable events and in 2002 received the Ebel Woman of Achievement Award, awarded by the watch company of the same name. While in New York Debbie was also a cochairperson for the Playing with the Masters Benefit at Carnegie Hall, where people were able to play musical instruments alongside such musical greats as Yo-Yo Ma and others. The show benefited the Knowledge Is Power Program (KIPP) Academy in New York. The program prepares young students for a college education. Also that year Debbie became a member of the Spring Branch Education Foundation's board of directors.

During Roger's final year with the Yankees, Debbie was able to work on the design and upload of her own website, which is intended to help women find their fitness goals and balance them with the needs of their families. The site also includes ideas on fashion, family life, and other goals and ways to make it all work in a fun way.

In honor of the Rocket's 300th win and 4,000th strikeout, both of which happened on the same day in 2003, she personally designed ornaments that were dubbed Rocket Rocks. An amount from the sales of the rocks went to the Roger Clemens Foundation for distribution to various children's charities. When Roger won his seventh Cy Young Award, she also designed an ornament for that event, and the proceeds also helped area charities. They also both took part in many golf tournaments that benefited charities across the United States. During 2003, Roger and Debbie also worked on the St. Francis Episcopal Day School program, helping to raise funds for the school via donated items in a silent auction.

The 2004 season brought Roger Clemens back home to Houston and to the Houston Astros. He and Debbie could work more closely with area charities after that move. When the All-Star Game came to Houston in 2004, Roger gave tickets for the FanFest to underprivileged children in the area and to M. D. Anderson Cancer Center patients. During that All-Star Game, Debbie helped design and build a booth about the Roger Clemens Foundation that helped increase the awareness of the foundation. She and Roger donated countless Astros tickets to area youth and charities for games and for the All-Star Week festivities.

In one of the highlights of the year for Debbie, the Linda Lorelle Scholarship Fund honored her service. When she launched her own designer jackets in 2004, called Jacket Happy, the line was accepted as part of the Bellagio Hotel Boutique in Las Vegas and many other quality fashion retailers in America, such as Harold's in the Heights of Houston, and the Houston Livestock Show and Rodeo, which is the largest rodeo in the world. Many similarly remarkable items are also available for sale on her website, and proceeds benefit charity. At a silent auction at Minute Maid Park, the home of the Houston Astros, one of her denim and rhinestone jackets went for a thousand dollars, and the proceeds benefited local charities. She recently told *Houston Woman Magazine*, "I realized that the marketplace wasn't offering much for female baseball fans. I've always loved fashion and been a very creative person. I guess you'd say I'm an artist at heart. So, I decided to design and manufacture specialty items that women would enjoy wearing—pink baseball caps and T-shirts with rhinestones at first and then denim and leather jackets."[5] Debbie's work on the project is full throttle. She enjoys what she is doing and also enjoys giving the proceeds to charity. One of her favorite designs is the butterfly. It is almost her "national bird" in that it reflects her free spirit and need for fun. The butterfly is actually one of the fittest of all creatures as it is almost constantly on the move. Yet, it is also one of the most delicate. This is probably why she uses it in many of her jackets, T-shirts, caps, and even her website. The cursor movement is followed by hundreds of butterflies in midflight.

In 2004 the Rocket signed up with the USO and was sent to visit the troops at Nebraska's Offutt Air Force Base in April.

In 2004 the Rocket signed up with the USO and was sent to visit the troops at Nebraska's Offutt Air Force Base in April. Roger has always deeply appreciated the work that the armed forces do to protect us and what they do for the world. His brother Richard served in Vietnam and his experience with war gave Roger an even better understanding of what military personnel go through in their daily lives. The troops were happy to see Roger there as they waited in line for his autograph and to take pictures with him. Roger toured the base and met with military officials and their families. It is difficult in many ways for families to deal with being away from each other for many weeks or months during the year. Roger empathized with this situation since during his own career he had been on the road for weeks at a time away from his family. The

meet and greet was a great success for the troops, and, to
an even greater extent, it meant a lot to Roger Clemens,
who saw in them many of the same things that he had
been going through. He made a connection with the troops
and could see that they felt the same way about him.

This was not the first time that the Rocket had enter-
tained the troops. He had also been sent to the Persian Gulf
area during the Christmas holidays in 2002. The troops had
been away from their families for many weeks, and Roger
thought nothing of giving up some of his off-season time to
be with them at various bases in Afghanistan, Qatar, and Ku-
wait and on an aircraft carrier in the middle of the ocean. For
several days he joined other celebrities, such as Drew Carey,
and military officials in bringing holiday cheer to the troops.

It turned out that the troops also brought cheer to
the Rocket. Roger told the *New York Times*, "I was over-
whelmed by that. You could feel the energy. These guys are
ready to jump in with both feet. Now that it's kind of gone
back to everyday life at home, people need to realize it's intense over here."[6] Many of the troops were not much older
than his oldest son, and that had an emotional effect on the
Rocket. He realized how important the guys and gals in uniform are to the world and that his family is safer at home
because of the work that they do so far away from their own
homes and families. Clemens recognizes the importance of
duty. Roger also told the *Times* at "each stop I was trying to
get the feeling and the mind-set of a lot of the soldiers. I
knew they were young. But I was thrown back by how
young. Just them saying thank you for coming was kind of
humbling."[7] He may have been thinking of the many fans
who show up at his games and that some of those fans may
well be those very soldiers. He wanted to thank them in return this time. "I would always anticipate who I was going to

see, how many guys I was going to run into, and never know what they say to you, and then hope you have the right answer. Because these are kids that might not come home."[8]

At each stop, there were the invariable requests for him to pitch a few for the soldiers. Some of the troops even met up with Roger while wearing baseball gear, hoping to get a few in before it was time to go. Roger happily obliged them. At first, his pitches were gentle, but the men in uniform kept egging Roger on for faster and harder pitches. Eventually he was pitching his regular, standard, major-league pitches toward the military catchers. They all did fine, and the biggest impact the pitching left was a memory that would keep them all going. When the USO tour was over for that holiday season, the publicity that Roger's tour generated wasn't necessarily for his own advancement, but it showed fans here at home just a small glimpse of what the daily life of the troops was like. Roger helped them realize just where the best pitches were coming from.

> *The 2005 season saw the Rocket make it to the World Series again, but for the first time in history it came to Houston and Roger Clemens participated in it in a National League uniform.*

Debbie Clemens could also relate to Roger's experience on the USO tour. She said, "It is difficult to travel with Roger a good portion of the baseball season, and that's tough. The kids have school and their own activities, so we stay home a lot. Only in June and July are we able to travel with him. Of course, we all love June and July!"[9]

Also in 2004, area teachers were honored with the SBEF Crystal Apple Award, which was chaired by Debbie.

When Roger became a spokesperson for a grocery chain based in the state of Texas he would help the grocery store find many needy families to whom groceries would be donated. This was in addition to Roger and Debbie Clemens serving as spokespeople for the area Houston Food Bank and its Strike Out Hunger campaign in the Houston and Harris County areas.

The 2005 season saw the Rocket make it to the World Series again, but for the first time in history it came to Houston and Roger Clemens participated in it in a National League uniform. This brought much attention to the Houston area, and, with that attention, the Learning Channel cable network series *While You Were Out* donated a home to a surprised family, with the coordination of the Roger Clemens Foundation. Roger had heard of a family in need and called on the producers with an idea that might help the situation get resolved. The program brought national attention to the Houston area again and to the Roger Clemens Foundation.

The start of the 2006 season was highlighted by contributions by the Roger Clemens foundation to the Memorial Hermann Hospital System in Houston for a wing for its main hospital at the Texas Medical Center near downtown. The wing was then named the Roger Clemens Sports Medical Hospital of the Memorial Hermann System. For Roger, this contribution was a way for him to return the fortunes that had been showered upon him by the sports world. The Roger Clemens wing helps to treat and to rehabilitate injured athletes from school age to adult.

Another charitable event in 2006, "An Evening with a Texas Legend," was a special evening that included Roger and Debbie along with other local celebrities. The fund-raiser brought in over $500,000 for the Texas Children's Cancer Center at Texas Children's Hospital.

Also in the summer of 2006 Roger and Debbie pledged $3 million for a pediatric wing and therapy center at Memorial Hermann Hospital Children's ward. This was in addition to partnering a sponsorship of a sports medicine performance center through the Memorial Hermann system that will bring to the area the largest and most comprehensive sports medicine program in the Southwest. To be known as the Roger Clemens Institute for Sports Medicine and Human Performance, it will be one of a kind in the country at its opening in January 2007 in the Texas Medical Center. In honor of Roger's uniform number 22, the hospital outlined 22 points in its mission statement, stating that it will catapult Houston's reputation for excellence in sports and medicine, perform world-class sports medicine and human performance research, have available the finest orthopedic and sports medicine physicians, and have access to a network of highly skilled athletic trainers and therapists. It would also have a network to include 26 sports medicine and rehab centers across the Houston area, attract elite athletes from across the nation and around the world to Houston for training and medical care, and offer practice facilities and exercise facilities and specialized sports programs for youth under the age of 18. It would also be designed to support youth sports leagues and school intramural team organizations, offer year-round facilities dedicated to the development of current and future Olympic athletes in such sports as baseball and track. The institute will create future facilities and programs tailored to sports enthusiasts and amateur athletes who thrive on competition, offer training and workout facilities for weekend warriors, and provide skill development opportunities for local and national baseball talent via the future Roger Clemens Academy minicamps. It will offer an expanded outreach program for underprivileged, at-risk, or special-needs children and add a new wing and therapy center to Memorial Hermann. Professional partnerships will be created with local school district athletic programs and offer medical and training oversight with college athletic programs. There will be on-going community education for preventative and healthy living and specialized sports employment opportunities. Young sports hopefuls will be given the opportunity to learn from the greats, as in the case of Roger Clemens. State-of-the-art conditioning programs designed to strengthen the whole athlete will be offered as well as certifiction programs in sports therapy and human performance. All will be available in three geographically dispersed locations to deliver the widest possible coverage.

Clemens spoke about the new partnership, saying at the press conference, "It's the right time and the right opportunity." The ace pitcher and seven-time Cy Young Award winner also noted: "Throughout my professional career and my life with Debbie and our four sons, I've tried to promote the importance of family, good health and fitness. I admire Memorial Hermann for its commitment to the health of the community. Together, I believe we can build an amazing program that will benefit not only professional athletes but youth and families as well. I look forward to being very hands-on in the development of the facilities and the programs and share Memorial Hermann's interest in funding outreach for kids." [10] The hospital system plans to develop, along with the help of Debbie and Roger, the Roger Clemens Academy, which will have baseball camps for various collegiate and high school athletes in the Houston area.

As time passed Roger Clemens would help in one way or another the Assistance League of Houston, the Children's Assessment Center, Texas Adaptive Aquatics, the Children's Art Project at M. D. Anderson Hospital, Children at Risk, the Arbor House, the Variety Club of Houston, the San Jacinto Museum Foundation, the DePelchin Children's Center, Cystic Fibrosis Foundation, the Twin Towers Fund, the Make-A-Wish Foundation, the Periwinkle Foundation, the National Paralysis Fund, and the Linda Lorelle Scholarship Fund. His foundation helped many times the Montgomery County Youth Services, the St. Francis Episcopal Day School, and the Texas Children's Hospital.

He has recently started yet another charity golf tournament. The Roger Clemens–Giff Nielsen Day of Golf for Kids contributes the proceeds to the YMCA of Greater Houston, the First Tee Houston at Redstone, and the Roger Clemens Foundation. Giff Nielsen is a former professional football player and now a local Houston sports broadcaster and personality. Funds raised during the golf tournament will be used to help the area charities and their work with the area's underprivileged children. Clemens also has announced that a Roger Clemens Lifetime Achievement Award will be given during a dinner of the same name and will include both live and silent auctions with autographed celebrity items and also luxurious vacations. For 2006, this award went to Lance Armstrong, the seven-time winner of the Tour de France. Like Lance, Roger is also a seven-time winner of an award, the Cy Young Award.

Johnny Bench is another baseball great who is now working with Roger Clemens for a charitable cause. They have recently put together the Johnny and the Rocket Golf Tournament. Bench is a Hall of Fame catcher, and joining him and Roger for the October 2006 tournament were Clyde Drexler, Truck Robinson, Gary Carter, Ron Streck, and Donny Anderson.

Roger has returned to his high school alma mater and helped to renovate the old weight room and field house at

Spring Woods Senior High School in west Houston. His collegiate alma mater is also high on his list, as he attends many of the Texas Exes Association functions from year to year. He has also teamed up with the mayor of Houston, Bill White, to help endorse the city of Houston's CleanUp Houston campaign, which was especially helpful during the various Super Bowl, World Series, and All-Star Games and other celebrations and conventions to give the visitors and residents a more favorable impression of the inner city. In fact, the area around Minute Maid Park had been rapidly deteriorating as a result of urban decay. At first, when city and county leaders took Astros officials on a tour of possible sites for a new baseball stadium in the late 1990s, both sides of the table were shocked at the site that was the front runner for the eventual Minute Maid Park. Crumbling abandoned buildings and squatters' flats were the norm for the area. Absolutely nobody who worked downtown would dare venture into the area. But when the new stadium finally opened, within a couple of years other businesses followed, and it is now a case of urban renewal rather than decay. People are actually on waiting lists to move into the newly rehabilitated area of townhomes, fashionable apartments, and condominiums, and two dilapidated historic homes that had been on the auction block were actually renewed as upscale restaurants. On the other side of the coin, some say that the area is experiencing growth because the city and county have set forth community

> *Roger chose his move to the Houston Astros wisely. He knew that he would not be the only one of the Houston Astros to set an example through hard work for his community.*

development money, such as new streets and sidewalks, and have encouraged businesses to relocate there from other areas of the city. In other words, they claim money has been taken out from one pocket and put into another. Whichever is the case, the results are stunning.

Roger chose his move to the Houston Astros wisely. He knew that he would not be the only one of the Houston Astros to set an example through hard work for his community. Astros great Craig Biggio is just one of the other team members who takes community involvement seriously. His dedicated work with the Sunshine Kids is truly inspiring. The organization was started in 1982 by a local volunteer at a children's hospital who saw that many children who were in for cancer treatment were often lonely and isolated, especially during long hospital stays. Even though the hospital staff worked hard to keep the children occupied, they still needed to get out for some excitement. The organization strives to give these children opportunities to take part in activities with other children or groups in order to help them take their minds off their hospitalizations, at least for a little while. During the decades that the Sunshine Kids program has been in existence, thousands of children from across the country have participated in these activities. Biggio, a longtime Houston Astro, is very involved in the Sunshine Kids. For many years each August, he has held a baseball camp and a day of entertainment at Minute Maid Park for hospitalized children. For them to play catch with an all-star or two is a dream come true for all of them. Craig and his wife, Patty, have been active in the organization each year since Craig started with the Astros back in the 1980s. According to Biggio, "This is one of the days I look forward to. It's a lot of fun to be able to come out here and do a little pitching and let them run around the field and feel what it's like for us. It's just an exciting day." He also went on to praise team owner Drayton McLane, saying, "There has been a lot of loyalty from Drayton. We started doing this outside, and it was hot. One day I asked him if we could do it inside, in the Astrodome, and he gave us the building. The rest is history."[11] All of the activities are free for the children and their parents. There are also excursions to local places of interest for the children, such as museums and parks, so that they can feel independent once again. Craig and Patty have also set up an annual golf tournament during the fall to raise funds for the Sunshine Kids organization, which is based in Houston. During that tournament, both local and national celebrities and, of course, many major-league baseball players show up to help with Biggio's endeavor to support a very worthy cause. It is often carried on the local news and is covered in several sports magazines and newspapers. The organization, as is the case with most charities, is also open for donations from the general public.

Roger Clemens is becoming one of Houston's most recognizable benefactors since the days of the great Jesse H. Jones (1874–1956). Mr. Jones was a dedicated philanthropist who made his fortune from the timber industry and various other endeavors, such as publishing the *Houston Chronicle*, developing real estate, and serving as part owner in several major corporations. Although born poor in Tennessee, he worked hard to achieve success. His most notable job was as the U. S. secretary of commerce under President Franklin D. Roosevelt. He was instrumental in helping to start up the Texas Children's Hospital, the Port of Houston, several of Houston's early skyscrapers, and Rice University. When he was at the height of his fame, the Great Depression struck. He immediately went into action and

worked endlessly in meetings with the city's power bro-
kers to work out a deal that would keep the area banks
solvent. As a result of his efforts, not one bank in the area
and not one major local business failed during the Depression. By working on building up the nation's infrastructure
during that period, he has been credited with helping to
save the United States from failing to meet the demands
World War II. When he died in 1956 the entire city of Houston observed a moment's silence in his honor. Today the
legacy of Jesse Jones continues in the Houston Endowment,
which he and his wife, Mary Gibbs Jones, established. His
donations to schools made absolutely sure that there would
be funds for minorities in a time when they were for the
most part overlooked, or looked down upon, because of
segregation laws. He made sure that blacks were accepted
equally into the charity hospitals and scholarships as whites.
The Houston Museum of Fine Arts, which also enjoyed his
patronage, named a new wing in honor of his late grand-
daughter, the Audrey Jones Beck Building. It houses many
of her art objects, which were donated to the public
through the museum. One of the lines in a speech Mr. Jones
gave closely resembles the work that Roger Clemens now
strives to attain. Mr. Jones said, "Success is measured by the
service you render and the character of citizen you make
rather than by the amount of money you amass."[12] He was
one to not only talk the talk but to walk the walk.

In addition to the Roger Clemens Foundation, in 2004
the Roger Clemens Award was announced. It honors the
top pitchers in collegiate baseball around the United States.
The award is administered through the Greater Houston
Baseball Association. The annual dinner is held each July,
and proceeds from its ticket sales benefit the Roger
Clemens Foundation, the Karl Young Summer Baseball

League, and Baseball USA. Clemens was a participant in the Karl Young Summer Baseball League during his college days, as were Mike Stanton, Doug Drabek, Chuck Knoblauch, Ron Davis, Chris James, and Craig Reynolds. Ironically today, its manager is Charlie Maiorana, who was the coach at Spring Woods Senior High School when Roger Clemens attended. Baseball USA, another beneficiary of the Roger Clemens Award Dinner, is based in the Houston area and offers year-round leagues for players with various skill levels to either learn about the game for fun or to increase their chances at getting to the college or professional level.

Near the end of the 2006 season, when he was still going full steam ahead at taking the Astros to the postseason in the pennant race, the Rocket was named the Houston Astros' recipient of the Roberto Clemente Award. Because of that, he became one of 30 nominees for the national award of that honor, which was given during the 2006 World Series. Each year, since 1972, the award has been given to the player who best sets an example of the values for which baseball stands: community involvement and exemplary sportsmanship. Roberto Clemente was a baseball great, a twelve-time all-star and baseball Hall of Famer, who was tragically killed in an airplane crash on New Year's Eve 1972 while he was carrying relief supplies to earthquake-ravaged Nicaragua. The award was originally called the Commissioner's Award, but after Clemente's death it was changed to the Roberto Clemente Man of the Year Award to honor the man and his values. Roberto Clemente had set such an outstanding example of goodness that the Baseball Writers Association of America decided to overrule the standard five-year waiting period for induction and unanimously elected Clemente to the Hall of Fame by the next August following his death. Each local nominee receives

$2,500, which can be donated to the charity of the recipient's choice. The national winner receives $25,000 that can be donated to the charity of his choice. In addition, $30,000 is donated to the Roberto Clemente Sports City in Puerto Rico in his name. The funds are raised each year via corporate sponsors. During the 2006 World Series, Carlos Delgado of the New York Mets was honored as the national recipient of the Roberto Clemente Award.

Roger and Debbie routinely will show up unannounced to join in on the efforts to help build affordable housing for the underprivileged. In 2005, Habitat for Humanity International dedicated its 200,000th home, which was in Knoxville, Tennessee. These homes shelter over a million people in over 3,000 communities around the world. The organization was founded in 1976 to renovate or build homes with qualifying families. In the early 1980s, former President Jimmy Carter and his wife, Rosalynn, brought the organization worldwide attention through their efforts to help low-income families of the world. Their efforts created a huge increase in area chapter membership. New chapters were created. Many decaying neighborhoods, either in the inner city or in desolate villages, were brought up to decent standards.[13] The Clemens family's involvement with Habitat for Humanity mirrors its generous spirit. In recent years, Roger Clemens has been working with Habitat for Humanity at build sites called the Roger Clemens Build. The program literally raises, from the ground up, a new home with the qualifying family. Debbie Clemens feels it is important to help families in need of simple, decent housing. Roger and Debbie have handed down these values to their sons as well.

In addition to all of the aforementioned programs and charity involvement, Roger Clemens leaves a legacy of good

sportsmanship to the next generation of athletes. Through
his example of fair play, tolerance of others, aversion to
cheating, and knowing his value, he has set the foundation
for others to follow in their quest for a career in sports,
whether in baseball or any other professional sport. Good
sportsmanship works equally well in any sport. Roger
knows the importance of playing fair and treating his opponents, and teammates, with respect. His example posi-
tively influences the children who are fans, those in the
various charities to which he has lent his name, and the
various corporations that
help out in those charities.
Even outside of the game, the
Rocket is friendly with just
about every major-league
player, coach, and staff
memeber. Nobody really becomes his enemy, even off
the field. He subscribes to the
view that sometimes you
win, and then sometimes you
lose. By staying clear of cheating, everyone remains friends
during and after the game. That's good sportsmanship. Roger
made it through the rough on his own efforts, not by cheating, using steroids, or stepping on others on his way up. If
he had done any of these things he would not have the
respect that he has built up and maintained for the past
quarter century. He strives to make sure that everyone has
a level playing field, whatever his or her social or economic
background might be. This is his entrenched version of good
sportsmanship. Outside of the game, he has not been one
to solely associate with the rich or powerful. There are
plenty of examples of him playing golf or a game of one on

> *Roger made it
> through the rough
> on his own efforts,
> not by cheating,
> using steroids, or
> stepping on others
> on his way up.*

one with people from all walks of life. This isn't just some publicity ploy in order to gain attention or to advance his cause. As a matter of fact, Roger and his wife, Debbie, sometimes volunteer at such places as Habitat for Humanity or food drives without being noticed. They feel privileged to help out the people who are most often their fans.

The Rocket also leaves a legacy of empowerment to anyone wanting to succeed in sports. Through his sports clinics and classes, he welcomes anyone who wants to better himself or herself, just as he did growing up. This is especially true with the underprivileged. While growing up Roger had only a fraction of what kids now have today. He got to the top with his natural, innate abilities and street smarts. Empowerment gives people the confidence to achieve their dreams, by recognizing their goals and working to achieve those goals and thereby arriving as close to the top as possible. The Rocket wants others to recognize the champions in themselves. In his own unique way, he helps the underprivileged find the steps to their own empowerment and goal recognition. He frequently discusses with them the importance of sticking with their desired goals and believing in themselves, practice, hard work, and, above all, their dreams. All of the Rocket's teammates have had positive things to say about Roger, such as how his fair-play personality is a plus to the team and how to a great extent they emulate the Rocket's example.

It's hard to imagine that in the decades that Roger has been in major-league baseball, the leagues are now scouting young men who had been in his first camps. Some who have made it into the major leagues were infants or in some cases not even born yet when Roger first stepped onto the Boston Red Sox mound as a pitcher back in 1984. The last opposing pitcher at his September 29, 2006, game was rookie

Chuck James, who was only two and a half months old at Roger's rookie debut. All his life he watched Roger Clemens and modeled his style and substance on him. When James retires, he will have influenced the next generation with the information that he gained from watching Roger Clemens, and so on, to the next generation of major-leaguers.

It's obvious that people feel privileged at the recognition and endorsement they receive from the Rocket, as if it is a high sign to keep doing what they have been doing all along. Roger shows appreciation to those who have helped him attain his goals. As an example, he can recall the names of the pitching coaches, trainers, and crew and has high praise for them many years after he worked with them. He is often quoted as saying he could not have succeeded without the help of people, especially the fans, along the way.

And it's not just the Rocket's fellow players who have praise for him. Fans also describe how incredibly proud they are to have him on their home team or even just to watch him on the mound as he visits their own home team. No matter how far up against the wall the team gets, he shows that effort will many times pay off in the end by never quitting or relinquishing a victory, no matter how hot the kitchen gets in high-pressure situations. Win or lose, he shows that hard efforts also work equally well off the field and that problems can be worked out when everyone does their fair share. His fans also follow the example that he sets in terms of volunteerism and other forms of community involvement. He can't change everyone, but he can do his best by setting an example and hope for the best.

In recent events, Roger has shown the ultimate sportsmanship by resisting the cheap shots thrown his way by his detractors. He doesn't return the cheap shots; he deals with them in a matter-of-fact manner. As an example, he has continually been subjected to accusations of steroid use. To people who know him and have always been around him, nothing could be further removed from the truth. Instead of ranting back with his own retorts, he dealt with the matter in a sportsmanshiplike manner. His professional responses to the accusations eventually brought even the doubters onto his side. Steroid use would be cheating, and cheating isn't something the Rocket wants to leave as his legacy. He knows that his best pitch is the one he makes about himself. In that case he doesn't throw a curveball, or a forked pitch. It's just a straight shot.

The dedicated hard work that Debbie Clemens does for the foundation is also widely appreciated throughout the community, both in Houston and around the United States. She sets an example, especially to the generation to which her boys belong, that there are more important things than material items. In a sports world that is sometimes hit with scandal or just plain materialism, she shows not just through her words but through her deeds that helping others to succeed is more important than getting to the top. In her interview with *Houston Woman Magazine*, Debbie said, "The Foundation provides us with a way to give back to the community. It is very important to share with others. A joy shared is a joy doubled."[14] Debbie also shared her thoughts on how Roger influenced her by showing her how working hard makes people feel better about themselves. "I've learned a lot from Roger, especially about what it means to have a good work ethic. Roger works hard. He keeps and honors all of his commitments. He is a great role model for me and our sons."[15]

The average fan and the people who know Roger and Debbie personally all realize the importance of the legacy of Roger Clemens. Not only has it helped their own community, but it also is prepared to help them when their time of need arrives. One never knows when disaster might strike, such as with Hurricanes Katrina and Rita in 2005 or with illness in the family. They might just be touched by what Roger and Debbie have been doing for almost the past quarter century with charities that stand at the ready for any of life's incapacitating events.

The legacy of the legend of Roger Clemens will continue for many years into the future. Though much of the younger generation is already having problems with name identification of many of the greats of baseball, including the ones who have recently passed away—such as Mickey Mantle and DiMaggio—this more than likely will not be the case with Roger Clemens. Still in his 40s and very young in spirit and body, he will have many years in which to work with the youth of America and with each new succeeding generation. He and Debbie will also have many years to work in their charity endeavors so that those generations will have some sort of safety net to turn to if the situation warrants it. It is quite possible, like many endowments, for the Roger Clemens Foundation to be helping people for many years, decades, or even centuries from now. Need does not go away on its own. Others will always require a helping hand. The Rocket is someone who realized this early on and will continue to work in alleviating hardship.

He might as well. He's too honest and up-front to run for public office. He is one to tell you straight off what's going on and what needs to get done, the exact opposite of traits needed to succeed in politics. The filibustering and stagnation in office would undoubtedly work against him. The Rocket wouldn't be good at political promises either because his constituents would instantly see right through him. But there are other ways to influence society for the good, and Roger and Debbie have chosen well in working out society's problems through their foundation.

Perhaps the most touching and wonderful aspect of Roger's legacy will be the way he is remembered for his family values. He puts his family right up there with him. Most important is the example he has set for taking care of one's parents. When he doted on his mom at Minute Maid Park, he was setting a great example. In today's world, there are too many children and grandchildren who stray far from what's important, while their grandparents sit at home with only occasional visits, if any, from them. When Roger showed the importance of having a parent throw out that ceremonial first pitch, hopefully it renewed for many people the importance of their families.

Throughout baseball history, there have been buildings and streets renamed after baseball's greats. The Boston area has named several places in honor of Ted Williams, for example, the Ted Williams Tunnel and the street Ted Williams Way. In the Houston area, officials renamed part of Highway 288 from downtown to Alvin, Texas, the Nolan Ryan Expressway, after their most famous Hall of Famer. Such honors aren't restricted to only ballplayers. In Las Vegas and Palm Springs there are numerous streets named after great entertainers, such as Frank Sinatra, Bob Hope, Gene Autry, Dinah Shore, Kirk Douglas, and so on. Also in Houston, an entire toll road system is named in honor of the hero of Texas independence, Gen. Sam Houston. It seems plausible that some time in the future one of Houston's busy thoroughfares could be renamed in honor of Roger

> *Perhaps the most touching and wonderful aspect of Roger's legacy will be the way he is remembered for his family values.*

Clemens. Possibly the stretch of highway from Houston to Roger's own alma mater, the University of Texas at Austin, could be renamed in appreciation of his efforts to keep Houston on the map when it comes to athletics, even after his retirement.

Baseball will then surely have an ambassador for the ages. So, in a way, Roger will never really retire from baseball, because he will always be working in some aspect of it. He may move to a different position in that great American pastime, but there will never be another Roger Clemens.

Chapter 2

—— DREAMS IN THE MAKING ——

On a cool autumn afternoon in 2003, Roger Clemens arrives at Yankee Stadium for what would be his final appearance on the mound there. As he had done many times before, he walks down one of the service halls along the inside of the building well before the game begins and peers out to see if the crowds have gathered there yet. Nobody but the wind. Exiting out of a service door, he slips unnoticed into Monument Park, the site dedicated to the legendary greats of New York Yankees baseball. Statues and plaques of the legends surround the almost cemeterial aspect of the area. He reads a few of the plaques and then, for good luck, rubs the forehead of the monument dedicated to baseball's greatest, George Herman "Babe" Ruth. He returns to the building and does his job. Then he walks off the Yankee Stadium mound for the last time.

A few days later, after he had pitched in the World Series, he would give a speech to his team, fans, and the listeners on radio and television that would announce his retirement from baseball at the age of 41. Retirement in baseball does not always mean retirement *from* baseball. He had thought long and hard about reaching this momentous decision. Although everyone knew it was coming, as he had virtually been on a farewell tour all through the year, he knew it would rattle some nerves but settle his. The most pressing reason for his retirement was his need to return home. He wanted above all things to be with his growing family that he had somehow missed out on for the past 20 years. Roger also wanted to be with his ailing mom, and he had asked her what she thought about his idea. He would now retire with her full support and understanding.

In a speech that some would view as his swan song, Roger said,

> I'd like to thank all of the baseball fans out there. Not only the ones in New York, Toronto and Boston, but in all of the baseball cities all over the world. I don't have to look any further than my World Series experiences in New York to know how much the fans have meant to me.[1]

Roger then added,

> I wanted to thank all of you fans, because it works both ways. You give me the inspiration when I go out to pitch, and it's been great support, even when I was a visitor here. It was meant to be. My sisters told me stories that when I was young, I would wear a Yankees hat and jacket, and that I was destined to play here. In college, guys called me 'Goose' after Goose Gossage. My mom says that everything comes full circle, so I guess that's true.

Being here, I've had an owner that wanted to win worse than I do, which, as a player, is all you can ask for. Playing for Mr. Torre, it's been incredible. He's been so much fun to work with, to watch him teach and pass along his experience to the younger players. It is inspiring. And what the fans have done for me, being a power pitcher for twenty years, is to help get me along.

Clemens also said, "I find it almost comical when we go out on the road, to hear and see the Yankee fans that are everywhere. The following we have out there is incredible. I love seeing the look on the faces of the new players on the team when they realize we have fans in all cities."

He stressed that "I could never have imagined that when I played Boston, I'd wear these pinstripes some day. When you're coming up, you always assume that you'll start and finish with the same club, and that didn't happen. It turned out that I got to experience Toronto and New York."

He was almost prophetic about his future when he stated: "I'll miss the competition the most. I still know that I can compete at a high level, which is why I came back. I didn't come back for a farewell tour or as a favor to someone, I came back to win."

Clemens finished the most memorable speech of his life by thanking all the fans, management, owners, and media for "making this whole ride as memorable as it's been. I couldn't have done it without you."

A few weeks later, he was in a Houston Astros uniform.

The New York Yankees, and much of baseball for that matter, were incensed. They felt that Houston had slapped them with some sort of conspiracy, especially after Andy Pettitte had been coaxed to join up with Houston a few days earlier. They felt humiliated in a very public way. They feared that the Astros had somehow used Pettitte to pressure Clemens to come out of retirement and join up with them. Or even worse, it had been a planned scheme by two of their most important players to somehow get back at them for some unperceived slight. As it turned out, none of this was true.

Baseball had come to terms with its own creation: it had become a two-way street. It's the nature of baseball today.

Although we will never be able to get inside of his dome and take a look around, the Rocket had a right to retire and then change his mind. Many people who retire don't stay retired. Even the player trades and moves are truly a two-way street. A team is able to trade its players and treat them as some sort of commodity, and a player knows that he has a right to do the same once free agency occurs. Player loyalty and team loyalty are no longer what they once were and have been slowly fading from the sport. Somehow in denial, the fans are slow to recognize this new reality. Roger needed to be at home in Houston. Pitching at his age is brutal. His mentor, Nolan Ryan, had made it to age 46, and Roger saw the toll it had taken on his idol. To feel comfortable at what one does, a person has the right to change jobs, to change cities, and to change his mind. Roger is no different than any of us and he will be the first one to tell you that.

> *Baseball had come to terms with its own creation: it had become a two-way street. It's the nature of baseball today.*

After he packed up and left New York for home in Houston, he mulled over what his future would be. He knew that he still had the drive and energy in him. Maybe being closer to a more stable family life, what he called his "home-town advantage," could work in his favor. He knew the world doesn't have much of a use for a baseball has-been. He didn't look forward to a life of erratic television commercials or car sales that so many previously retired athletes engaged in after their retirement.

Every generation deserves its icons, and once each generation, sometimes twice if we are all very lucky, there comes along an athlete with such an outstanding talent and presence that the experience seems to change our lives. At least for the few hours when we watch a game in the ballpark or listen to it on radio or visualize it on television we can all escape the world. Then, in some way we all become part of the game. Whether the athlete is hyped up from nothing or actually consists of real talent seems to really matter to the majority of people. If this athlete merely shows up to do his job, waves at the crowd, and then disappears until the next time he is needed in the lineup, somehow the icon status is not fulfilled, regardless of the person's statistics. The athlete has to have an unwavering presence, a presence that can't easily be cut down by scandal or gossip or bad press. He has to be beyond reproach in his public and private life. That's why these guys are so rare, especially in today's instant and all-encompassing media, where the slightest step out of place at home or failure in the game is instantly known. With such dauntingly high standards, few make it to this status. For our generation we are lucky enough to have such a great athlete who is a hero to many. And for the ones who do not see him as such, they still respect him as a great athlete. But many can agree as to who this person is: Roger Clemens. He has had a career that has lasted long enough to encompass the careers of two or three baseball stars, given that the average career lasts between eight to 12 years. It is a rare thing indeed for someone to have lasted almost a quarter century in major-league baseball. This is when a player becomes that icon to many, and then that icon becomes a legend. Roger Clemens is older than almost any of the major leaguers, and the majority of today's players was not yet born or was still in diapers when he first stepped onto the mound on that spring day back in 1984. Atlanta Braves right fielder Jeff Francoeur was just four months old at the time, as was Scott Kazmir, pitcher of the Tampa Bay Devil Rays.

It's hard for writers to talk about, much less put into words, a career such as Roger Clemens's. He was a dynamic athlete in an even more dynamic time in baseball. Never before in baseball history have so many dichotomies existed. During the reign of Roger, baseball was in a time period of great records made and then broken; yet, it was also a time of great scandal. Steroids, strikes, gambling, hormones, dishonorable personal conduct in public and in private, and the manipulation of taxpayers to fund and build palatial stadiums to enrich the team owners—all had taken their toll on the fans and the game. These unsavory issues began to leave a foul taste in the mouths of fans, and attendance at games, if not declining, was leveling off. At least one person during this time span stood above it all, above the fray. A popular vote on who this person might be would invariably lead to Roger Clemens.

Indeed, all generations demand to have their role models or icons, and ours is no different. Societies live for their heroes, and whether they are wrong or right, it's hard to let them go. Roger Clemens was given many gifts in life and, as we will see, was also saddled with many burdens. He bore them with grace and strength because he knew that he had to set an example. He is the first one to say, "Hey, I'm not perfect," but for those quarter century of summers, he was perfect enough for us all. For his fans who had watched him grow up through high school, then his college years, and then to the major leagues, he became "our Roger."

It is often difficult to even begin to write about such a legendary player with such an illustrious career. On one hand, pointing out the duplicity of many events in his career might seem to upset a few readers; on the other hand, reasoning with these differences would show that things have a way of working themselves out for the better. I tossed around many ideas and methods for writing this book. One method would be to arrange everything by listing his career statistics or by interviewing key people or other baseball legends in his life. Another method would be to watch reels and reels of old film clips and video of his performances on the mound and write about how he set an example for his team and for the fans. A chronological order to his life would seem to be a unifying thread. No matter what individual method would be used to compile all the information into a book, it would fall short. Using a combination of all of these methods would still seem to fall short of the goal, even with all of them tied into each other. His career is indeed an anomaly. Although all the approaches were turned upside down and dissected and discussed, in the end I decided to start at the most logical spot, where all of the great books have started. Simply start at the beginning.

He was born in the age of the rocket. William Roger Clemens entered the world in the emotional and eventful way in which we all do. Of course, no tabloid reporters waited in the hospital wings to mark the event. That kind of attention would come years later. Born on Saturday, August 4, 1962, in Dayton, Ohio, on a warm sunny evening where the future Houston Astros, known back then in their

pre-Astrodome days as the Colt .45s, played the St. Louis
Cardinals in the old Sportsman's Park, the predecessor to
the 1966 Busch Stadium. The Cardinals scored 2 runs while
the Colt .45s scored 0. His future New York Yankees were
playing the Chicago White Sox; that score was White Sox
2, Yankees 1. The Washington Senators scored 5 runs while
the Boston Red Sox scored 3. Roger's Toronto Blue Jays didn't
exist until 1976, as an expansion team. Globe-girdling sat-
ellites had just made live television a reality in everyone's
living room, but most fans still listened to the games on
the radio. American royalty was in full regalia, as President
John F. Kennedy was in his second year in office, and with
First Lady Jacqueline Bouvier Kennedy, they were the nation's
most popular couple. It was Camelot. It was the Space Age.
The word "Roger" had recently become NASA jargon for "understood," "known," and "got it."

But the day would still forever stand out in the minds
of the entire world, not because of Roger Clemens, but
because on the very evening that he was born, arguably
the greatest film star of all time, Marilyn Monroe, the former
wife of baseball great "Joltin' Joe" DiMaggio, lay dying in
her home in Brentwood, California. She was in her bed-
room, alone, her life ebbing away from a self-administered
overdose of sedatives, either accidental or intentional. She
would be found very early the next morning on August 5
by her housekeeper and psychiatrist and pronounced
dead by the authorities at that time. Her death has been
blamed on a variety of reasons. Friends who had failed her,
an industry that had used and then deserted her, medica-
tions that had only made matters worse, and the fame that
had smothered her all contributed to her early demise. Immediately after her death was announced to the world, it
was clear that she would live forever as a legend. It's difficult

to comprehend that, had she lived, she would now be a woman in her 80s. Fame, which had just destroyed such an innocent life, was now watching a new life enter the world. But this time, this new life, Roger Clemens, would be in complete control of his fame. Fame would never be able to control Roger Clemens. He would take it on by the horns and run his fame the way he saw fit. Roger doesn't let his deeds define him; rather, he defines his deeds and mostly well ahead of time.

But meanwhile, fame would have its focus on other matters of the day. The impending Cuban missile crisis was beginning to stir behind the scenes at the White House. The manned space program was sending rockets to orbit the earth and eventually the moon. These new inventions brought legendary fame and attention to the men who risked everything to get there. They even surpassed baseball heroes, for a while. At least for the time being, if the words "the rocket" were mentioned, it meant only one thing back then.

> *Roger doesn't let his deeds define him; rather, he defines his deeds and mostly well ahead of time.*

In some ways Roger Clemens would become a paradox of a legend. He would become known as arguably the best pitcher in the history of baseball when all of the parameters were compared and the candidates studied. Yet, ironically, he would be one of a handful of players who would never hit a home run in his professional career. Nor would he ever pitch a no-hitter. But he shouldn't feel so bad about any of that. The other great pitcher of our time, Roger's mentor, Nolan Ryan, has never won a single

Cy Young Award. Contradictions such as these make a legend even more intriguing. There has been so much in the media during his career about his early life and childhood—even when he was a rookie—that it has now become part of the legend and lore of Clemens just as much as his career statistics are.[2]

Roger was born into a family that had waiting for him two sisters and two brothers. His mother, Bess Clemens, was a strong-willed mom who raised her children with the firm discipline of the late 1950s and 1960s. Not too long after Roger was born his parents separated, which left Bess to raise the five children alone. This was extremely difficult for a single mom in the early 1960s to do. Roger would later say that he really never knew his biological father because he was out of the picture so early.

People today tend to forget that for any single mother in the early 1960s to raise that many children alone would have almost certainly been catastrophic to the family budget, and the stress would even possibly endanger the mom's health. There were few "equal rights" for women in those days, and the glass ceiling we speak of so often today was a closed and locked steel door back then. Women and minorities would have had an uphill battle just to keep food on the table with the prejudices and laws that existed in those days. Just as with today's controversies, the lawmakers in those days excused their biases with the claim that their laws created a society the way that the founding fathers of this nation would have wanted it to be. In some areas lunch counters, waiting rooms, and drinking fountains still had segregated signs for whites or blacks attached to them. These would not completely disappear until the mid- to late 1960s. Also very striking, a single mother, or any female for that matter, was not able to obtain a loan in her own name without a cosigner, even if she had the collateral to back it up. In addition to that hardship, the laws stated that the cosigner had to be a male, not a female, over the age of 21. She would not be able to get credit or even a charge card in her own name. Moreover, no matter how hard she would work, any chance at a promotion or job opening would first go to a man, whether he had a family or not. Many of the want ads of the day in the newspapers or flyers simply stated "Help Wanted—Male" or "Help Wanted—Female."

Without a doubt, Bess Clemens faced these exact same difficulties. She had to fight to overcome the odds of being a single mom in America. She worked hard and had more than one job to make ends meet. In 1962 even the oldest of the children was too young to work, so all income came from her. According to the great broadcaster, Hall of Famer Milo Hamilton, she "undoubtedly had a difficult time, and she did her best."[3] Milo would later become a good friend to the family, especially during Roger's days with the Houston Astros.

By 1965 Bess had met and married Woody Booher, a friend from previous years. All of the children became exceptionally close to Woody, including Roger. Later, the youngest of the children, Bonnie, was born. This completed the family with three girls—Janet, Brenda, and Bonnie—and three boys, Richard, Gary, and Roger, the youngest boy.

Roger looked up to his stepfather, as Woody was the only father figure Roger had really ever known. Woody was as dedicated to the children as Bess was, and it was obvious that the hard times were getting a little easier for now. It was around this time that Roger, as with most boys, began to notice sports, albeit on a child's level. Physical activity was about the only outlet for kids in those days, before home computers, video games, cable television, or other distractions came into existence. To get to a friend's home, you walked there or rode your bike. There was no text messaging back then. The games played were physical and challenging to the imagination, and there weren't any prepackaged Game Boys back then either.

Eventually, T-ball and other sports began to enter Roger's life. He credits Woody for being there for him and for introducing him to sports. Today, Roger remembers something odd that happened to him when he first went out for baseball at a tender young age. Roger reflects, "When I first went out for baseball, the coach said that I wasn't any good at it, and that I should pack it up and go back home and find another sport to play."[4]

This didn't faze Roger in the least, because in his early forceful way he didn't back down and he wasn't deterred. At least not for long. He was soon in Little League and had somewhat distinguished himself through practicing at it. It seemed as if his life and baseball were finally starting to amount to something or at least seemed to point in some iconic direction. But about that time came a crushing blow to everyone.

Around the time of Roger's ninth birthday, their beloved Woody passed away from a heart attack. Woody had suffered from previous heart problems, and although the family knew that there was a possibility of a severe setback, his last illness was a complete surprise to all. It made an impression on Roger that would last for the rest of his life.[5] Now, still a child, he had no father, he had just lost his stepfather, and his mom was now a widow.

It all seemed to fall back to square one. Bess was now again the focus and center of the family. Roger has always said that she was the inspiration for all parts of his life, especially those early days when life was so hard. Roger looked up to his mom, and after the death of his stepfather, she became a source of inspiration and encouragement during that stage and all subsequent stages of his life. When his enthusiasm for study or sport waned, Bess was there to encourage him to take another step toward success in whatever his goals were at the time. She did this for all of her six children. She instilled in them a secure sense of family. They would know that no matter how uncertain things became, family was their anchor. In good times and in bad, that anchor was always there. Even in later life, Roger would credit his mom as the reason he came out of retirement, saying, "I get my determination from her . . . she told me to go to work."[6] Undoubtedly this motherly encouragement also occurred during his childhood, too.

In 1969, the family received a shock. His brother Richard was watching the local draft board call-up on television when he saw his number posted on the bulletin board. The family was in a state of shock. Richard was being called up to fight in the Vietnam War.[7] As a member of an ever-responsible family, Richard fulfilled his tour of duty, and this made Roger appreciate what military men and women go through in order to protect our country and our freedoms. Years later, Roger would honor their sacrifices when he and other sports stars would make celebrity tours to visit American troops fighting in Iraq and Afghanistan and recall the way in which his brother Richard served his country.

The family had its trying times, but that didn't stop Roger from beginning to excel in all of the sports he wanted to play, especially baseball. He had everything that he thought he needed. Somehow, ends would be met, and he would get his sporting equipment. What they lacked in money, Bess made up for in devotion and hard work, and by the mid-1970s the kids had jobs to help with whatever was needed.

The story of Roger Clemens and his childhood is just one of the many stories that major-league players have about their own childhoods. Many of them were brought up in single-parent households and went through much the same hardships as Roger and his brothers and sisters. These hardships, beyond the obvious ones, were such things as not having the correct or inappropriate supplies for training properly in baseball. Somehow they made it through. One story is of a youth who didn't have a bat or baseballs for practice, so his mom improvised by pitching him tennis balls while he used a stick as the bat. This scene has been repeated time after time in many players' lives.

Around the time of the mid- to late 1970s, most of the country was in an economic downturn. Well-paying jobs were hard to come by. Inflation was rampant, and the dollar didn't go as far as it once did for the Clemens family or anyone for that matter. The one pocket of resistance to the economic downturn was Texas, one of the largest petrochemical areas on earth. Thriving on its banner industry, oil, it was supplying this precious commodity to the world from its ports. Roger's older brothers, Gary and Richard, obtained jobs in the Houston area. Richard was by now finished with his tour of duty with the armed services. Texas was also the nation's epicenter in high school sports, which attracted Roger's attention. He probably visited his brothers at their new homes in Houston and apparently liked what he saw.[8] He asked his mom if he could stay there with his brothers and attend a sports-friendly high school. Bess eventually agreed to this in 1977.

Roger seemed to meld into the population of Houston and Harris County, which was burgeoning during this time period because of the oil boom. Its metropolitan area population grew dramatically from 1970 to 1980 with the influx of workers from other states and countries. Almost overnight it went from a cow town to the oil capital of the world. Often it was said that the construction crane was the official state bird of Texas because of all of the expansive growth during this time period. Jobs seemed to be everywhere for the taking. It was also the famous period of time known as the "Love Ya Blue" frenzy. The Houston Oilers, now known as the Tennessee Titans after the team's well-publicized riff with the city and county, tried to make it to the Super Bowl for several years in a row. Even in the years in which they played lackluster, they were still popular with the fans and the political forces that financed them. Earl Campbell of the Oilers, known as the "Tyler Rose," was equivalent to the Roger Clemens of the day. Even today, Campbell's popularity rivals that of Clemens and other athletes, according to a newspaper poll listing the all-time great athletes of Houston.[9] Other center stage characters during this time were Bum Phillips, the team's colorful coach, and Bud Adams, the team's owner in Houston. In Texas, sports were more than a team effort. It was a religion, and football was its god. In the public schools, budgets often spent more on the football stadiums than on classroom space. Coaches in schools were routinely paid higher salaries than regular teachers, and it eventually negatively affected entrance test scores.

Undoubtedly, the oil boom and its economic outcome brought Roger Clemens to Houston. Within a short while this boom brought Bess and her girls to town, also, from Dayton, Ohio. They all settled in a working-class area in northwest Houston known as Spring Branch. Bess still worked two jobs to meet her budget, and the children also were now bringing in their share by having part-time jobs themselves.

Now in his teenage years, Roger saw himself markedly improve on his skills in sports, especially in baseball, where once he was told that he "was not good enough." His pitching skills were unmatched. He also excelled in football and in basketball. He was now enrolled in high school at Spring Woods Senior High in west Houston. He unknowingly chose a uniquely qualified school, as this was the territory of the Spring Woods Fighting Tigers, and it had the reputation of being the best in everything: football, basketball, baseball, and track and field. The foundation for his future success was being laid down carefully. As an added benefit to all the sports that Roger was interested in, this was the hometown of his idol and role model, Nolan Ryan. At that time, Ryan was with the California Angels. He would soon leave the Angels for the Houston Astros after a dispute with the Angels' management. Whenever Nolan pitched, Roger would save up his money and go down to the Astrodome—hyped as the eighth wonder of the world— with his buddies and watch it all unfold. The Astros in those days were not quite as popular as the Oilers, but they had their loyal followers. While watching those games, Roger must have imagined being Nolan, as did countless other young hopefuls in the stands.

It was during his junior and senior years at Spring Woods High School that friends and coaches began to notice Roger's athletic abilities. His high school teams faced such crosstown rivals as Klein, Bellaire, Katy, Cypress

Fairbanks, and Galveston Ball High School (which was the high school of fellow Astros pitching great Brandon Backe, who was born as Clemens was arriving in Houston), to name a few. It was not uncommon for these games to be on radio or even television. Weekly newspaper articles in the sports sections of the *Houston Chronicle*, the *Houston Post*, and neighborhood papers routinely covered the games and more than once mentioned the name of Roger Clemens. In football, he was known for his size and strength. He garnered three years of letters as a defensive end and helped the team make it to all-district. As a center and forward in basketball he lettered for two years. But, realistically, he had to choose a sport in which to focus his abilities in order to have a chance at a college scholarship or even a career in professional sports. After coaches and teachers had told him that he would most likely make it in baseball, he zeroed in on it. Roger played first base and also pitched on his high school team, and his squad also made it to all-state and the American Legion State Championship.

> *Roger, like a hatchling just out of a nest or a rocket just off the launch pad, was learning how to take flight.*

To Roger, pitching was now his domain. In baseball in general, pitching is the most important position for any team. It is the engine that runs the show, and Roger, like a hatchling just out of a nest or a rocket just off the launch pad, was learning how to take flight. All young players, regardless of their position, fantasize about being the star pitcher, because the entire game is centered on them. Most coaches focus a larger percentage of their time on training the pitcher, because no matter how sharp the opposing team is, the home pitcher can keep them at bay with his inventory of pitching surprises. Some teams in high school even had coaches for the different team positions. Much as the quarterback in football, the pitcher will quickly end up shouldering any team's wins or losses.

Around the time of his high school graduation in 1980, several scouts from the Philadelphia Phillies and also those from the Minnesota Twins approached Roger in hopes of signing him to their farm system. Clemens was leery of such offers. Many young high school hopefuls who were sent off to the farm systems, at least in those days, did not achieve what they had hoped and often ended up getting injured early on, thus eliminating any chance at ever making it to a major-league career.

Clemens also found himself in the middle of a time period that was also known as the heyday of the "urban cowboy" craze, which got its name from the 1980 mega hit movie of the same title, starring John Travolta and Debra Winger. The movie centered on Mickey Gilley's nightclub in Pasadena, Texas, probably the most famous club of the time. It was especially known worldwide for its mechanical bull-riding machine, on which countless patrons had themselves photographed. Celebrities from around the world were spotted in the joint, and more than likely Roger and his buddies, just as others his age, enjoyed the atmosphere and concerts from such noted performers as Willie Nelson, George Jones, Charlie Daniels, Johnny Lee, and, of course, Mickey himself. It was often said around town that before the urban cowboy craze, the only people who wore cowboy hats were fans of country music and cowboys. During the craze, it seemed as if everyone wore them.

Roger had hoped to get into the University of Texas in his freshman year on a scholarship but the offer was not extended. The high cost of attending such a large university was out of the question for him. He settled instead for a local community college across town in Pasadena by the name of San Jacinto Junior College because of its lower costs and its good baseball program. Serendipity aside, he couldn't have chosen a better place in which to hone his sporting skills.

The San Jacinto Gators had the soon-to-be legendary Wayne Graham as their baseball coach. His coaching skills were spectacular. He eventually piloted the Gators to five national championships during his 11-year stay there. He had also been elected Coach of the Century at the junior college level in honor of his remarkable series of successes. Today, when one thinks of coaching great college baseball, the name Wayne Graham comes to mind for many. An entire book could be written on this man. He has the magic touch when it comes to coaching a collegiate player and turning him into a major-leaguer. Eventually such names as Roger Clemens, Andy Pettitte (who also attended San Jacinto College under Wayne Graham from 1990 to 1992), and Lance Berkman of Rice University would fill Graham's portfolio, just to name a few. As of the 2007 season, more than 30 of his former players were playing baseball on a professional level. Coaching a team to a national championship or conference title and molding players into pro draft picks or All-Americans are Graham's special forte. Coaches such as Graham have the innate ability to communicate workable success skills to their players in ways other than what is spoken.

Graham had the credentials. When Graham's University of Texas Longhorns college days ended in 1961, he spent over a decade in professional baseball leagues with the Philadelphia Phillies and the New York Mets. Two of those years were at the major-league level. He brought those base-ball skills to teach for ten years at Houston area high schools and then became coach at San Jacinto Junior College in 1981. It was there that his reputation began. His first year he coached freshman Roger Clemens and the rest of the baseball team to second place at junior college conference titles. After his groundbreaking stay he moved on to Rice University, compiling an extraordinary record and building the team into a national collegiate powerhouse in baseball. Not surprisingly, Graham was elected to the Texas Baseball Hall of Fame in Ft. Worth in 2003 and the Texas Sports Hall of Fame in 2005.

Roger Clemens concentrated his freshman year on perfecting his workout regime. More than likely he devised it from watching how other professional athletes, such as Nolan Ryan, maintained their workouts.[10] Roger added to it to create for himself his own form of grueling exercises that would make boot camp seem elementary by comparison. Others on his team could not keep up with Roger when he worked out, and he focused his increasing strength into improving his pitching. He increased his speed of pitch to well over 90 miles per hour and improved his windup. His college pitching career was well under way, and in 1981 he accomplished 9 wins against 2 losses for the season. At San Jacinto, Roger, wearing jersey number 26, distinguished himself as a star pitcher; he was very popular with the local media as well as with friends on campus and teammates.

> *Others on his team could not keep up with Roger when he worked out, and he focused his increasing strength into improving his pitching.*

His outstanding performance that year certainly got the attention of major-league scouts, and in June 1981 he was drafted in the 12th round of the amateur draft by the New York Mets. Again, as in the case with the scouts at Spring Woods Senior High School, he did not sign. Had he signed at that time, he would have been a rookie with another up-and-comer who also would become famous: Dwight Gooden, the uncle of another baseball great, Gary Sheffield. "Doc" Gooden would debut in 1984 with the Mets, deliver a 15-year career in the major leagues, and eventually retire in 1999 from the Cleveland Indians.

If there is a hallmark of Roger Clemens, it's his use of caution and not rushing into a quick decision about things. Not signing on the first offer that came his way showed that he had already begun to develop into a mature decision maker.

Chapter 3

THE FORMATIVE YEARS

There are many reasons why a senior in high school or a freshman in college would pass on being signed to a farm team of a major-league baseball organization. One of the biggest is that he needs to hone his skills while performing on a team that is on his level. If he has confidence in his ability to grow as a player, then he would more than likely choose to stay in school. Another reason could be his dreams and aspirations or loyalties were to another team that had not chosen him at that time; in other words, he's waiting for something better. The majority of players just wanted to get their education behind them and get on with life, be it in the majors or as a workingman.

This was especially the case in 1981. Major-league salaries were not comparable to today's scandalous incomes, and certainly farm team salaries back then were not enough to be rewarding if a player were to choose it, or to chance it, only to be released several years later with no degree and with limited skills for the real world's workforce.

Wisely, Roger decided to move on to showcase his talents on an even grander scale at the University of Texas in Austin. In later years, he told his University of Texas alumni newspaper, "I know where I've come from, where my background is. I always tried to not leave a stone unturned, and I feel that way right now. I'm never satisfied, and I'm never gonna get complacent until I know this career is over."[1]

Clemens knew that a noted exception to the worst-case scenario in risking a chance in the major leagues while still in school was National Baseball Hall of Famer Nolan Ryan. Ryan was a spectacular high school pitcher in Alvin, Texas, a small town just south of Houston. His pitching abilities on the mound, together with his stamina, fastball, and his team-building skills, got the attention of major-league scouts. In 1965 he was drafted by the New York Mets, and while he was attending Alvin Community College that summer he was called up to the majors in September 1966. At that time, at the age of 19, he was one of the youngest players ever in the leagues. But even then,

> *"I'm never satisfied, and I'm never gonna get complacent until I know this career is over."*

at least to start with, and as so many of the young when catapulted into the majors, he had problems with his delivery and was sent packing down to the farm system on more than one occasion. His attempts to correct himself continued, and it wasn't until the 1969 World Series between the Mets and the Baltimore Orioles that he made a name for himself. He shut down the mighty Orioles in three innings in Game 3, thus paving the way for the Mets to win the 1969 World Series. He has the unofficial world's record, at least at that time, of serving the fastest pitch ever, at just over a hundred miles per hour.[2] When he joined the Houston Astros in 1979, he became the first million-dollar player in major-league baseball history. This was the first of the payroll milestones passed since Joe DiMaggio became the first player to pass the $100,000 mark 30 years previously in 1949. Nolan's nickname quickly became "the Express," and in his hometown area it was the "Alvin Express." He became so popular that in 1998, Texas officials renamed part of State Highway 288 from Houston to Ryan's hometown of Alvin as the Nolan Ryan Expressway. The Boston area already had its Ted Williams Tunnel, and the Houston area naturally wanted something larger and more imposing, so they came up with the Nolan Ryan Expressway. However, Nolan Ryan's last pitch was for the Texas Rangers on September 22, 1993, at the age of 46, after a falling out with the Houston Astros a few years earlier on a payroll issue. Nolan ended his major-league career after 27 years, 5,714 strikeouts, 324 wins—a tie with Don Sutton at 12th place—and eight all-star teams. Five years later on January 5, 1999 (the first year of his eligibility), Ryan was elected to the National Baseball Hall of Fame in Cooperstown, New York, by the Baseball Writers' Association of America. He was the oldest Texas Rangers' player in their history, and he is the only player in the history of major-league baseball to have had his uniform retired by three different teams: the California Angels, the Houston Astros, and the Texas Rangers. He was many times in the running for the Cy Young Award but never won that honor. His storied history was an inspiration for Roger Clemens to follow, and the many similarities at the end of their careers are striking. Today, Nolan Ryan is a consultant for the Houston Astros.

Another great whom Roger looked up to as a role model was New York Mets pitcher Tom Seaver. His nicknames of "the Franchise" and "Tom Terrific" just about say it all. In the 1960s and through the 1980s, Seaver was most associated with the Mets but later played for the Cincinnati Reds. He spent his last season with the Boston Red Sox, a season, ironically, that would have Roger as one of Seaver's teammates. He went on to win 311 games, strike out 3,272 players (a mark that Clemens would eventually surpass), and win the Cy Young Award three times. At the height of his popularity, Seaver had more Opening Day starts than any other pitcher in history with 16. He would be elected to the Baseball Hall of Fame in 1992, six years after the end of his major-league career, which started in 1967 in Shea Stadium. Roger Clemens, Nolan Ryan, and Tom Seaver had very similar careers, and Clemens still admires both of them. Just as Clemens, Seaver was extremely competitive and was once quoted as saying to a reporter, "There are only two places in the league, first place and no place."[3] Sadly, a torn ankle ligament kept him from being in the Boston Red Sox World Series in 1986. He was, however, given a standing ovation during the player presentations at Game 1 of the Series.

For Roger's next step, the university that he could not afford to attend during his freshman year and that had not offered him an athletic scholarship at the end of his high school days was now accepting many prospective athletes such as Clemens. Roger began his sophomore year at the University of Texas as a business major. Although he was there for baseball, he knew eventually that he would put to good use what he learned in those business classes. He knew ahead of time that he was a product that needed to be marketed in just the right way. Roger has always known exactly what his value is; he knew this from his college days up to the end of his career. And he always wanted to go to the University of Texas because he knew that it would offer more for his pitching talents.

Roger arrived on campus that fall as an impressive, 6-foot-4 athlete who attracted a lot of attention. Athletics at UT had always distinguished itself. The football rivalry between the university and their "down the pastures" neighbor Texas A&M University was legendary. In the fall semester of 1981 when Roger Clemens arrived on campus, such sports as swimming, tennis, track and field, football, and baseball all had an honorable and storied history that Roger found important in his own quest there. During Roger's stay at UT, he would change the baseball program in his own way. Before Roger, football towered over and dwarfed the baseball program. After Roger, the baseball program was lifted to a higher level of respect, especially after the 1983 College World Series.

At UT, Roger would befriend teammates Calvin Schiraldi, Mike Capel, and Spike Owen, all of whom would have their own careers in major-league baseball. Two, Owen and Schiraldi, would become teammates of Clemens with the Red Sox during their careers.

Roger's new teammates nicknamed him "Goose" because of his resemblance in style and physique to Rich "Goose" Gossage. At the time that Clemens was at UT, Gossage was the relief pitcher for the New York Yankees. The Yankees and Gossage are credited with formulating in the 1980s the current pitching arrangement of starter and relief, or closer, that has come to replace the older method of using a pitcher until exhaustion and then sending in a relief pitcher. Gossage eventually pitched in over a thousand games, made an amazing nine All-Star Game appearances, and pitched in the World Series three times. He then went on to several other teams in his 22-year career before retiring in 1994. He still awaits his election to the Hall of Fame.

As an obvious star pitcher for the Longhorns, Clemens was coached by the great Cliff Gustafson, who had an almost 30-year career at UT from 1968 to 1996 and remains one of that university's most winning baseball coaches with 1,427 wins. He is still the coach with the most wins in the NCAA's Division I. During his stay as the team's skipper, he took the university to two College World Series. In the 1983 College World Series, Clemens was on the mound for the win.

Clemens and Gustafson eventually formed a wonderful friendship that lasts to this day. Roger told his campus newspaper, "Yeah, I loved Coach Gus. I would have thrown my arm out for him! And I always felt joy, whenever I'm back on that campus."[4] According to Roger's alma mater, Coach Gustafson said of Roger: "He had size, he had power, and he had a naturally good delivery. Roger was a power pitcher but with exceptional control. And he was highly motivated. To me, he seemed like a guy who was on a mission. If you put it all together, it adds up to quite a package. Roger was the best pro baseball prospect I ever coached."[5]

It was at UT that Clemens was exposed to the routine rituals of the local and sometimes state and national press. But to succeed, Roger had already learned how to concentrate on his game. He was known for his size, now topped out at 6-foot-4 and already over 200 pounds. But size was not his only asset, as he had form and delivery with power. Roger's star power was setting in; his heat of delivery fanned batters out of the box as if he had a flamethrower and a gas can attached to a delivery hose under the pitcher's mound. Quite readily he was the team's ace hurler, but he never allowed this to go to his head. Once an athlete allows this to happen, as has been the case with some, he or she is finished.

An amusing story from this time period in Roger's career is that when he was on a roll, the letter "K" (for strikeouts) would disappear from signs, billboards, and marquees so that fans could use them during one of Roger's appearances. Desperate business owners eventually figured out what was going on and made appearances themselves to the college baseball games, if only at to identify and pick up their missing property.

Clemens looks back on the two years he spent at UT with fondness. His two-year record there saw 241 strikeouts in his 275 innings pitched. His final record there was 25 wins and 7 losses over both years. In that amazing feat, it was said that while in college, the aluminum bats were supposed to go "ping," but with Roger, the only sound they made was "swipe." Aluminum bats have been used in college baseball since 1974 in the belief that they, much more so than wooden bats, help the batter perform better at their level. Controversy has followed this theory ever since. Some claim that aluminum bats are more dangerous for the pitcher because of the speed of impact on the ball, thus making it harder for the pitcher and others on the field to react to a low hit ball.

In the summer of that year, Clemens was the winning pitcher during the 1983 College World Series in which UT defeated Alabama 4 to 3. In addition, he and the team had All-American honors. He often returns to campus for various alumni functions, including season baseball games and alumni games. When he became one of the Houston Astros, he helped organize Longhorns Night at Minute Maid Park. It pays tribute to the team, former UT students and alumni, and their families. His return to the Astros for the 2006 season happened to coincide with Longhorns Night, which added to the magic of the return. Clemens is

often seen about town wearing UT "Hook 'em Horns" baseball caps and shirts and other burnt orange accessories, in
addition to wearing his major-league clothing. Roger is
known as the only University of Texas alumnus to have
had his number, 21, retired from service. Years after his
college days, when UT made it to the Rose Bowl in 2006,
for the second time in a row, Roger took his 19-year-old
son Koby for the experience of a lifetime there.

Because of his record at the University of Texas and
his status as star hurler, he received the attention of scouts
from the Boston Red Sox. On June 6, 1983, while he was
with his friends and family and waiting on the 1983 draft,
Roger was selected as the 19th pick of the first-round draft.
On June 21, 1983, he was signed to the Boston Red Sox minor-league system. The Clemens family's reaction in Houston
was ecstatic. Although not large, especially when compared
with today's amounts, his signing bonus alone signaled to
them that their years of hardships were finally going to
ease somewhat. Roger was at the center of attention in a
very public way this time. Not only was he drafted by the
Boston Red Sox, but he was able to show off his talents to
a now very attentive crowd. Upon winning the College
World Series that summer, he recalls

> I remember my team at UT jumping on me after get-
> ting that final out against Alabama to win the National
> Championship in '83. You know, in 1982, the year we
> came in tied for 3rd, we probably had a better team—
> I mean as far as talent. When we came back the fol-
> lowing year and won it, our pitching staff was a little
> more experienced and it was such a thrill. Going to
> Omaha for the College World Series—the people
> there are tremendous—huge crowds and a lot of

excitement. I still remember those days—you make a lot of friends that you never forget when you win a championship like that.[6]

He knew that he would have many more experiences just like this, except that now it would be on a national scale in professional baseball. Had he been drafted by, and accepted a contract with, his hometown Houston Astros, as he had hoped for, he would have rookied on the 1983–84 team that featured some of his role models, such as Nolan Ryan, Alan Ashby, José Cruz, and Phil Garner. If there was any disappointment on Roger's part, it was undoubtedly dissipated by the joy of now being in the major leagues.

Roger had finally made it to professional baseball. His first contract was with Class A Winter Haven, where, after only four starts under his belt and garnering 3 wins to 1 loss with an amazing ERA of 1.24, he was quickly promoted to Double A New Britain. Roger showed even more promise there and exhibited that he could handle more pressure as a pitcher. During his short stay at New Britain he struck out 15 batters and accomplished a 1.38 ERA while going 4 to 1 in just seven starts. Toward the season's end, his opponents' batting average was just 1 one hit per 10 attempts, a .167 ERA average. He was on one of his proverbial rolls. In recognition of his first professional season's accomplishments he garnered two starts during the playoffs in the Eastern League Championships. There he allowed only 1 run for his opponents in 17 innings. At the end of 1983 his name was well known in baseball circles, it was also gaining momentum in all forms of media, and, most important, he had the attention of the upper management at the Boston Red Sox.

In the late summer of 1983, Roger got a call from home, telling him that a severe hurricane suddenly popped up in the Gulf of Mexico outside of the Houston/Galveston area and was heading inland. Hurricane Alicia struck full force on the entire Houston area, severely damaging buildings and homes. There was no electricity for days, and phone service had also been cut off. This was all before cell phones, the Internet, and e-mail, and it took most people several days before they could know for sure the fates of their friends and relatives. As if that disaster was not enough, four months later a Christmas Day freeze, the area's first real freeze in decades, burst the plumbing pipes in many of the same homes, destroying much of the repair work that had been done on carpets and walls.

The year 1984 would prove to be a banner year for Roger. It was the year of promotion from Double A to Triple A and then to the majors. He would shatter many categories of records. This would also be the year that he became a family man. At the age of 22 he married Debbie Godfrey in Houston after his debut professional baseball league season ended in the fall. Thus the number 22, his age at his wedding, would become his lucky number, especially in his later years in the major

> The year of 1984 would prove to be a banner year for Roger.

leagues. He and Debbie originally met while in high school, but according to Debbie, "we went to high school together, but we didn't date." She continued, "I was dating someone else, and he was new there."[7] But a few years later, while she was working for Pennzoil in downtown Houston in 1984, she and Roger met again. "We met in January, we were engaged in April and married in November," she said.

"I must say it has been a whirlwind ever since."[8] Debbie is reflective on her life with a famous athlete: "He's been recognized everywhere he went for 20 years," she said. "It would have been really hard living under the microscope. But I have a good tune-out system, I think. I'm conditioned to that. What you see is what you get with us."[9]

Clemens began the 1984 baseball season in the minor leagues with Triple A Pawtucket. Because the team is owned by the Red Sox, the Pawtuckets are known as the Paw Sox. Located in Pawtucket, Rhode Island, they have a storied history with the Red Sox organization. Many have started their professional baseball careers there. Now it was Roger Clemens's turn to begin what would turn out to be an almost quarter century of major-league service. Just off his College World Series jaunt, Roger quickly gained control of the pitching for the remainder of the Pawtucket 1983 season. In the three games in which he appeared and the 29 innings in which he pitched, he performed a respectable 3 wins and 1 loss, striking out 36 players and allowing only 22 hits. The number 22 again worked its way into Roger's psyche.

Spring training in 1984 assured Roger that he was on his way. In many instances the minor-league teams trained with the major-league players, although their games were still in their separate classes. Walking into spring training that March he saw and met many of the players whom he viewed as role models during his high school and college playing days. The Boston players that he met were Wade Boggs, Al Nipper, Oil Can Boyd, and Jim Rice, to name just a few. On opposing teams, he met and actually befriended many more players whom he found to be just as down to earth as anyone else he had ever met. The manager for the 1984 Red Sox was the famous Ralph Houk, who would introduce to the world of baseball such young players as Clemens, Wade Boggs, and Marty Barrett.

On May 11, 1984, Roger was called up from the Pawtucket Paw Sox to the Boston Red Sox, the big time, for good. This promotion was in part a result of his record strikeouts of 50 players in just 39 innings. He became the fifth person in major-league history with the name of Clemens. His first major-league appearance was against the Cleveland Indians on May 15, 1984, at Cleveland Stadium. It was a game that the Bo Sox would lose 5 runs to 7, but on May 20, thanks in large part to Roger's stamina and the abilities of the entire team, Roger would have his first win, over the Minnesota Twins. In seven innings, Roger would strike out seven opponents and would win the game 5 to 4. The efforts of Clemens and other key players were beginning to lay the foundation that would eventually lead Boston to its greatest attempts at the World Series in years.

There are many theories about what it takes for a young man who wants baseball as a career to make it into the major leagues. Ask any number of players that question and you will have that many answers. But there is a common thread to all of them. It goes back to the old adage of "practice, practice, practice." I don't mean in the derogatory sense of the word as used by a famous athlete, Allen Iverson, who, to avoid a practice session, sarcastically said something along the lines of, "How the hell can I make my teammates better by practicing?"[10] Instead I refer to practice as a respectable way of bonding into a team.

I asked a few major-league players about their secrets: how they made it into the majors while many of their former teammates and friends didn't make it. I did not just concentrate on the big names; rookies, call-ups, has-beens, and others were asked as well. These interviews took place "on the battlefield," while their pulses were living and breathing major-league gusto so that their answers were firsthand and as close to reality as possible. It's amazing to note that they all pretty much had their answers figured out, and not because they had been asked the question before, but because they had often wondered, "Why me?" The question of just why they made it to the big time was often asked in their subconscious and eventually worked its way up to their conscious minds, and they were ready to answer if the question should ever come up.

One of the greatest of pitchers today outside of Roger Clemens is San Diego Padres pitcher Greg Maddux. When this interview took place, he was after his 325th win, this time trying to do it while up against the Houston Astros. On the opposing mound was Clemens. It was a game to remember for both pitchers and their teams. Clemens was the winning pitcher in the game, though, where the Astros won it 4 to 2 on July 19. Maddux said, "A person should not be afraid to change because change allows one to experiment and eventually to have a better chance at succeeding to the top. Because of this I was able to throw harder. I liked to pitch the most of all the positions and also enjoyed trying new pitch selections and experimenting with them. Because of this, I believe, I was drafted into the majors and succeeded to where I am today."

Maddux also said something amazing. "I was 22 years old before I realized for sure that I really wanted to be a major-league baseball player. I know that so many kids have the dream early on, but it took me a while to know it for sure. But I began to entertain the possibility of being part of major-league baseball around the age of 18, when the scouts began to show up at my games."[11] Roger Clemens has great admiration for Greg Maddux, and Clemens has been seen, while in the dugout, watching the pitching style of Maddux intensely.

Phil Nevin, Greg's teammate, seemed to be at a complete loss of words to accurately describe how his struggles helped him make it into "the Bigs," as the players often call it. After a few moments of thought, and lots of cajoling from his fellow team members, he reflected, "It was pure luck that gave me the ability to get here. Sometimes that's all that it is, anywhere. We all played baseball all the time, while others played with the same buddies and developed strategies. I received a scholarship, which helped a lot, and then I was drafted into professional baseball."

Steve Finley of the Colorado Rockies seemed to nail the issue down when he said, "Success is based almost entirely between the ears. It's how you deal with the pressures. For anyone to succeed at what they're doing, and to do it well, there has to be a desire deep inside. A burning passion will take you far."

Finley knows what he is talking about because he has survived in this game far longer than the majority of other players. He has now been in the majors for over 20 years.

"You can't teach passion and you can't be taught the will to win. It has to be already ingrained into your psyche, waiting to be rubbed the right way by what appeals to you," adds Steve. "You have to find it on your own. There are so many start-up players in high school, college, the minors, just trying to find out what it takes to stay in the game. If you can't polish it to the surface, it isn't there.

"The biggest and most important ability is to learn from your mistakes. This is also the mental versus physical aspect of the game. Train your mind to recognize an approaching error and the physical part will then take over," the five-time All-Star says.

Andy Pettitte has been a close friend of Roger Clemens's for years. He grew up in Deer Park, Texas, a town near Houston, and attended San Jacinto Junior College, as did Clemens. Andy is certainly one of the most soft-spoken players in the majors and has a way of remaining a fan favorite wherever he goes. Millions of fans know him as the "good guy" and an all-star, both on and off the field.

When younger he said, "I really didn't do anything different from my classmates or teammates that set me apart from them in sports. I just practiced and realized there was a burning passion inside me for the game of baseball. I had that desire to succeed and to make something out of myself." Also in his earlier years, he realized that he was left-handed, back in the days when left-handed kids were almost always forced to write, play sports, and to do everything with their right hands. But in baseball, being left-handed has its benefits. "What helped me was that I was left-handed, and there weren't that many left-handed pitchers in my area. Most of my pitching teammates were being trained as right-handed pitchers." Andy's nickname to this day is still "Lefty."

Speaking of his time at Deer Park High School, he said, "I trained and worked out a lot harder than the other guy, and it seemed to come naturally to me. Maybe hard work is genetic for me." Pettitte knows a lot about hard work. "I'm convinced that hard, hard work got me to where I am today. There are no lucky breaks in baseball. To be really successful at what you do, your mental shape has to be as good as your physical shape," he's fond of saying. "In many ways this can work in reverse. When a player is injured, it affects their emotions as well. They are not going to be a happy camper, especially the ones dedicated to their career."

The off-season is not a time to slack off, either. "I stay in great shape during the off-season. Working out every day is necessary for success. Don't slack the physical aspect during the off-season. People outside the game don't realize that baseball is a 365/24/7 job. It's not a 40-hour-per-week job because there are workouts, interviews, meetings with coaches and staff, and agents and media. There is more to baseball than what you see on television," said Pettitte.

Another great pitcher, and sometimes adversary of Roger Clemens's, Kyle Farnsworth had a lot to say about this issue: "I'd say once a game starts, the mental aspect takes center stage as the most important thing going for a pitcher. Quite a few hitters try to distract my concentration with sideshow antics. That doesn't work on me, and it only serves to make the hitter's stance a more difficult one for himself. Concentration is the key once I'm out there, and no one's going to take that away from me, because I never let them do that to me, ever," Kyle said with confident experience.

"For now, baseball is just about everything to me, it's my life at this point. There eventually will come a time when I can slow my life down and take some time off and get settled. But for now I can't, and I don't know of anyone in this career who can really settle down and take it easy," he added.

Khalil Greene of the San Diego Padres is a very humble and intelligent person. Visiting with him gives one the impression that he has been in his career for many more years than he actually has been. He is fond of saying, "I never thought I would never be here." In other words, he knew that baseball was going to be his career since childhood. Getting to the major leagues has always been a goal of his. "I actually knew that I had made it just out of high school and just before college, with the scouts and all," he said. Khalil, in the ancient translation, means "friend of Abraham." He is as insightful and thought provoking as is his namesake, the writer Khalil Gibran. "I felt as if I was destined to be a major-league baseball player."

But Greene didn't take it for granted. He said that those who take it for granted "are the ones that lose out on a gift." He had a burning sense of desire for the game, and he prepared for his career each day, even as a kid. "Although," he said, "I did get here a lot faster than I thought I would, probably because I put my mind to it. You know, a person can go far when they put their mind to just about anything."

He wanted to add more on this "mind and body" subject: "A person's mind is what should control his body. A player should take a mind over body stance, not a drug or steroid stance. Those drugs are just poisons to the body and mind. It's only recently that people realize what those non-natural and human-made chemicals do to their well-being. Remember those old advertisements and commercials that said that chemicals are our friends? Well, we now know a whole lot more, and they're not a friend. Most should be held at arm's length away.

> A person's mind is what should control his body. A player should take a mind over body stance, not a drug or steroid stance.

"Preparation for the game is more than just being here, it involves concentration and dedication, as far as the mental aspect goes, and as far as the physical aspect goes, a player has to stay in shape every day of the year to stay ahead of the curve," he said.

For game time, he adds, "I use a lot of instinct before and during a game, and once out there I try not to think too much. I let everything I've prepared for fall into place." Instinct is just one of the talents that Greene uses. "For the game, I've become very good at visualizing every possible scenario on the field before it happens. It's almost a déjà vu mentality," Khalil stressed. In many ways, this can work for many careers other than baseball.

Carlos Beltran of the New York Mets said, "Hard work is what set me apart from my teammates in my early years." Beltran added, "I always came in early to practice for the game, and to this day I still do. That's because you might have talent, but you still have to practice it. No matter how far I go in the game, I'll always believe that. Thankfully, all of my teammates that have made it to the top think the same way. Baseball is a sport almost like a ballet. You need to practice constantly. One or two days off can hurt you, and you have to repair that time off with even more work-outs. That's why I work out every day, sometimes twice a day, to keep up with the demands on my body."

He realized he enjoyed baseball at the age of 14. He and his father would play many sports, but eventually his father gave him a gift of a bat and ball and told him that baseball would be his life. "That's when I decided to play baseball and not the other sports. I was better at it and had that fire in me." Beltran added that his family and friends back home in Puerto Rico call him "Ivan," not Carlos, be-cause his full name is Carlos Ivan Beltran and they want to distinguish it from his father's name, also Carlos.

Tom Glavine is one of the longest-tenured veterans of the major leagues. His perfection at his skill has amazed fans for two decades. Although he is currently teamed up with the New York Mets, he was originally drafted by the

Atlanta Braves in the second round of the 1984 amateur draft. After a few stints on various minor-league teams, he made his Braves' major-league debut in August 1987. His departure from the Braves for the Mets was a severe blow to his Atlanta fans, who worshipped him for years.

Baseball is just one of the sports in which Glavine excelled. As a kid, he puttered around the baseball fields and also the hockey rinks in Massachusetts. In high school, he was voted to the All-Star team, and in hockey, he was an All-Conference honoree. He loved to play both of these sports. But he really did not realize just how good he was until just after high school, when, because of his multisport interests, he had the unusual situation of being drafted by two professional sports at the same time: in baseball by the Braves, and in hockey by the NHL Los Angeles Kings.

While a pitcher for the New York Mets, Glavine was involved in a minor taxi accident in Manhattan just before a game. This resulted in an unusual interview as he had to write the answers to the questions, after having had his two front teeth knocked loose and then reimplanted. As is usually the case, Tom was a real trouper in keeping his word to go along with an interview. When asked what he did differently from his high school teammates to get into the major leagues he wrote: "I don't think it's really different. I work out year-round. It's a combination of hard work and God-given ability that has allowed me to be where I am today."

He also elaborated on the hard work required by the job that he has. Tom said, "A baseball player's work just isn't showing up on the field, doing the job, and leaving for the day. A player has to get up very early, sometimes going to a meeting at the hotel, then bus it over to the ballpark. From there, get to an early workout; training room;

maybe another clubhouse meeting; pitching/batting practice, which is universally called BP; then maybe a bite
to eat; somehow work in a few early press interviews;
then the game. After a game there are the ubiquitous
locker room interviews, discussions of mistakes, then
back to the hotel and getting ready for the next road game.
The entire day might be 12 hours in length. There are usually 165 games in a regular season, a few more games in
the playoffs if the team makes it there, and, of course, there
is spring training, which also has its 12-hour days." From
the outside looking in, a baseball player has a great job,
but from the inside looking
out, a baseball player's job
isn't as glamorous as it
seems.

> *From the outside looking in, a baseball player has a great job, but from the inside looking out, a baseball player's job isn't as glamorous as it seems.*

How does he keep it all
together? "Concentration is
very key. Every pitch is important, and you have to
block everything out and
execute that pitch. Also,
with technology the way it
is today, I watch a lot of
video and break down the opponents and study the
scouting reports." In other words, he learns to know the
enemy well ahead of time. However, the term "enemy" is a
bit harsh. The opposing team is usually made up of many
former and current friends of his, given his long tenure on
the field.

Barry Larkin encourages up-and-comers to stay with
their dreams. "I stuck with it. I worked at it hard. You have
to be determined to achieve your goals and dreams. A person has to anticipate and prepare for a situation before it

happens, whatever the scenario. That's how I got into college, and that's how the scouts found me."

John Smoltz of the Atlanta Braves is a very good example of how a player prepared himself to be in major league baseball. Smoltz told me he

did not let anyone dictate my goals to me. There was never any peer pressure for me to choose to play or not to play baseball, on a college or professional level. I started playing baseball at the age of 7, and by the end of 10th grade I knew that I could make it to the major-league level and that I had as much a chance as anyone. I stay focused on my goals. Once a person loses that focus, especially while out on the field during a game, they are done for. I have never done what is popular or what is pressured. I knew what I was getting into. Baseball is a game of failure. One has to accept that and view those lessons as positive reinforcement. I view failure as a lesson and that is what got me here.

Smoltz also added, "Failure motivates me, because failure can ruin you or make you better. Pressure also motivates me. It would be very difficult for me if there was no pressure in this game."

So what does Roger Clemens believe helped him get into the majors? Obviously a lot of things combined to make him a force to be reckoned with, much as the formation of a strong tropical storm or hurricane. Roger himself seems to have attained his place in baseball through the old method of constantly practicing and improving himself. On his off-days he is training. He is training just as fiercely as when he was a Red Sox rookie. He has always trained and worked out with far more intensity than his teammates have. Roger often says that the only off-day he has from training is the day he pitches, and even then that's not really an off-day.

Roger realizes what is expected of him. He once told a reporter, "It took a lot of work from a lot of guys in this clubhouse. It made it worth the wait. It made it worth my decision to come back. Playing this time of year never gets old."[12]

Roger Clemens knows that he made it to the majors on his own abilities.

Chapter 4

ONE FINE SUMMER

Now a part of Major League Baseball, Roger Clemens suddenly found himself living in what turned out to be a very tightly controlled organization and had quite a few adjustments to make both personally and professionally. Personally, he had to find his own place to live on a permanent basis away from home for the first time in his life. Social adjustments were sometimes daunting. Boston was very different from Texas. Bostonians perceived themselves as refined in their own certain ways. Texans also considered themselves refined in their own unique ways. Although Roger had heard of these differences, the most surprising thing to him was the different attitude of the Boston Red Sox fans, who were a very different group of people than any of the Texas fans he had met or played for during games. Boston fans were rowdy, very rowdy, and considered rude, especially when compared to the more genteel Texas fans of Roger's youth. This rowdiness was exacerbated when they played their rival, the New York Yankees. There was an unexplainable difference between their cool, public demeanor and their sometimes barbaric antics during games. This puzzled Roger and other visiting players, as well as the fans from other cities, and it still does today.

When Roger arrived, Boston seemed also to be consumed with their champions in another sport, the National Basketball Association (NBA) Boston Celtics, and another year of winning. For several years in a row, the Celtics either won the division, conference, or went all the way to the championship. Larry Bird was in his heyday and, along with the rest of the team, seemed to far overshadow the Boston Red Sox in many ways. To Roger, this was comparable to his arrival in Houston several years earlier as a teenager, when the Houston Oilers and their fever seemed to catch hold of everything in his new area. Eventually, the Celtics would go on to win an unprecedented 16 championships, the most of any NBA team in history. In addition to the Celtics, Doug Flutie of Boston College was another celebrity giant of the day. Flutie was at the start of his heyday and would win the 1984 Heisman Trophy. The trophy was named after John W. Heisman, who spent the last four years of his galactic career at Rice University in the 1920s. Wayne Graham, one of Clemens's coaches, would also end up at Rice in the last years of his career.

Roger quickly gained new friends in Boston. Good movies to grab during the 1984 year were *The Natural*, starring Robert Redford, Glenn Close, and Kim Basinger. This movie about baseball would have piqued the interest of Roger and his new friends, as it did with the entire country. Also, the hilarious *All of Me* hit the big screen, starring Steve Martin and Lily Tomlin, along with the Tom Hanks flagship movie of *Bachelor Party*, also starring Tawny Kitaen and Adrian Zmed. But the movie to take the lead that year was *Ghostbusters*, which starred the *Saturday Night Live*-famed Dan Aykroyd and Bill Murray and introduced Rick Moranis. The theme song of the movie played throughout baseball stadiums for the entire year, and then some, and it became the theme for the San Diego Padres during the 1984 World Series.

Roger was newly engaged. This showed that he was prepared to settle down in his personal life, and it reflected the maturity that he would need while in professional baseball. This and all other aspects showed Roger had a level of seriousness well ahead of his age.

Today, just as it was back in the 1980s, a player's life is dictated by an unyielding schedule from spring training until the very last game of the season. A description of this will help aid a better understanding of what Clemens would have been going through. This schedule not only governed what time the players had to be at the ballpark, eat, work out, and practice, but it also seeped into their personal lives. Unless there was a grave illness or death in the immediate family, there was very little time to spend with family during the season. Even when there were home games, the player had to be at work early. Sometimes, the games and postgame duties lasted until past midnight. Then, the entire process started all over again in the morning. As in many other high-pressure jobs, this took

> *Roger was newly engaged. This showed that he was prepared to settle down in his personal life, and it reflected the maturity that he would need while in professional baseball.*

its toll on the family lives of many players and was also to blame for breakups of marriages.

A typical day for any player is a well-known routine. Whether the game is a homestand game or an away game, the players arrive within an appointed window of time, usually four hours before game time. The earlier the player gets there the more he has time to chill out, eat a meal in the stark team dining room, or to catch up on e-mail with family and friends. The home team has parking under the building near the service ramp, while the visiting team gets there by taxi, private car, or, most often, the team bus from the hotel. The hotel is not usually as luxurious as one would expect.

The first place a player goes to in the ballpark is the team clubhouse. Although the general public often views this clubhouse as a mysterious and luxurious hangout, it is nothing like that at all. Located under the stands and just up the ramps from the dugout, it is a beehive of pregame activity. As you walk in just behind the dugout is a service area with bottled water, sunflower seeds, and other supplies. A small restroom for dugout emergencies is a sparse convenience. The dugout after a game is a hideous sight, especially considering that grown men have just been there. Candy wrappers, bags of chew, spit, and other spilled fluids are spattered all around. It has to be pressure washed after each game. Anyone who has ever seen a postgame dugout soon realizes that a bridge party has not just happened there.

Up the concrete-walled access stairs is the clubhouse, behind closed, steel double doors. This area can be compared to the back stage of a concert or play. In a way, baseball has been compared many times to a form of ballet. Technically, the clubhouses are supposed to be equal in size and amenities for both visiting and home teams, but the home team invariably has the superior digs. Behind the steel doors there is a carpeted hallway that spiders off and leads to several offices for coaches and managers. Alongside the hall, a player dining room awaits with a buffet steam table that's occasionally waited on by a chef. The players and staff refer to this food as "the spread." It has been toppled over in anger one too many times by upset players or managers after an upsetting loss. Soft drinks, juice dispensers, and microwaves are there for those bringing their own meals. One might get quite a surprise to walk by and see Morgan Ensberg toasting his own

> *Although the general public often views this clubhouse as a mysterious and luxurious hangout, it is nothing like that at all.*

waffles and pouring on syrup, alone, under a burned-out light fixture, looking quite content with the snack that he had managed to put together. Or to encounter the very naturally enthusiastic Brian Giles discussing various things with his fellow team members while gulping down a snack.[1]

Across the hall from the dining room is a small gym for last-minute warm-ups and a physical therapy room where the cold or hot packs are applied or a rubdown is given. Nearby is the player locker room, including a big-screen plasma television with just about every channel or technology on earth connected to it. There are also computers for surfing the Internet. Personal laptops seem not to be a priority for baseball players. Leather sofas, lounge chairs, and coffee tables with current magazine subscriptions are for relaxation. This contrasts with the sparse sling-back director's chairs at each locker. The entire locker room seems to be the center point for the players to relax and enjoy a few things before the game. There is still time for a card game or a game of checkers. Horseplay and razzing abound. Off to the side is a small, tiled hall leading to the private restrooms and showers, which are off-limits to anyone but the players. Along the tiled walls and sinks, hundreds of new or used bottles of soaps and colognes are scattered, as if in some quirky dollar store, for the next group of players to use.

Just down the carpeted hall is a door to the batting cages and the eventual bullpen. It's interesting to note that the term "bullpen" didn't get its meaning from the players penned up inside there. Rather, it was originally an unused holding area that took its name from an early advertiser in baseball sponsorship by the name of Bull Durham Tobacco. Even back then, the naming rights' game had begun. Ironically, given the once close association of baseball with tobacco and alcohol, both are banned below deck with severe punishment for those who violate the rule. Also strategically placed within the clubhouse walls is a small press conference room, where coaches or managers and sometimes players answer to the press before or after a game on posted issues or matters of the moment. If a major development unfolds, a larger press conference room is used in another part of the building.

At the end of all the rooms, past all nooks and crannies of the clubhouse, the carpeted hallway ends in another set of secured, double steel doors that open up into the service level of the building. Here a security guard stops all who enter and leave. Golf carts, luggage buggies, security vehicles, and maintenance equipment line the circumference of the entire stadium. The private parking area for players, owners, and staff terminates this level leading up onto the street.

But even with all the apparent luxuries, the painted concrete block walls are a reminder of where one happens to be. Everyone is walking underneath tons of steel and concrete.

The true major-league baseball fan believes you can never really experience the fullness of a game by just listening to it on the radio or by watching it on television. However, according to what the great Baseball Hall of Fame broadcaster Milo Hamilton has always said, "Baseball is a game for radio."[2] Of course he would be very happy to see you there at the ballpark in person. One has to catch the essence of the game, the aroma of the grills at the food courts, and the sights and sounds that just can't be captured on radio or television. You have to be there in person. There are barks and sounds of kids as they hold out a ball for Albert Pujols or Jim Edmonds or another great player to sign. And then there are the smiles on their faces from that experience. "There you go, young man, this one's for you," Pujols says as he hands the ball back to a kid. Mike Grimman brought his two sons from Austin to Houston for the St. Louis Cardinals vs. Astros games. "With experiences like all this, it doesn't get any better for anyone!" he says. The sound of the first pitch being caught by the catcher, or that pop of a bat that announces well ahead of time that, yes, indeed, it is a grand slam, would cause the great Milo Hamilton to say at that point, "Holy Toledo!"[3]

What goes on when the public sees baseball owners and managers having a good time with the players during press conferences and such is often quite different than what happens behind the scenes. There is tension, big tension. Even in happy times the stress works into all aspects of team life. The handshaking at a press conference that the public sees when a player is signed to a team is often in stark contrast to what has just occurred on the other side of the conference room doors. There are many unkind words during the negotiations. The player is often worked over about his abilities and value to the potential team. The owners continually bring up failures and errors, while the agents have to remind the owners of successes. This process often takes days, weeks, or even months before a negotiated settlement is reached. Then, the media is called in, and the wonderful saga of baseball continues with a barrage of flashbulbs, handshakes, and bear hugs. Once the cameras are gone, the tension continues on both sides of the sword. It does not end.

Whatever tension Roger was feeling must have been quickly alleviated by his sense of history when he first walked into Fenway Park that May of 1984. As a pitcher he was obviously proud that he had made it to the home of the great Cy Young. Fenway Park opened in 1912, just five days after the sinking of the ocean liner *Titanic*. The *Titanic* disaster was so enormous that it captured all media attention for weeks, making it hard for the ballclub to make front-page news. Through Fenway Park's history it has served up quite a few greats in baseball lore. In addition to Cy Young, there have been the legendary Babe Ruth, Jimmy Collins, Duffy Lewis, Joe Cronin, Bobby Doerr, Johnny Pesky, Ted Williams, Carlton Fisk, Jim Rice, and Carl Yastrzemski, and now, he hoped, Roger Clemens would add his name to that spectacular list. At the time of his debut, Fenway Park was and still is the oldest ballpark in existence.

One of the first things that amazed everyone, and probably Roger, about Fenway Park, besides its well-seasoned age and history, was that it still used its ancient manual-drive scoreboard.[4] This was 1984, and all stadiums and ballparks used state-of-the-art scoreboards, especially after the opening of the Houston Astrodome in 1965 with its animated scoreboard. Fenway's appeared to be digital but instead used solid-state equipment, so each movement was controlled with a light bulb. More than a million bulbs created motion or a rehash of the score.

Roger's first manager was the infamous Ralph Houk, whom he called "the Major" and for good reason. Actually, everyone called Houk "the Major." Of all the nicknames in baseball, his was the most appropriate. Houk was in the minor leagues with the New York Yankees when World War II broke out. Houk wasn't drafted; rather, he enlisted, as the majority of young men did back then during a national crisis. He soon found himself in battle and was promoted to major. When the war was over, his uniform had a decorated chest "that looked like the Fourth of July," with metals such as the Purple Heart, Silver Star, Bronze Star, and the appropriate metals of his rank. Clemens, who was very keen on respecting what servicemen have done for the world, held Houk in high esteem. Houk immediately returned to professional baseball when his war service was over and soon attained major-league status in the Yankees' organization. He debuted in the same year as Yankees great Lawrence "Yogi" Berra. His greatest accomplishment during his major-league days as a player was an overall batting average of .272. He appeared in two World Series. The Boston Red Sox courted Houk for years, even after Houk had officially retired. After the Red Sox fired manager Don Zimmer, they contacted Houk, who

> *Clemens, who was very keen on respecting what servicemen have done for the world, held Houk in high esteem.*

immediately took the job of skipper for the Red Sox. He was demanding but was known as a player's manager rather than someone who kowtowed to owners or to the press. When Houk took over the Boston Red Sox in 1981 as manager, the team had already lost such core greats as Fred Lynn and Carlton Fisk. His job was going to be one of rebuilding, and he quickly sought out and began to build up players such as Marty Barrett, Bruce Hurst, Wade Boggs, and now Roger Clemens.[5]

It was obvious that Roger had a very high degree of respect for Houk. As much work and loyalty that Houk demanded from Roger, Roger demanded even more from himself and also of Houk. Roger saw in Houk his chance to succeed, but the difference was that Roger was one who appreciated all opportunities given to him or, rather, the opportunities Clemens garnered through hard work. Houk undoubtedly must have seen in Roger his control and his confidence, two major things that are key to the success of any player. Roger devoured each chance to succeed, and this did not go unnoticed by the powers that be. Even after Houk retired in October 1984 at the age of 65, relinquishing his duties to John McNamara, Roger kept in touch. Houk had left the team with three years of over .500 records.

Major-league baseball meant major-league pitching to Roger. Although he was confident of his abilities, he feared that he was still pitching in a minor-league fashion. To remedy this fear, he practiced longer than the other team members and even worked out at home. He worked as a possessed fanatic to find his own style and to become more comfortable with what he believed to be that major-league style. While he wasn't yet known as the Rocket at this time, he wanted to feel worthy. He concentrated on his pitching mechanics, focusing on the form and function of his pitch. He analyzed the first part of his pitching, called the windup. The pitching coach had his ideas, and the other team members of the pitching crew lent their ideas. Roger had his own. He had his arm swing, the second mechanical component, filmed and dissected in one analytical review after another. The arm acceleration received the same treatment, as did his follow-through, or delivery, which created the result of a curveball, a slider, or any other of the inventory of pitches that Roger possessed. He didn't invent these pitches—they had been around since the 1870s—he just improved them for his own unique form. He worked on all this until he was confident that his mechanics suited him and his individual style. But most important, he knew that any miscalculation of strength or in his style could be potentially disastrous for him physically. Even the slightest error in any of these areas, albeit minor and undetectable, would show up after a few hundred pitches. A damaged shoulder or other injury would not do him or his team any good.

Years before Roger rose to the major leagues, pitchers would routinely pitch the entire game. Today, that rarely happens. Coaches make use of closing, or relief, pitchers in addition to the starting pitcher, which is the most revered and sought after of the position titles. With today's use of so many pitchers, they still see the rewards, because once a pitcher reaches the magical 300-win mark, he is ceremoniously eligible for the Hall of Fame. This benchmark has been a standard for years, and this notch might have to be tweaked just a little to adjust for modern times. Since many more players are used on the pitching roster than in previous years, a pitcher might only get to pitch every fourth or fifth day. This dramatically reduces the frequency of his wins, even if his pitching is equivalent to that of a great potential Hall of Fame inductee, such as Clemens or Maddux.

Around this time, film was gradually being replaced by video and would eventually be replaced by digital video. These technological developments made Roger's review of films of the habits of his opponents much easier. Roger would watch films and videos of upcoming hitters and study their style. He concentrated on their stance and their habits while they were at bat. Moreover, he studied their body language. To this day it's known that he studies boxes of videos, whether he is pitching or not. But on the opposite side of the coin, Roger also worked on how to avoid tipping his pitching, because just as a pitcher can decipher a batter's style and habits, he knew that the batter had also been watching films and videos of him and his habits. Clemens was meticulous about this aspect of his job. A pitcher might unconsciously exhibit a certain stance or style and be quickly figured out by the opponent. Roger had to guard against that. Cleverly, he knew that he could also use that aspect as a ploy to confuse a batter. The way he held his arm, his leg movements, body language, and so on could be used to make the batter think that a certain pitch was about to fly out, only to have another style come at him. All the practicing on his pitching style paid dividends nicely.

> *Throughout the years, one of the hallmarks of baseball has been superstition, both for the players and for the fans.*

Throughout the years, one of the hallmarks of baseball has been superstition, both for the players and for the fans. Roger almost immediately picked up on these superstitions and honored them with the pride of his predecessors, possibly to be accepted as part of the pack or to find some sort of meaning in it all. It is important to note that a baseball player will usually deny having any superstitions, because one does not talk about his fears or insecurities during the game. Of the players asked about this aspect of the sport, none admitted to having any superstitions. To them, it is reality. To break the code by admitting to having a superstition would be to crack their luck, even if they have been on a losing streak.

One of the earliest superstitions Roger adopted was not speaking to anyone at the stadium on the day he pitched. This is common to almost all pitchers. They claim this is needed to help them "stay in the zone" of concentration and not be distracted by executives, media hounds, and fans. Some would avoid talking about the subject of winning, especially when they were on winning streaks, in order to avoid jinxing the lucky situation in which they had found themselves. Other superstitions have something to do with the fixation on an object or a practice. Some wear their lucky jersey, unwashed. Some have a pregame ceremony of putting on an article of clothing backward. Some eat a certain food or meal before a game. Khalil Greene is known to eat tuna fish right out of the can before a game; however, he told me that this is because of his intense dietary regime, not because of a superstition. Many superstitions get started because of earlier habits that might reassure a player that he is doing the right thing. Subconsciously a player might choose to do something to calm himself, and that calming might be all that it takes to attain the winning edge. Or, for the more wary, it serves to shake off the evil spirits and allows him to get on with the game and to win.

Admittedly, most superstitions are based on some truth. As an example, prehistoric humans were superstitious about thunder, and they would hide in their dens until the monster cloud was gone. Anyone caught out during such thunder ran the risk of not coming back. This fear came from the misunderstood reality of the cause of thunder, which obviously is lightning. The experience of having some of their crew struck by lightning, followed by thunder, gave rise to this superstition. It is true that there is a difference between cavemen and modern baseball players and their respective superstitions. However, superstitions help to muster the confidence of a player, and confidence is one of the basic building blocks of a player's success.

Roger was nearing the age of 22 when he rookied in 1984. He found himself in the American League, which prided itself on being better than the National League. Ironically, the National League was the older of the two, resulting from a split starting in the late 1800s. Back then, the National League controlled all major teams. When some of the teams were dropped for the new 1900 season, they formed themselves into the American League, which then attained more teams by 1901. This league rivalry would play a role in the last part of Clemens's career, when he would come out of retirement from the American League and join the National League in 2004. Some viewed that "un-retirement" as a swipe at his past teams. Others viewed it as a factor of changing times. In any case, Roger arrived as the youngest member of the Boston Red Sox for that year and wore the number 21, the same number that he had worn during his University of Texas days. Teammate Charlie Mitchell, number 38, also born in 1962, was just 41 days older than Clemens was. Mitchell's career would take him through just one more season; his career cut short by injury. Mitchell's experience was an early warning flag to Roger, and it probably left him with a lasting impression. The oldest member of the team was Rick Miller, born in 1948, making him 36 at that time. Miller's baseball career would take him just one more year, when he retired with a 15-year career at the end of the 1985 season. Ironically, Roger arrived in the majors as the youngest on his team. Toward the end of his career, he would consistently be the oldest member of the teams on which he played.

Clemens quickly attained the confidence of his fellow teammates, and especially important was the support of his fellow pitchers. Pitchers for the 1984 Red Sox team were Dennis "Oil Can" Boyd, whose career would last until retirement in 1991. Because he was the second Dennis of the team, they used his nickname of Oil Can instead. Dennis Eckersley, the first Dennis, who was known as "Eck," would retire in 1998 after a stellar 24-year career. Al Nipper, nicknamed "Nip" by his teammates, also a rookie that year, would go on to Chicago and Cleveland before retirement in 1990. He eventually came back to the Boston Red Sox as a coach. Bobby Ojeda would have his final major-league game in 1994. Bob Stanley would stay in Boston for the remaining five years of his career. Bruce Hurst would eventually move on to the San Diego Padres and retire 10 years later. Steve Crawford would move to the Kansas City Royals five years later and would retire in 1991. Mike Brown would have just three more years in his career. Mark Clear soon moved off to the Milwaukee Brewers and retired in 1991. Jim Dorsey would end his major-league career in 1985, as would Charlie Mitchell, and John Johnson moved off to Milwaukee for his last year in 1987. Rich Gale's career would end with the close of the Bo Sox 1984 season.

It has often been said that the catcher is "the third arm of the pitcher." The catcher's roster for that year included Jeff Newman, who would retire at the end of that season after an eight-year stint. Also in the roster was Gary Allenson, who would retire after a move to Toronto in 1985. Rich Gedman, who would move on to St. Louis and retire in 1992. There was also Marc Sullivan, who would stay with the Boston Red Sox and then retire in 1987. Roger knew that a catcher's ability to communicate with the pitcher, both in words and actions before a game and during practice and workouts and in the unspoken signals and actions during a game to avoid tipping the opponent, was paramount. In every team that Roger has played on, he has built working relationships with the catchers in order to secure a better chance of success on the field. Since the old days of baseball, this relationship between the pitcher and the catcher has been called "battery mates."

Roger Clemens almost certainly knows of a baseball legend who originaed many of these pitching, catching, and field signals, potential future Hall of Famer William Ellsworth "Dummy" Hoy. He played major-league baseball from 1888 to 1903. At only 5-foot-6 in height and a gaunt 162 pounds, Hoy was deaf and mute. In those days, his condition was called "deaf and dumb," hence the nickname of "Dummy," although most people called him William or Bill. He not only accepted his fate of becoming deaf in early childhood but also of not learning the ability to communicate the spoken word because of it. It was a time period when people with disabilities were often subject to ridicule. His ability to play baseball far exceeded his disabilities, and, while unknown at the time, his signals were to become the foundation for the signals used to this very day by umpires, players, and catchers in baseball. In the new American League, he was the first player ever to hit what is now termed a "grand slam." His fans have made sure that his legacy survives. He died in 1961 just short of his 100th birthday and a few weeks after he had ceremoniously thrown out the first ball in the third game of the 1961 World Series, where his Cincinnati Reds were up against the New York Yankees. To the very end, he was often invited to throw out the first pitch or officiate at ceremonies in recognition of his accomplishments. Followers still support the idea that he is worthy of a place in the Hall of Fame, and he has already been installed in the Ohio Baseball Hall of Fame and the Cincinnati Reds' Hall of Fame.[6]

In addition to the pitchers and catchers, Mike Easler was the most utilized designated hitter by the Red Sox. In the American League, pitchers rarely come up to bat. Their place in the lineup is filled in by using the DH, or designated hitter. The hitters, or batters, for the 1984 lineup included Marty Barrett, whose career would eventually end with the San Diego Padres in 1991, and Wade Boggs, who would go on to even greater fame in years to come with a career that in many ways would rival that of Roger's. Boggs would go on to the New York Yankees with Roger and then to the Tampa Bay Devil Rays until his retirement in 1999. Bill Buckner would leave, then come back to Boston, and retire in 1990. Jackie Gutierrez went off to the Baltimore Orioles two years later and then to the Philadelphia Phillies before ending his career in 1988. Glenn Hoffman would change to the California Angels and retire in 1989. Ed Jurak's career would end with the San Francisco Giants in 1989. Jerry Remy, known as "Rem Dog," was in his last year of major-league service. Dave Stapleton would stay his entire career with Boston and retire in 1988, and Chico Walker would bounce from Boston to the Chicago Cubs and to the New York Mets until he retired in 1993.

On his June 6 appearance against the Milwaukee Brewers at their then County Stadium, Clemens helped defeat the opponent 6 runs to 2. On June 7, he suffered his first loss, which was against the Brewers, 6 runs to 3. He had his first credit as a Fenway Park winning pitcher on June 22 with an 8 to 1 defeat of the Toronto Blue Jays. It would seem as if his arm would never give out, with wins against the White Sox on July 26, 7 runs to 0, and his defeat of the White Sox again on July 31, 14 runs to 4. The August 6 game against the Detroit Tigers resulted in another amazing defeat of the opponent, 10 runs to 2. The August 11 game in Arlington was a defeat for the Rangers, 5 to 4. Perhaps a precursor, or an omen, of what was to come in his career happened on August 21, where Roger was the winning pitcher in a game against the Royals. There he struck out 15 Royals and walked none, resulting in an 11 to 1 win for the team. It amazed the crowd and attracted press attention. During his 1984 debut season, Clemens struck out an amazing amount of batters, 126 of them, which was the most by a Boston Red Sox rookie since the 1970 major-league

> *During his 1984 debut season, Clemens struck out an amazing amount of batters, 126 of them, which was the most by a Boston Red Sox rookie since the 1970 major-league season.*

season. He had 20 starts for the club with 21 appearances, resulting in a record of 9 wins to 4 losses. Five of these games were complete games for him, where he pitched all innings. He had a total of three games of 10-plus strikeouts. In his last six starts, he was 6 to 0, resulting in an ERA of 2.63. The first shutout was on July 26 at Chicago in a 7 to 0 win, and he struck out 11 hitters. The first and only relief appearance for his career as a Red Sox was on July 18 at Oakland, where Boston lost 7 runs to 2. Because of all of Roger's accomplishments that year, the Boston Writers Association named him the Co-Rookie of the Year, an honor shared with his pitching teammate Al Nipper. It was easy to see how his nickname would eventually become the "Rocket." Clemens looked upon his debut in the major leagues as a successful event. Although he saw his ERA become a corpulent 4.32, it was well known that it was because of an injury and that he had years ahead of him to prove otherwise that a legend was in the making.

In late summer, the first of several small mishaps befell Roger. He was put on the disabled list from July 3 through early August of that year because of an injury to his right shoulder. He probably viewed this as a warning shot for his abilities, as it had begun to draw down on his ERA, and worse yet, any more severe injuries could cut short his career. But on August 26 of that year, he suffered the worst of the many injuries in his career. While pitching to Cleveland, he suffered a forearm and shoulder injury that proved to be so severe that it cut short his year. Clemens would have to have to undergo surgery in September, and the resulting physical therapy and healing process would place him on and force him to remain on the disabled list for the rest of the 1984 season.

The 1984 All-Star Game took place in San Francisco's Candlestick Park on July 10. The National League was on a winning streak and won the game 3 to 1. Gary Carter of the Montreal Expos, now called the Washington (DC) Nationals, was voted MVP. For the 1984 season, Ryne Sandberg of the Chicago Cubs was voted the National League's MVP, and for the American League, Willie Hernandez of the Detroit Tigers received the honor. Roger Clemens would miss out on being chosen the Rookie of the Year; the American League honor went to Alvin Davis of the Seattle Mariners. The National League honor went to Dwight Gooden of the Mets.

Roger Clemens watched intensely the playoffs for the 1984 season, in which the Detroit Tigers of the Eastern Division of the American League faced the Western Division's Kansas City Royals. The Tigers would win 3 to 0. In the National League, the Eastern Division Chicago Cubs would play the Western Division champion San Diego Padres. The Padres would go on to win 3 to 2. The Detroit Tigers won the resulting World Series for 1984 on October 14 in Game 5 over the San Diego Padres, 8 to 4. They won the Series 4 games to 1 and gave Detroit its first World Series victory since 1968. The one game the Padres won, Game 2, is widely known as their only win in their history of attempts at the World Series; they won it 5 runs to 3. Kirk Gibson of the Tigers was given the nod as the World Series' MVP. An unusual note to their victory is that from day one the Tigers sailed through the entire season ahead of all the rest of the American League, giving them the best performance of the 1980s.

For the 1984 season, Boston finished fourth in the final standings in the American League, just below their rivals the New York Yankees. In second place were the Toronto

Blue Jays with Detroit at the top of the heap. The Red Sox had missed out on the playoffs, but Ralph Houk could boast a record of over .500. The fans, as could be expected, were unhappy that the team failed once again, as they had since 1975, to compete in the postseason. There was no "wild card" standing in the 1980s as there is today. The worst game of the year was on April 8, 1984, where Boston lost to the Oakland Athletics, 2 runs to 14, in a game that some could view as a massacre. Boston's record was improving by the summer after Roger appeared on the mound, and its best game of the year was the July 31 win over the Chicago White Sox, 14 to 4. The last Boston Red Sox game of the 1984 season was on September 30 and left them with 86 wins and 76 losses. Their home winning percentage was a respectable .507; they won 41 games and lost 40. Their away winning percentage was an excellent .556, having won 45 games and lost 36.

It was not until after the season ended that Roger's greatest accomplishment of the year occurred. Earlier in the year he had proposed to his steady girlfriend, Debbie Godfrey, and married her on Saturday, November 24, 1984, over Thanksgiving weekend. Roger's close family attended the charming wedding, an event that was not possible to arrange during any other time of the year because of the demands of baseball. Roger was 22 when he married, and it obviously made him the happiest man in the world. Thus, the number 22 began its subtle association with Roger; toward the end of his career it would have major symbolism. After the wedding, when the couple returned to town, they shopped around the Boston area for a home and found a small Cape Cod–style home not too far from Fenway Park. They reassured friends and relatives that their main home would always be in Houston so that they could be with the rest of the family. The new Boston house would remain their home there for years until Roger moved on to the Toronto Blue Jays in 1997.

Debbie Godfrey Clemens was born in Arlington, Texas, in 1963 and, as was the case with many Dallas citizens of the day, was not too far from the eventful motorcade of President John F. Kennedy and Texas governor John Connally when it passed on November 22, 1963. Although she had met Roger while they both were at Spring Woods Senior High, her family moved a lot, and she graduated from Cypress Fairbanks High School a few miles north of Spring Woods. After college and after Roger was drafted into the leagues, they met again and the rest is history.[7] Debbie's warm personality and style quickly gained her friends from all parts of their new "away" town of Boston; her friendliness also helped to garner friends in whatever city to which she and Roger moved. The two would set an example of a stable marriage and a loving family unit in a baseball world that was sometimes known for its unstable and dysfunctional family life.[8]

> *Sports in general were becoming more commercial than they ever had been in the past; players participated in more advertising spots and the number of commercials during a game increased.*

At the time of Roger's debut, when a baseball star pitched products in advertising, his words were respected. One of Roger's first advertising gigs was with an athletic shoe manufacturer. Sports in general were becoming more commercial than they ever had been in the past; players participated in more advertising spots and the number of commercials during a game increased. It was the start of the overcommercialization of sports. In years past, fans would go to a game or watch it on television or radio and be out of there and on with their lives when the game was over after a couple of hours. Today, a game might last five hours even when a deadlock doesn't require extra innings. Commercials are taking up more time during the innings' breaks. Fans sitting it out in the stands during these longer breaks were often directed to buy the products offered at the stadiums, such as the food, drink, and souvenirs. Today, an All-Star Game has much more commercial advertising, and other sports, such as football, basketball, and hockey, are also beefing up their advertising inventories. Billboards have been a staple of baseball advertising since the beginning. Today, they encircle the stadium both inside and out like a vacuum-packed candy wrapper. The invention of the changeable billboard one sees on television saw a boon of ad revenue to team owners, not to mention the naming rights for the ballparks, their suites, and even the parking areas. Advertising has always been around, but in some ways the game is cheapened by it.

Since Roger first stepped onto the mound back in 1984, team loyalty has also changed dramatically. Baseball has always morphed to keep up with the times, but loyalty seems to be more challenged today. Loyalty for a player back then was to stay with a few major teams. Today, a player will leave his team just as quickly as his team owner would trade him. However, now there is more of a chance for a player on a smaller franchise team to become a legend, and for a smaller, less-financed team to succeed and make it to the World Series. In addition, a lack of team loyalty can inadvertently worked in a fan's favor. A favorite player on a team across the country could pull up stakes and end up on a closer team, with a hometown advantage. On all sides, there seems to be an increasing amount of abbreviated appreciation.

But Roger was, and still is, obviously a responsible person when it came to his newly found fame and income. In all of his life, since childhood to newly married adulthood, he never had substantial amounts of money to spend freely. Old habits are hard to break, especially if they have been ingrained in a person. A few of the other players who showed up to camp may have had sports cars and other forms of bling-bling, but not Roger Clemens. The most he would splurge on would be a golf vacation for himself and his new bride. (They have always been and are still very avid golf fans.) The purchase of a house, an appreciable asset, showed Roger's responsibility for the future and to his family. He would also get things for the rest of his family back in Houston, especially his mom. She had always sacrificed so much for him and his brothers and sisters. Now it was his turn to return the joy.

To Clemens, it was all about the fans, especially the little fans. He often is quoted as saying, "What the fans have always done for me is to help me get going."[9] He thrived off the crowd and their unwavering support. During his stay in Boston he and Debbie devoted much of their time and donations to various children's charities. He wanted to ease their suffering, because in some primal way, he related to their hurt. Roger would many times buy tickets for local needy children so that they could experience a real, live baseball game for the first time in their lives.

And now, with his debut major-league season over, his new status as a married man, and finding himself now in the national media focus, Roger Clemens had a great sense of what changes were to come in his life and career. He knew that handling it all would be one of his greatest challenges.

Chapter 5

———————— ROCKET ROGER ————————

With the completion of the dramatic 1984 season, Roger Clemens had received his first full year of what would turn out to be over two decades of fame. He may have looked upon it as bittersweet. His hard work and his impressive show during the season brought him the attention of media and fans, but he also suffered an injury that laid him off for a good chunk of the season, something no one would look upon as good for his career. Roger knew that he was called up to the majors from the minors after Oil Can Boyd had been sent down to the minor-league Paw Sox for a rehab assignment during the spring of 1984. He was wary not to let that happen to him.

Far into the winter of 1984-85 he was recovering from his orthoscopic surgery, which left him stiff and out of shape. The recovery process also entailed lots of physical therapy immediately after surgery. Orthoscopic or not, it was a painful procedure to go through as the surgery had not yet advanced to the point it is today. When all of the healing and physical therapy were complete, Roger was able to get back into his monstrous routine schedule of workouts and practice, which he kept up even in the off-season. Although the thought of injuring himself through a rigorous practice session had crossed his mind, he was able to stay focused and keep his training in "the zone."

The 1985 Boston Red Sox roster saw a few changes. Roger's pitching teammate, Dennis "Eck" Eckersley was traded in the previous year to the Chicago Cubs for Bill "Billy Buck" Buckner. The pitching roster was expanded for 1985 from its size in previous years. This was the plan of Major Houk, who believed pitching to be a team's greatest chance at success. He would be proven correct. He would bring in several new pitchers. Added to the pitching roster for the year were Bruce Kison from the California Angels and Tim Lollar from the Chicago White Sox. Tom McCarthy was a rookie that year, as were Jeff Sellers, Mike Trujillo, and Rob Woodward.

Skipper Ralph Houk retired from baseball for good at the end of the 1984 season, leaving the Red Sox with three memorable seasons of above .500 averages. His successor, John McNamara, was 14 years younger. McNamara's playing career had taken him only to the minor leagues as a catcher, but his managing skills, although sometimes controversial, were what got him into the majors. He originally managed the Oakland A's in 1969 at the age of 37, one of the youngest skippers in the American League at that time. After moving on to the San Diego Padres in 1974, he lasted there until the middle of the 1977 season and didn't manage again until the Cincinnati Reds hired him in 1979. He then moved on to the California Angels until he was hired to replace the retired Houk in 1985.

For his second year in the majors, Clemens was well aware of what was termed the "sophomore slump." The term is mainly applied to musical performers and the release of their second album and to athletes at the start of their second year. The honeymoon that he experienced as a rookie was over. Although Roger had not received any sort of special treatment during his rookie debut, he would now have to prove that he was not a flash in the pan pitcher. With his surgery behind him, he practiced and worked out to avoid such a slump. All athletes, especially in baseball, dread being labeled as some sort of flavor of the month. But it would turn out that Roger would not have to worry about his sophomore slump, at least not for another few months.

The season for Clemens, and the rest of the Red Sox, got off to a terrific start. The first three games were a homestand against the rival New York Yankees. The series was a complete shutout against the Yanks. Oil Can Boyd pitched the opener on April 8, 1985, winning it 9 to 2. Bruce Hurst pitched the next day, winning it 14 to 5. Roger's first game of the year was the next game, where he led the team to victory 6 runs to 4. The Red Sox's next victims were the Chicago White Sox, who lost to the Red Sox 7 runs to 2. Boston now had 4

> *For his second year in the majors, Clemens was well aware of what was termed the "sophomore slump."*

wins and 0 losses. But the next day the White Sox won and then won again. Soon the Red Sox's stellar start became a dead even heap and stayed that way for the entire year, with them constantly fighting to maintain the .500 mark.

Roger fared the same. His win against the Yankees for his first start was followed by a loss at his next start against the Kansas City Royals on April 16 in Kansas City. Boston lost 2 runs to 0. Roger again was the losing pitcher in the

April 21 game against the hosting Chicago White Sox at Comiskey Park, losing 7 to 2. By midseason Roger's record was dead even also, with 4 wins and 4 losses. Part of the situtation could be attributed to lack of run support by his teammates, similar to what would occur in the later years of his career. But much of it could have also been placed on the constantly growing pain in his right shoulder; his previous surgery may have caused him to overcompensate during training rehabilitation and pitching.

Roger continued with his scheduled pitches, and everyone was convinced that he was on a positive turnaround when he completely closed down the Cleveland Indians during the May 17 game, his first professional shutout and 10-strikeout game. Unfortunately, after the game, the shoulder pain increased, leaving him wrapped in layers of ice packs and undergoing additional massage therapy. He was able to pitch in only a few more games, but each time, he suffered more pain. The dreaded "bad arm" rumor that had dogged him since the time of his college days began to pop up again in media circles. His last game of the year was August 11 against the unrelenting New York Yankees; he would be the losing pitcher, 3 runs to 5. Two and a half weeks of pain were alleviated with physical therapy, cold or hot packs, and anything that was available in the mid-1980s. Finally on August 30 Roger checked himself in to have orthoscopic surgery to scrape off shards of cartilage in his right rotator cuff. Again, as had been the case with the previous season, he missed the remainder of the 1985 games while on the disabled list. The dreaded sophomore slump had indeed proven itself in a very public way. It has been said that the 1985 season for Roger was one of the worst in his career, with only a sparse 98.3 innings pitched and a 7 to 5 win-to-loss ratio.

Clemens again watched the 1985 All-Star Game as a fan and not as a participant. He did, however, see three of his teammates get to play in the game. Wade Boggs was there as pitcher, Jim Rice as outfielder, and Rich Gedman as catcher. Roger's idol, Nolan Ryan, appeared on the roster for the National League. The game was played in the Metrodome in Minneapolis, Minnesota, on July 16. The National League was still on its roll and it beat the American League 6 runs to 1. It was the 13th win in a row for the National League at the All-Star Game. New for the 1985 All-Star Game was the Home Run Derby. Held the evening before the main game, it brought in additional ticket sales from fans who wanted to see many of their favorite players up at bat, even some pitchers who rarely went up at bat.

Nolan Ryan, just a few days previously, made history on July 11 by becoming the first player ever to reach the 4,000-strikeout level. The Astros faced the New York Mets and won the game 4 to 3. Ryan struck out the Mets' Danny Heep to attain the illustrious standing.

On August 4, the 23rd birthday of Roger Clemens, two more incredible events occurred in baseball that would change the record books. On that day, Tom Seaver became the 17th pitcher attain the 300-win mark with a win against the Yankees at Yankee Stadium, and Rod Carew of the California Angels became the 16th player to attain the 3,000-career-hits level off the Minnesota Twins. Incredibly, in Chicago, Dwight "Doc" Gooden won his 11th straight victory when his New York Mets beat the Chicago Cubs 4 to 1.

But a few days later a black mark would scar baseball for years to come. The Major League Players Association staged a walk-off strike in order to change the compensation rules. This time the strike only lasted one day, unlike the previous 1979 strike that lasted 50 days. The lost games would be made up during the regular season. The sudden settlement left some issues unresolved, and they would eventually come to a head a few years later in the catastrophic 1994 player strike.

As if to rub salt in the wounds of the Red Sox, suffering through a flatter than usual year for the team, it was a year of records for the leagues in general. On October 6, the last day of the regular season, Phil Niekro of the New York Yankees attained the 300-win level. At 46 years of age, he was and still is the oldest pitcher to have attained that mark, and while doing so, he threw a shutout game against the Toronto Blue Jays. The career of Niekro is also remembered because he reached 121 career victories after the age of 40.

The best of seven showed itself to be controversial or at least provocative that year in the series between the Kansas City Royals and the Toronto Blue Jays.

For the entire year, the Red Sox ended up with 81 wins and 81 losses, with 1 tie. In their best games, they won the May 3 game at Oakland with their 10 runs to 0 for the Athletics. A spectacular defeat of the Cleveland Indians came on August 29, 17 to 2, with Bruce Hurst as the winning pitcher.

The baseball postseason that year marked the first time that the format for the American League and the National League Championship Series was changed from a best-of-five format to a best-of-seven series. The new baseball commissioner, Peter Ueberroth, and others in Major League Baseball supported this change, because more games meant more money and the newer expansion teams might have a better chance of attaining playoff status. The added revenues would total in the millions for 1985 alone. And, because the average player's salary was just over $370,000, the added revenues went far. The divisional series still remains in the best-of-five format.

The best of seven showed itself to be controversial or at least provocative that year in the series between the Kansas City Royals and the Toronto Blue Jays. It took all seven games to knock off the Blue Jays. However, had the best-of-five format still been in effect, the Blue Jays would have won and then gone on to the World Series with the St. Louis Cardinals. But as it turned out, the Royals won the American League Championship Series 4 games to 3. In the resulting World Series for 1985—sometimes called the "Show Me State Series" because both teams were from Missouri—it took all seven games for the Royals to knock out the Cardinals, ironically winning it 4 games to 3 as had been the case with the league series championships.

By the end of the postseason, Roger Clemens was healing, progressing rapidly in his rehabilitation on his shoulder, and preparing for the upcoming season and spring training. Already irked by his sophomore slump, he was intent on a successful and injury-free upcoming season.

The 1986 season would be one of the best, if not the halcyon, year of Clemens's career. He helped lead his team to the postseason championship and then to the joys and heartbreak of his first World Series. Little did he know at that point that he would have many more World Series ventures in which to showcase his talents. If a sophomore slump occurs in the second year, then three would be the charm in his third year. Roger knew that he would not be in complete control of all the variables that determine whether a player has a great year. He could be in perfect shape, pitch perfect innings, and influence his team members to do better, but without run support it would not amount to much.

That year Roger would become the first player in the modern era to strike out 20 men at bat in the same game, a feat that would not be matched for 10 years and then by his own performance. It would also later be matched by the up-and-coming legendary Chicago Cubs rookie, Kerry Wood. Wood had his major-league debut in 1998 and within a few weeks threw a 1-hit game while striking out 20 Houston Astros batters on May 6, 1998. Roger's 1986 20-strikeout game easily matched one of the best games ever pitched in the history of the leagues. It led to Roger attaining the ultimate nickname in the history of baseball, or organized sports in general. The nickname of "the Rocket" became his second nomenclature and the nickname to which all others in the sport would be compared. He attained his first Cy Young Award by unanimous vote and also was voted onto the All-Star team. It was also the year for the Boston Red Sox, a team that would lead the American League East for almost the entire major-league season, especially dominating in the last half. Roger indeed smelled blood in the water and had the instincts to go for it. The team had the potential to be the best in the American League and maybe the worst nightmare for any of the National League teams.

The year started off with a lot of changes for the team, especially in the pitching roster. Joe Sambito came to the team after a long history with the Astros and the Mets. Calvin Schiraldi, Roger's good buddy, and Wes Gardner also came from the Mets. Sammy Stewart joined the Red Sox from the Baltimore Orioles. But the biggest surprise would come later in the season when one of

Roger's role models and idols, Tom Seaver, was traded to the Red Sox from the Chicago White Sox. Tom and Roger immediately became good friends, as Roger was friends with just about all of his teammates. However, their playing time together was short lived: "Tom Terrific" Seaver ended up getting injured near the end of the season and was not able to play in the 1986 World Series. The Red Sox declined to renew his contract at season's end, and a spectacular career drew to a close. This possibly left Roger with a negative impression of the managerial processes in Major League Baseball.

The 1986 season didn't start off with a bang as it had the previous year. The first two games were losses to the Detroit Tigers; both scores were 6 runs to 5. It turned around almost immediately for the Red Sox when Al Nipper defeated the Tigers the next day. The following day was Roger Clemens's first time to pitch for the season, and he defeated the Chicago White Sox 7 to 2 at the historic Comiskey Park. Roger remained on a roll, and so did the rest of his team, for the remainder of the season without any real competition other than their rival's, New York Yankees in the East and the California Angels in the West.

Roger worked himself into a roll when he pitched four games straight of 10-plus strikeouts, starting with the April 22 defeat of the Detroit Tigers 6 to 4. But the game for which he would always be remembered, and perhaps the most important day in Roger's career, occurred on April 29, 1986, in a three-game homestand at Fenway Park. The destruction of the Seattle Mariners during those three days would show the world that Roger and his teammates were headed directly to the big-time World Series. The April 29 game wasn't a sellout, as it happened in the middle of the week when most people were returning home from the workday or preparing for the next day of school and final exams. But in this game Roger Clemens struck out 20 Mariners in a 3 to 1 victory and became the first pitcher in the history of major-league baseball to achieve that level of strikeouts. Roger broke the previous record tied by Nolan Ryan, Tom Seaver, and Steve Carlton of 19 strikeouts in one game. Fellow Red Sox players and fans, and even the jaded media, who are used to their team's successes, were amazed at what they had witnessed. After the game, Roger's team commented on how he not only fired up his gas can on the mound but used it with the fury of a rocket, blasting off his opponents on the launch pad. Earlier in the day, Elton John's song "Rocket Man" was played over the loud speakers at the stadium, and the team used that song's title to describe what Roger Clemens had just done. Roger Clemens was now the Rocket Man, not Elton John. Shortly after this they just started to refer to him as "the Rocket." He liked and accepted the nickname. Previously in college at the University of Texas his most glamorous nickname had been "Goose," after Goose Gossage, and many of his friends still called him that. Somehow, the Rocket sounded better than the chants from when he was on the mound during his college days: "The Goose is loose, the Goose is loose!"

There are many stories explaining how Roger ended up with the Rocket nickname. The 1986 game against the Mariners is one that stands up to most inquiries, as the name doesn't appear in any comments or press releases, or in any form for that matter, before that game. It is also the one usually used to explain the name by the people surrounding Roger today, such as his teammates, reporters, family, and friends. Other stories are that his name, Roger, when yelled across the field, sounds equally as good as

Rocket, and it being the case that many major leaguers end up with a nickname, it might as well be something that matches his name. Still yet another is the countdown theory, where fans and team members would count down during his pitches, which more often than not ended with a strikeout. The countdown was as if a rocket was taking off. With Roger's roots in Houston, still known as Space City back in the 1980s, it would seem logical to give him a nickname that suits his heritage. Even still, the name didn't appear in print before that Mariners game.

Roger Clemens was now the Rocket.

Previous to Roger's 20-strikeout game, pitching great Tom Seaver, who was now Roger's teammate, had pitched a 19-strikeout game, a tie with Steve Carlton's record, against a battered San Diego Padres in 1970. After Roger Clemens, Kerry Wood equaled Clemens's record in his rookie year with the Chicago Cubs by striking out 20 Houston Astros in 1998 during his fifth career start. He

An unfortunate side effect of the new nickname was that the song "Rocket Man" was played endlessly during Fenway Park events . . .

did it so quickly, it was thought that he might actually get one more in for the record books. Randy Johnson also attained it in 2001 against the Cincinnati Reds. His 20-strikeout game was controversial from the start. Although he struck out all 20 in nine innings, the game went into extra innings, and baseball officials would not accept his record as part of a regular nine-inning game. Since that time, baseball has reversed its decision, and it now lists Randy Johnson along with Roger Clemens and Kerry Wood in the 20-strikeout club.

An unfortunate side effect of the new nickname was that the song "Rocket Man," either in Muzak form or directly from the Elton John album of the same title, was played endlessly during Fenway Park events, sporting news shows, and other recaps. It still does today wherever the Rocket appears, either on the mound, at a charity event, or by singing fans. Occasionally as Roger took the mound as the starting pitcher, the song would begin to play, or it would play during the pregame activities. To him, it became a staple of his life, much as the music to "Thanks for the Memories" was played when the famous entertainer Bob Hope appeared on television shows or in person, or the Johnny Carson theme music was played whenever Mr. Carson walked into an event. In Roger's case, the song's appeal waned with time and it was played with less frequency, but the nickname of the Rocket remained with him wherever he went.

Word soon went out about Roger's game against the Mariners, and the next day, which was in the middle of a workweek, a sellout crowd showed up to see the Red Sox, even without Roger as the pitcher. Sammy Stewart of the Red Sox was the pitcher on that date and defeated the Mariners 9 to 4. The May 1 game on Thursday had a similar outcome: Oil Can Boyd performed nearly similar antics to Roger's of just two days earlier, defeating the Mariners 12 runs to 2. In any case, the fate of the fame of Roger Clemens was now sealed. Whatever he did in the future, he would not be forgotten.

In all the excitement, the season continued. On May 4 Clemens pitched a near perfect game against the Oakland Athletics, winning it 4 runs to 1. Then on May 14 Roger defeated the Red Sox's nemesis California Angels 8 to 5.

The attention drawn to his 20-strikeout game would be one of the reasons that Roger would be voted onto the 1986 All-Star Game roster. Clemens was beside himself with pride that he had made it onto the list and would be a starting pitcher. The game was held in his hometown of Houston, Texas, at the eighth wonder of the world, the Astrodome. Other Boston Red Sox teammates joined him there, including Wade Boggs, Jim Rice, and Rich Gedman. Although Roger had already by that time met his idol, Nolan Ryan, this was the first time he would pitch in a game that also included his role model, even if it was on the opposing league's team. But Roger by then already had interleague friends such as Ryan. On July 16 Roger's career was on the rise, and Ryan was on the afternoon side of his yardarm, although it would have been difficult to see the differences between the two players at that time. Roger's entire family and growing list of friends attended the game. His mother, all of his sisters and brothers, and his wife were there to support him. That year, the American League won the All-Star Game in one of the few times in a 14-year drought. They beat the National League 3 runs to 2. Roger found himself voted Most Valuable Player for the game, although mostly it was in recognition of his 20 strikeouts on the Mariners earlier in the year.

Oil Can Boyd, upon hearing that he had not been selected to the All-Star team, protested rather strongly and had such a fit at Fenway that he was suspended from the team for a few games. He then was admitted to the hospital for a short stay and observation because of the stress-filled incident.

There was even better news than making the roster for Roger: around the time of the All-Star Game he and his wife, Debbie, announced that they were expecting their first child, due to arrive during the Christmas season.

Commercialism has almost always been a part of baseball. Following the fame of the Cy Young Award, the MVP, and other prestigious awards was the honor of the "Rolaids Man of the Year Award," which in 1986 went to the American League's Dave Righetti of the New York Yankees and to Todd Worrell of the St. Louis Cardinals in the National League. The first year of the award was 1976.

In midseason and for the next few months the Red Sox fought off the New York Yankees. Their win-to-loss average stayed well above an amazing .700 in a game where staying afloat above .500 is a great feat. On August 18, Tom Seaver pitched a winning game against the Minnesota Twins in what would turn out to be his 311th and last win. The Red Sox would win the game 3 to 1. An injury to his ankle would put him on the disabled list for a while but would eventually contribute to end his career. Other memorable games for the Red Sox were several wins over the White Sox, the Twins, and the Brewers. But, troubling losses to the Yankees on many occasions were staggering for the Red Sox. This was also the case in several losses to the California Angels. But fortunately for the Red Sox, the Yankees had their own problems with losses, as did the Angels. Regardless of the losses, Roger and his team carried on, especially with the confidence of the April 29 game behind them.

There was a growing fear that the Boston Red Sox would not be able to overtake the Yankees for the pennant and make it to the American League Championship Series (ALCS). But Roger's team would overtake the Yankees for the American League East title, and the California Angels would get the pennant in their domain.

For the National League, the Houston Astros would go on to the playoffs for the first time in their history after

defeating the San Francisco Giants in the Houston Astrodome. Mike Scott, the Astros' pitching ace, threw a 2 to 0
no-hitter against the Giants, and he himself became the
stuff of legends for the Astros. The champagne celebration
in the Astros' home clubhouse that year was as close as
they would get to the playoffs or any chance at a World
Series game for the next two decades, but little did they
know it at the time. They made the best of it. For many
years, this clubhouse celebration was looked upon as a
pivotal point in the history of the team. That is, perhaps a
great chapter in baseball that is often overlooked in the
Astros' fight with the Giants in the 1986 pennant race. Mike
Scott's no-hitter indeed became a moment remembered by
all Houston fans. Though there had been previous no-hitters in the leagues, Scott's was important in that it clinched
the National League West title for Houston and led the Astros
to take on the Mets, to whom they would lose in one of
the most spectacular games in recent history.

The Astros faced the New York Mets in the National
League Championship Series, losing 4 games to 2. Game 6
was a knock-down-drag-out fight that lasted for 16 innings,
which was the longest game in baseball's postseason history, and the Mets squeaked by and won over the Astros 7
runs to 6. It was a heartbreak that Houston would never
forget, even as late as their spectacular 2004 and 2005 seasons. The old newsreels of the 1986 loss were played repeatedly by the media as a reminder of how much they
had lost, and gained, over the past years.

The Mets' win over the Astros had the Boston Red Sox
facing the Mets in the World Series. The Mets had not been
to the fall classic since 1973 and were looking forward to
winning. It may have been Roger's dream to have faced the
Astros that year, but it would not be for him. He would have

loved to have played his hometown team and pitched opposite his mentor, Nolan Ryan, and Mike Scott. Without a doubt the reverse was also likely true, and Ryan would have seen it as a challenge to have pitched opposite the rising star of Roger Clemens.

In the ALCS it took Boston all seven games to defeat the Angels. If the format was still best of five, as it had been recently, the Angels would have won the championship. The new rules allowed Clemens and his team to clinch the series with their wins in Games 6 and 7. One of the most decisive moments in the series was in

An awestruck Roger Clemens, at the ripe young age of 24, was going to the World Series . . .

Game 5, when Boston was behind the Angels and was ever so close to elimination. Roger's teammate Don Baylor blasted a home run, bringing two in and thus chopping away at the Angels' lead. Don Henderson slammed in a home run against the Angels and put the Red Sox into the lead, allowing room for the next two games and a Red Sox win. Roger was the losing pitcher in Game 1, but the winning pitcher in the most important and decisive of the games, Game 7. His bitterness about losing the first game had all but disappeared with the final win. In addition to the exhaustion of overtaking his rivals in the series, Roger had taken ill a few days earlier and was much too worn out to celebrate the victory with team members. He was instead in another room, working to gain enough strength just to make it home that evening.

An awestruck Roger Clemens, at the ripe young age of 24, was going to the World Series as an ace pitcher for the Boston Red Sox.

The Red Sox's record of 95 wins to 66 losses and a
.590 average facing the Mets' record of an incredible 108
wins to 54 losses and a .667 average was slightly lopsided
in any analysis. The resulting World Series of 1986 would
cap off a spectacular season for Roger and the Red Sox.
The team hadn't made the scene there in many years. They
had not won a World Series since 1918, when Babe Ruth
was on the mound and pitched his team to a victory over
the Chicago Cubs. The World Series gets its name because
in the beginning it was a series of games to determine once
and for all the best of the teams for that season. There were
no championship series in the leagues leading up to the
World Series in the old days. That didn't start until the 1960s.
For 1986, it was the best-of-seven games, and it took all
seven that year to prove it.

But for this year, it was Roger Clemens who was on
the mound for the Red Sox, not Babe Ruth, and Doc Gooden
was pitching for the Mets. Because of this matchup, it could
have been said that the Rocket's red glare was about to get
"doctored" a bit. Tom Seaver was still out of the lineup for
the World Series because of his ankle injury. He did, however, receive an enthusiastic standing ovation from the
crowds in the ballpark in recognition of his long and brilliant career. "Tom Terrific" had such an impact on the game
that former player Reggie Jackson once said of him: "Blind
people come to the park just to hear him pitch."[1] In Game
1, however, McNamara used Bruce Hurst to pitch a great
show against the Mets. Roger watched the game intensely
because he knew he would be up to pitch in Game 2. The
Red Sox won Game 1 with a single run against the Mets,
who had no runs to their credit. By then, the Mets were
on the warpath for Game 2 and put Doc Gooden on the
mound. His nemesis, Roger Clemens, was placed on the

mound for the Red Sox. Although the press had hyped it as a battle of the giants, nothing even came close to that description. Gooden would become the losing pitcher in that game as he allowed 6 runs by the Red Sox. Clemens fared so poorly, not even lasting six innings, that he couldn't even claim the spot of winning pitcher. That honor was given to fellow teammate Steve Crawford, when the Red Sox pulled another win out of the hat, 9 runs to 3.

With the Mets down two games in a seven-game series, they were compared to a disturbed hornet's nest, swarming out for revenge in Game 3. They took the lead almost immediately from Boston's starting pitcher Oil Can Boyd. In an interesting twist of events, the players the Red Sox had traded with the Mets earlier in the season turned out to be those who helped to score against their old teammates, the Boston Red Sox. The Mets scored 7 runs to the Red Sox total of 1 run. The winning pitcher for the Mets was Roger's old teammate Bob Ojeda, and the losing pitcher was Oil Can Boyd.

For Game 4, the Mets were able to succeed in moving up and tying the series in a dead even heap. Al Nipper was the pitcher for the Red Sox and allowed Gary Carter to pop two home runs and three runners batted in for the lead. This allowed the Mets to win it 6 to 2.

The October 23 game at Fenway allowed Bruce Hurst to stave off the advancing Mets and brought Boston to within one game away of winning its first World Series in nearly 70 years. Hurst was able to pitch the entire nine-inning game, although Roger was eager to pitch as much as he could in as many games as he could. As for the Mets, Gooden wanted to prove himself worthy after messing up Game 2, but he fell short of that goal when the Red Sox won 4 runs to 2 and moved into advantage territory above the Mets. By winning Game 5 the Red Sox were 3 games to the Mets' 2 games, and they eagerly awaited Game 6. They were ready to prove that they had what it took to win.

Game 6 was one of the storybook baseball matchups of all matchups, and it was played out on October 25, 1986, at Shea Stadium in New York. Roger was in enemy territory, and the Red Sox were ready to deal with the butterflies in their collective stomachs. This time, Boston was on the warpath to defend what the Red Sox believed to be their World Series. Clemens saw in this game their chance to clinch it once and for all. Boston rapidly scored two runs for the lead, and it took five innings before the Mets could even out the score with two runs in the fifth inning. Boston came back with a run in the seventh, but Mets players also scored to make it even in the eighth inning. Clemens was doing a spectacular job on the mound, pitching a no-hit game for the first four innings and then giving up only four hits later into the game.

It is at this point in the game that a controversy ensued. McNamara removed Roger in the middle of the eighth inning after Clemens developed a blister on a finger on his pitching hand. Roger adamantly said that he didn't want to leave with just a blister on his hand and that he could handle what the Mets were doing. McNamara removed him anyway even though the blister wasn't hurting Clemens, and he was admittedly and obviously still pitching like the Rocket with a 3 to 2 lead in the game. The skipper sent Calvin Schiraldi to the mound, and shortly after that move the Mets scored a run off the Red Sox from a Gary Carter sacrifice fly for a 3 to 3 tie. Noting that Schiraldi was in shaky territory, McNamara changed his mind and sent Bob Stanley to do the job. Things got even worse for Roger's team, as a scoreless ninth inning sent the game into extra innings. In the tenth inning, the injured Red Sox first baseman Bill Buckner made an error—perhaps one of the most famous errors in the history of baseball and certainly that of the World Series—and allowed the Mets to score yet again, ending the game in favor of the Mets, 6 to 5. Buckner somehow allowed a very slow rolling hit from Mookie Wilson to escape his glove near first base, and by the time he had retrieved it the Mets' Ray Knight had flown through home plate, allowing the Mets to win Game 6. As was the case in the AL playoffs, Roger and his team felt let down after blowing what they thought would be their game. It would all be decided in Game 7 at Shea on October 26.

Fortunately for the Rocket and the Red Sox, a cold front was making its way through the northeastern states, causing a one-day delay of Game 7 because of rainy weather. The delay was a bonus for the chances of the travel-weary Boston Red Sox, allowing them one more day of rest while they cared for their injuries. Roger wanted desperately to pitch in the October 27 and last game, but McNamara put in Bruce Hurst as the starting pitcher. Oil Can Boyd and others were also desperate to pitch. They believed that they could change the outcome of the game. It appeared as if things got off to a great start for Boston: in the second inning they scored three runs while the Mets did not score until the sixth inning. Then they tied the score 3 to 3. McNamara called in Schiraldi to the mound in the seventh when the Mets scored three more runs, making the tally 6 to 3. Boston retaliated in the eighth inning with two more runs, which cut the Mets' lead to a nail-biting 6 to 5. But the Mets gained two more runs off Red Sox reliever Al Nipper to win Game 7 and the Series, 8 runs to the Red Sox's 5 runs in the ninth.

For the New York Mets it was the most glorious of their World Series wins. For the Boston Red Sox it was the most tragic of losses. Roger Clemens got himself to the World Series at such a young age and it was the joy of his career so far, but losing the Series was at the other extreme of his sorrow.

There were many scenarios, intrigues, and comparisons in hindsight explanation for why Clemens and the Boston Red Sox lost what perhaps would be the most memorable of all the World Series. The most famous intrigue was Roger's sudden exit in Game 6 from the mound to be replaced by the reliever, Calvin Schiraldi. Clemens, blister or not, was said to have been relieved too early and while he was still on a roll. Clearly he could possibly have held off the next few points attained by the Mets. Ironically, Schiraldi was brought in to pitch in Game 7, which resulted in the same outcome. Clemens, wanting to pitch, may have been proven correct that he could have won the game and the Series.

More speculation surrounded the way Roger acted when he left Game 6. He is known, and is still known today, not to shave on his pitching days. When he was suddenly removed from the game he went back into the clubhouse to shower and shave before the end of the game, which, to some who were leery about superstitions, resulted in an unfortunate outcome.

Yet more controversy follows McNamara's other key player decision. There is still talk about just why McNamara allowed an injured Buckner to stay in the game in Game 6. His most obvious reason was that he wanted a veteran player to be in the game when the hoped-for win would become a reality, even if he had to chance an injury.

Roger knew that he had many years ahead of him, and somehow instinct told him that he would have many more chances at the World Series in which to prove himself. Indeed, that would turn out to be the case. But, if Roger had signed with the Mets during his earlier days when the opportunity arose, he would then have had a World Series win under his belt.

Returning home to Houston after the loss, he and his wife, Debbie, prepared for an even bigger event than the World Series: the birth of their first child. On December 4, 1986, Debbie had a boy they named Koby. The "K" in his name was for all of the strikeouts that Clemens had in his career at that time. Roger had at least made it through an injury-free season, save for a little blister on his finger that might have, or might not have, cost him and the Boston Red Sox the World Series for 1986.

In November 1986 he had received good news. He had won his first Cy Young Award, and this, to go along with being voted the American League's Most Valuable Player, capped a year that seemed to heal any wounds. He was only the eighth player in major-league history to have won both the Cy Young Award and the MVP in the same season.

As most young baseball players, Roger had always dreamed of winning the Cy Young Award. The annual award is handed out to the best pitchers in the American League and the National League. It's named after the man who is arguably the best pitcher, if not the most hallowed pitcher, in the history of baseball, Denton True Young. He was nicknamed "Cy" Young early on because his fastball resembled the furor of a cyclone. Born in Ohio in 1867, Young worked his way up to the major leagues, and at the age of 23 he was called up to the Cleveland club in 1890. In his first game he threw his famous fastball, and only three batters were able to get a hit. This was in the age when a pitcher would pitch the entire game, only to be relieved by what would be called a "relief" pitcher when exhaustion took over. Because of this extraordinary amount of pitching, most of Cy Young's statistics remain records to this day, such as the 7,356 innings he pitched, sometimes pitching no-hitters, and the 511 games he won in a career lasting 22 years. He also holds the record for the most losses,

> *At first, the Cy Young Award was given to the one best overall pitcher in all of baseball.*

313 of them. His other noted accomplishments are his major-league record of 751 complete games pitched, 20 or more wins for 16 seasons, 30 or more wins in five seasons, and three no-hitters with one as a perfect game. He led the leagues in shutouts for seven seasons, and for four seasons he led the leagues in wins, averaging 27 wins per year. His career ERA was 2.63. When he finally retired in the early 1900s after a two-decade-long career, he was 45 years old in an era when the average man lived to only 50 years. He died in 1955 at the age of 88. Cy Young was elected to the Baseball Hall of Fame in 1937.[2]

In 1956 baseball commissioner Ford Frick announced that the late baseball great would have an annual award named in his honor. At first, the Cy Young Award was given to the one best overall pitcher in all of baseball. In the late 1960s it was decided that the award would be given to the best pitcher in each of the two leagues. It is voted on by a select group of the Baseball Writers' Association of America. Originally the writers just placed a vote for the pitcher they believed to be the best, with one vote per writer. In 1970, the association changed the voting to a first-, second-, and third-choice format with the winner in each league announced first, followed by revealing the voting to show the runners-up. This more inclusive voting format serves to recognize that sometimes there are more factors in creating a winning or dominant pitcher than just popularity.

As Roger looked back on his 1986 season, he saw success. His first All-Star Game, and his award as that game's MVP, was icing on the cake. His season of 24 wins to 4 losses was the highest since Mel Parnell went 25 and 7 in 1949. He led the AL in wins, ERA, winning percentage, and lowest hitter's average.

After all, to everyone he was now the Rocket.

Chapter 6

CANNON FODDER

The Boston Red Sox's series of great successes in the 1986 season, even with the World Series loss, brought in more fans than in previous years. The Red Sox had been struggling to stay in the area of the 1.5 million mark in attendance for several years, but with the excellent performance during the 1986 season, the number of fans finally popped above the 2 million mark annually and stayed there for years. The higher fan attendance and the revenues produced by such would prove a point of tension for players and management in the upcoming year.

Season tickets and game days became sellouts long before the 1987 season began. The team may have lost out on the World Series, but it won the most important trophy, the paying fan. The fans were just as heartbroken over the loss as Roger and his teammates were, but they still believed in the team. With the increase in fan attendance there was a proportional increase in revenues but not an equitable increase in player salaries. This upset the players, who felt they—and not management—had pulled it off in the first place. This tension came to a head when the players complained and, as in Roger Clemens's case, refused to show up until an acceptable salary was in place. Roger has always known exactly what his value is.

Roger's 1986 salary was around $220,000, which was well below the average player's salary of about $370,000 annually. Without a doubt, Roger Clemens was an above-average performer with above-average abilities and talent. Before the season began, word leaked out to the press that things were getting out of hand between Clemens and the Red Sox's management. The Red Sox's owner would not budge, and by the time of spring training, Clemens was demanding over $1 million for the upcoming season, with opportunities for bonuses. The ownership balked, and Roger walked. Eventually, Roger walked off spring training and did not return until he received what he believed was his fair share of the revenues. The walkout lasted for nearly one month, when Major League Baseball stepped in for mediation between the two feuding sides. When they finally reached an agreement, management met Clemens halfway: Roger would receive $500,000 for the 1987 season and over $1 million for the next season, with incentives. In the end, the Red Sox would pay Roger $650,000, which included the incentives, for the 1987 season.

Other Boston Red Sox players were making substantially more than Roger: Jim Rice was paid over $2 million at the time, Wade Boggs made $1.6 million, Bob Stanley and Dwight Evans each earned $1 million, and management paid $700,000 to Bruce Hurst. The Red Sox's management had let Tom Seaver go earlier in the year because of his injuries. Roger saw a player with decades of talent sent unceremoniously on his way, and Seaver's dismissal affected him. He likely resolved not to let this happen to him and not to let team management treat him as some sort of commodity that could be bought or sold or sent away on a whim.

Even though he won at the salary negotiations, the 1987 season as a whole would be a forgettable one for Roger, the team, and the fans. The Red Sox earned a win-to-loss percentage of just .481 by winning 78 and losing 84 of their games. The first game, just two days after Roger's contract was approved, was a disappointing fiasco against the underdog Milwaukee Brewers. It was a shocking 5 to 1 loss for the Red Sox, who

He likely resolved not to let this happen to him and not to let team management treat him as some sort of commodity . . .

would go on to lose the entire opening series to the Brewers. In the past the Red Sox had had little, if any, problems in handling the Brewers. Roger's first appearance on the mound was on April 16 at Toronto, ending in an embarrassing 11 to 1 loss to the Blue Jays and with Clemens as the losing pitcher. But a few days later in the April 20 game, Roger was able to pull off a win over the Kansas City Royals and be credited as the winning pitcher, 8 runs to 0. But the press was all over the losses. A turnaround later in the month got the Red Sox to a .500 average they fought to maintain, but then they quickly lost it again. It was as if Roger and the team had given all they had in the preceding season's fight to stay afloat in the American League and the World Series and had nothing left for the current season. The media started the tittle-tattle that Roger was out of shape because his salary negotiation walkout left him basically without any spring training. They didn't discuss, even though they were aware of it, that Roger continued to train while he was gone through his usual intense pitching work-outs. But that was of little consequence because Roger did indeed have a slow start for the season, as reflected in a poor average, especially by Roger's own high standards. By midseason he ended up with a not-so-great, for Roger, 3.51 ERA and a record of just 5 wins to 8 losses. Roger was in the hot seat, and he knew it.

Roger recognized the problem, worked hard on it, and corrected it. One of the best games of Roger's season was on April 21, when he and the Red Sox defeated the Kansas City Royals 8 to 0 at Fenway. Ironically, the April 30 game saw them lose to the Mariners 11 to 2 in Seattle almost a year to the day after the Rocket had performed his 20-strikeout game against that team. This time, Bruce Hurst took the fall as the losing pitcher of the game. Another great day was the August 21 game, where Roger defeated the Twins 11 to 3 as the winning pitcher. However, of all the wins under Roger's belt at this time, the most pride came from the July 26 game at Fenway, and he was the winning pitcher, smashing, again, the Mariners. The Red Sox won it 11 runs to 1, and it was the 50th win in Roger Clemens's career. Roger was again on a roll, and during his last 23 starts his record soared to 16 wins and 3 losses with a 2.68 ERA by the end of the season. For the year, he racked up 20 wins, the most ever in one season and a tie with Dave Stewart of the Oakland Athletics for the record. Curiously, as time went on, Stewart would have a 7 to 1 all-time career record against Clemens.

Clemens was not selected to appear in the 1987 All-Star Game in Oakland for that season. That show-down, played out on July 14 in County Stadium, was one of the longest All-Star Games in history at that time, run-ning for 13 innings and lasting well into the evening. The

National League won the game 2 runs to 0. The Most Valuable Player in the game was Tim Raines.

In September of that season, Nolan Ryan, now with the Houston Astros, surpassed the 4,500-strikeout level when Houston beat the San Francisco Giants 4 to 2. Amazingly he struck out the last 12 batters in a row, finishing the seventh inning for the win. Ryan would eventually become the all-time strikeout leader with 5,714 under his belt. A few days after Ryan reached this benchmark, Roger's teammate Wade Boggs garnered 200 hits for his fifth straight season.

In any case, the Red Sox finished fifth in the standings in the American League East and were out of contention for the playoffs early. The AL championship, which saw the future Houston Astros' pitching coach Gary Gaetti chosen as MVP, was won by the Minnesota Twins over the Detroit Tigers 4 games to 1. In the National League playoffs, the St. Louis Cardinals won over the San Francisco Giants 4 games to 3. In a shocker, the Twins won the ensuing World Series. The St. Louis Cardinals lost the fall classic 3 games to the Twins' 4 games.

After the season ended, Roger again received great news to cap off another year in the majors. He had won the year's Cy Young Award for the American League, making it two in a row for him. For the National League, Steve Bedrosian of the Philadelphia Phillies won the honor, mostly in recognition of his 49 saves during the year and a 5 to 3 record.

New to the Boston Red Sox's pitching roster in 1988 was Mike Boddicker from the Baltimore Orioles. Joining the roster in early June was Zach Crouch, a call-up from the minor leagues as was Steve Curry. Steve Ellsworth joined the pitching roster on Opening Day. Dennis Lamp moved over to the Red Sox in 1988 after a long career with the

Chicago Cubs, Chicago White Sox, Toronto Blue Jays, and a year with the Oakland Athletics. John Trautwein joined the team, and Mike Smithson joined up after a career with the Rangers and the Twins. Lee Smith got on board with the Red Sox after a long career with the Cubs. Mike Rochford joined the team early in September and had a three-season career with the Red Sox. Most of these players were a year or so younger than Roger was, and he saw in this that he was starting to advance in his career not only based on his talent but also now on his seniority. In previous years, the pitching staff had averaged about a dozen on the roster, but with 1988, there were a total of 17 pitchers for the Red Sox. The most notable absence for 1988 was Calvin Schiraldi, who had moved on to the Cubs for that season.

The season had a certain takeoff to it that led Roger and the fans to believe it would be another successful year and would make up for last year's fiasco. One of the most significant games was in April with a great 15 to 2 win against the Texas Rangers. This was soon followed on April 21 with a 12 to 3 win over the Detroit Tigers and a few days after that a 16 to 3 win over the Chicago White Sox. When Joe Morgan debuted in the July 15 twin-bill game against Kansas City, Roger put on an excellent show with his second 16-strikeout performance of the year, winning the game 3 runs to 1.

> *The season had a certain takeoff to it that led Roger and the fans to believe it would be another successful year and would make up for last year's fiasco.*

Detroit came back in August with an 18 to 6 win over Roger and his team to end an incredible 23-game winning streak for the Red Sox. August of that season was one of Roger's worst. He lost all five of his starts and ended up with an overly bloated 7.33 ERA by the end of the month. The Rocket had no injuries or soreness as an excuse, just bad luck. On September 10 Roger pitched what would become the closest to a no-hitter he would ever achieve, when he pitched a one-hitter against Cleveland. Dave Clark was the only hitter in that game to reach base. Roger's best day undoubtedly came on September 20, where he defeated the Toronto Blue Jays 13 to 2. For the season, the Red Sox won 89 to 73 losses and placed first in the standings in the American League East with their .549 average. Roger and the Boston Red Sox were again headed to the playoffs.

Roger was again selected for the 1988 All-Star Game, which was held on July 12 at Riverfront Stadium in Cincinnati, now known as Cinergy Field. Joining him in Cincinnati were teammates Wade Boggs and Mike Greenwell. Clemens pitched one scoreless inning with two strikeouts, helping in the win. That year the American League held up for a 2 to 1 win over the National League.

During the 1988 All-Star break, on Bastille Day, the Boston ownership fired controversial manager John McNamara because of his lackluster performance for the year. Even when his management was superior it was marred by bad decisions, such as his pitching decisions during the 1986 World Series. The 1987 season that had just ended was an embarrassment to the ownership and to the outraged Boston Red Sox fans, and although they were able to give McNamara another chance at proving himself during the 1988 season, by the middle of the year it was all over for him. The All-Star break has usually been the time of the season when teams make important midyear decisions that they believe will increase their chances at success.

After considering several candidates the ownership decided to hire on a temporary basis their bullpen coach, the much-liked and respected Joe Morgan. The fans saw him as the workingman's skipper and as dedicated to the Red Sox.

Morgan was a native of Massachusetts, and almost all of his baseball experience was with Boston Red Sox organizations. He was manager of the Pawtucket Paw Sox for almost a decade from the early 1970s to the early 1980s. The Boston ownership made him a scout for the Red Sox in 1982, and Morgan just missed out on being the skipper for Roger Clemens in his minor-league rookie year with the Pawtucket Paw Sox. After a couple of seasons as a scout, management made him a first-base coach with the Major-League Red Sox in Boston in 1985. When he was promoted to skipper in 1988, he knew that he was to serve on a temporary basis until a permanent manager could be hired. Others who were being considered as a permanent replacement were Lou Piniella and Joe Torre. When the negotiations broke down with the more permanent candidates, Morgan was already on a roll that impressed the Boston ownership, and they didn't want to break it. Morgan had steered Roger and the Boston Red Sox into winning 19 of the first 20 games. When he was fired from the Boston Red Sox in 1991, he had an impressive major-league record of 301 wins to 262 losses resulting in a .535 record.

Joe Morgan took the Red Sox on an incredible ride after he was hired in midseason. They finished first in the American League East Division, while in the AL West Division the Oakland Athletics finished first. Roger Clemens and the Red Sox were going to the championships for 1988.

In the American League Championship Series, the Oakland Athletics seemed to have the upper hand even before the first pitch of Game 1 on October 5, as they were the favored team. On the opposing team was Roger's old teammate from his rookie year, Dennis Eckersley. There were three scoreless innings before the Athletics scored a run in the fourth. It wasn't until the seventh inning that Boston was able to score a single run, but then in the eighth inning the Athletics scored the final run and won it 2 runs to 1. Hurst took the credit as losing pitcher for the Red Sox, and José

> Roger and his team were really in the hot seat now and needed to at least avoid being swept by the Athletics . . .

Canseco of Oakland took the credit in making their only home run. Game 2 was a virtual duplicate, but with Roger Clemens pitching, the Red Sox were able to stave off Oakland's advance and Boston was able to score first with 2 runs in the sixth after five scoreless innings. But the Athletics came back with a vengeance in the seventh, scoring 3 runs to Boston's 1. In the ninth inning the Athletics made one more run for the kill and won Game 2, 4 to 3. Roger had done his best in attempting the win. In Game 3, Roger didn't pitch; it was left up to Mike Boddicker and Bob Stanley. Even though Boston came on strong in the first inning, Oakland matched its offense with even more power from the A's arsenal of hitters and pitchers. Bob Welch and Gene Nelson were pitchers for Oakland, and they won Game 3 10 runs to Boston's 6. Roger and his team were really in the hot seat now and needed to at least avoid being swept by the Athletics in Game 4, but that wasn't in the cards. With Boston's pitchers Bruce Hurst and Mike Smithson, the Red Sox just couldn't keep pace with the Athletics' strong advances in all the innings. The final score in Game 4 was a 10 to 4 win for the Athletics, an outcome unbearable to Roger, Morgan, the team, and especially the Boston fans whom they had to face in the aftermath. Another year had just slipped through their grasp while trying to atone for the 1918 failure, again. The Oakland Athletics were going to the World Series, and they were not.

Game 1 of the resulting 1988 World Series, held at Dodger Stadium in Los Angeles, found the Los Angeles Dodgers behind the Oakland Athletics until the ninth inning. Then the Dodgers somehow eeked out a 5 run to 4 win over the Athletics. Game 2 saw the Dodgers coming on even stronger, winning it 6 to 0. But the Athletics came on strong in Game 3, beating the Dodgers 2 runs to 1. The Dodgers retaliated in Game 4 with a 4 to 3 win over Oakland and finalized the Series with a 5 to 2 win in Game 5. The Dodgers won it, 4 games to 1, on October 20, 1988. When the season was over, the Cy Young Award for the year went to Frank Viola of the American League and Orel Hershiser of the National League. Roger Clemens had, however, come in close in the voting. The MVP of the year for the AL went to José Canseco for his attention-getting and outstanding performance for the year; for the National League, Kirk Gibson was MVP.

The late 1980s saw baseball in high gear as its popularity soared. Baseball topics garnered tremendous box office money for both 1988 and 1989. The years were dominated with such movies as *Bull Durham* and *Eight Men Out* in 1988, and in 1989 the movies *Major League* and *Field of Dreams* were dominant. All won or were nominated for Academy Awards and other honors. During the premiers of the movies, famous baseball stars of the past and present were in attendance in order to drum up hype for the movies.

In May 1988, Roger became a dad again with the birth of his second child, a son named Kory. The choice to use a name beginning with a "K" was another sign that Roger's career would have a many more strikeouts well into the future.[1] For the year, he didn't receive as many awards as in previous years, but he led the league with his 291 strikeouts, which was a record by any Boston Red Sox pitcher. This achievement marked his third consecutive season of 200 strikeouts and above. He led the AL in his total shutouts with 8.

Early in 1989, Bruce Hurst, as a free agent, signed on with the San Diego Padres. Roger Clemens had lost one of the best on his pitching roster and faced the upcoming season with a new roster of more relative unknowns. The pitching roster had changed substantially in the few years that he had been with the Red Sox. By the start of the season the team was showing diminished capabilities, and it barely resembled a forceful threat to opponents. Roger was the most dominant pitcher on what was once one of the most dominant teams in baseball, almost like a lone tree left somehow miraculously standing after a forest fire. This was a fire of anger and distrust, mostly on the part of the fans who were being alienated one by one. It would be another average year for Clemens, for his team of tagalongs, and for Joe Morgan. But average for Roger Clemens is spectacular for the rest of baseball. This would be the year that he would reach his 1,000th career strikeout, would be second in strikeouts for the year in the leagues with 230, and would pitch his fourth straight year of 200-plus strikeout seasons.

The Red Sox's first four games in 1989 were losses, big losses. The fans were already on the warpath, as was the press. After each game, they hounded the players for explanations of their mishaps. They were, however, able to at least maintain their average above the .500 mark, if only for the time being. On April 13 Roger was able to record his 1,000th strikeout in a game against the Cleveland Indians. Brook Jacoby was his victim in the 9 to 1 win for Roger. On April 19 he again defeated the Indians as the winning pitcher in an 8 to 4 win. These were some of the few wins early in the season. On April 30, he took a bow to his iconic role model, Nolan Ryan, when Clemens became the losing pitcher, 1 run to the Texas Rangers' 2, in the game Ryan won at Arlington Stadium. However, Roger was able to turn it around one week later by becoming the winning pitcher against the Rangers, 7 runs to 6. A spectacular win against the New York Yankees, 14 runs to 8, occurred on June 10 at Yankee Stadium with Roger as the winning pitcher. In a Fenway game on June 21, Roger gave up Sammy Sosa's first career home run. At the time Sosa was with the Texas Rangers, and during the game Roger didn't take revenge out on Mr. Sosa or any of the Rangers for the home run against him.

By midseason, Roger was in a sort of a free fall, with an ERA of 4.00 and with 7 wins to 8 losses in August. Part of this could be attributed to soreness in his right elbow, which lingered for a while. The Rocket missed out on an August 2 start versus the Orioles, and he had to leave the August 6 game versus Cleveland in the first inning because of the soreness. By the season's end, he had won a total of 17 games and lost 11 and had an ERA of 3.13 with 35 starts for the team.

The Rocket was not selected to the 1989 All-Star Game, which was played on July 11 at Anaheim Stadium. Clemens had a couple of teammates on the All-Star roster, including Wade Boggs and Mike Greenwell. The American League won 5 runs to 3. The MVP for the game was Bo Jackson.

The Red Sox closed the year with 83 wins and 79 losses, resulting in a respectable .512 average but leaving them out of the postseason playoffs. Boston ranked below the Baltimore Orioles and the first-place Toronto Blue Jays in the AL East. The Blue Jays went on to lose to the AL West Oakland Athletics in the ALCS, 4 games to 1. In the NL, the Chicago Cubs lost to the San Francisco Giants, also 4 games to 1. The resulting 1989 World Series was played between the Giants and the Athletics and was known as "the Battle of the Bay," or "the Bay Bridge Series," because the Oakland Bay Bridge was the only thing that separated the two cities. Unexpectedly, the Series also became known as "the Earthquake Series," because the massive Loma Prieta earthquake struck just as Game 3 was about to get under way. Oakland would sweep the best of seven in just 4 games.

Oakland won Game 1, 5 to 0, with winning pitcher Dave Stewart at Oakland Coliseum. Game 2 was also won by Oakland, 5 to 1, with winning pitcher Mike Moore. The Series traveled to San Francisco's Candlestick Park for Game 3 on October 17, 1989. In the pregame activities, such as batting practice and in the press boxes, it was business as usual. The pregame was televised and included interviews with the players and other dignitaries. Baseball commissioner Fay Vincent was also present and had only been in office for a month after the death of his predecessor, A. B. Giamatti. The world will never forget ABC network commentator Al Michaels's coverage of the game and his last comments as the ground began to shake at 5:04 PM with the approach of the earthquake, "I'll tell you what . . . we're having an earth—"[2] and was cut off in mid-sentence when the power went out. For a few moments, viewers from around the world could only guess at what had happened. The network put up a plain image of the World Series' banner on the screen, but shortly after that, backup broadcasting informed the viewers that a strong earthquake had just hit San Francisco and stopped the World Series in its tracks. This was also reported on other networks as they broke into their own regular programming to inform viewers of the disaster. The earthquake measured 6.9 on the Richter scale and lasted for just 15 seconds, but it was strong enough and long enough to cause massive amounts of damage around the Bay Area.

Many players were still on the field, either giving interviews or talking with family and friends. When the rumbling began, most people on the ground felt suddenly dizzy or weak on their feet, especially those who were not used to earthquakes. Fans in the stands felt it the most, as the concrete and steel beams began to wobble as if they were made from rubber. Some said that they felt as if they were having a seizure when the rumbling began, but then they noticed everyone else also having problems and quickly realized something else was going on. Panic resulted on all fronts, but there was an orderly evacuation of the stadium when security announced the orders for everyone to leave. Players who were in the clubhouses or offices ran out onto the field in panic, and the dugouts were cleared instantly. It can be said that the 1989 World Series had the first and only bench-clearing episode in history.

Fans in the stands felt it the most, as the concrete and steel beams began to wobble as if they were made from rubber.

The earthquake not only put off the World Series but also caused damage throughout much of the Bay Area, including the collapse of part of the Oakland Bay Bridge.

Coverage from a news camera as it was heading into town shortly after the quake showed an unfortunate couple driving off one of the broken pavements onto the lanes many feet below. Part of the double-height freeway system collapsed, crushing cars that were stuck in traffic and resulting in many heroic endeavors to save as many motorists as possible. In the Marina District, a fashionable residential area not too far from Candlestick Park, fires started in some of the collapsed buildings and combined into a larger fire that threatened to engulf the entire city as it had done in the great 1906 earthquake. Baseball great Joe DiMaggio was said to be seen walking nearby, looking for his sister to make sure that she was safe. In those days before the Internet or common use of the cell phone, most communication had been cut off. Those outside the area had much difficulty in finding out about the safety of loved ones.

When the word of a postponement was made official, the Oakland Athletics gathered their gear and other items and headed for home, either in their own cars or team buses. It took them several hours to reach home, in part because of the closing of the damaged Bay Bridge and the heavy traffic of people trying to get out of town. Many of the baseball players were not able to change back into their street clothes and had to drive off or walk in their baseball uniforms.

If Game 3 had actually been in play, it would have complicated things even more. Luckily, the first pitch had not yet been thrown, and the consequences of the earthquake were a lot easier to work out. The day after the earthquake, it was announced that the games would resume in five days; however, when the true devastation was revealed, the games were not able to resume until October 27. Candlestick Park was deemed too unsafe and required safety engineers to examine chunks of concrete in order to clear the structure for use. But eventually Game 3 was able to resume in Candlestick.

Ironically, the World Series may have actually saved many lives. Because the quake struck at rush hour and because many workers had already left work early either to attend the game or to just avoid the predicted area jams, the streets around the city had only small amounts of traffic. Possibly, since many people were at home and not on the double-decker freeways or on bridges, lives were presumably saved.

When Game 3 did proceed, it was with subdued enthusiasm. The Bay Area didn't want to forget about the people who were in need of help or those who had been injured or killed. But, San Franciscans didn't want the area represented as a dangerous place to live, work, or visit in the future, especially if an aftershock hit during play. Oakland would again prove to be the dominant team, and the A's won over the San Francisco Giants in nine innings, 13 runs to 7. The winning pitcher was Oakland's Dave Stewart. Game 4 was almost a duplicate, and the Athletics ended in a four-game sweep of the Giants. At the time the October 28 game would be the latest game date ever in the history of the World Series, until the 2001 World Series, which was delayed because of the September 11 tragedy.

The Cy Young Award for 1989 went to Bret Saberhagen of the AL and Mark Davis of the NL. Roger was not selected as MVP in his league this year; the honor went to Robin Yount of the AL and Kevin Mitchell of the NL. The Rocket had made it to the postseason, and his year, although 17 to 11 in wins to losses with a 3.13 ERA, was a respectable one for his 35 starts for his team. He passed the $2 million

mark in salary and incentives for the first time in his career during this season.

Chapter 7

——— LIKE A SHOT FROM NOWHERE ———

For spring training in 1990, Roger worked out and practiced as if he again smelled blood in the water. The season would turn out to be one of his greatest of all. The Rocket would attain his first 100-win level and become the Red Sox's all-time strikeout leader by surpassing Cy Young and reaching the 1,341 mark.

The most notable loss to Roger's team this year was the loss of Oil Can Boyd, who as a free agent had signed with the Montreal Expos shortly after the end of the 1989 season. Even though he sometimes had the reputation of being unpredictable and short with some of the team members, he had incredible value as a pitcher. This was one more in a series of pitching losses for the Red Sox. However, Jeff Reardon arrived onto the Boston Red Sox pitching roster from the Minnesota Twins and would pick up much of the slack. The pitching roster had swollen to almost 20 members, and again Roger was the most dominant pitcher on a team that desperately wanted to overtake the ALCS and retake the World Series.

Early in January, the Baseball Writers' Association of America elected two-time National League MVP, also having the name of Joe Morgan, to the Baseball Hall of Fame. Jim Palmer was also voted into the Hall of Fame for the American League. Palmer was a three-time Cy Young Award winner during his long career.

Indeed, the season for the Rocket and the Boston Red Sox started off just like a rocket. Roger was the starting, and winning, pitcher for the first game of the season. On April 9, the Red Sox defeated the Detroit Tigers 5 runs to 2. They would go on to defeat the Tigers in the next two games, and Roger would again be the winning pitcher for the April 14 game against the Brewers and the game four days later versus the White Sox. However, one of the worst losses in the history of the Red Sox franchise came on April 16, when they had trouble with and succumbed to the underdog Milwaukee Brewers, outscored by 18 runs to the Red Sox's 0. Despite this devastating loss, the team would surpass the .500 mark early in the season and never lose it. Roger himself reached a momentous milestone by becoming a member of the 100-wins club at the May 9 game against the Seattle Mariners. The Red Sox defeated the Mariners 4 runs to 1 and brought the Rocket's win-to-loss record for the year to 5 and 2. By midseason they were steaming right along and trophied a 13 to 1 win over the Twins on May 19, only to suffer an embarrassing loss to them one week later 16 to 0. The fans, while they may have forgiven the team for their losses in previous years, had not forgotten and were back in droves in the stands. The

> *Indeed, the season for the Rocket and the Boston Red Sox started off just like a rocket.*

Rocket was bringing them in and was worth his paycheck. By the season's end the Red Sox had 88 wins under their belt compared to 74 losses for the year. The postseason was a gift waiting to be unwrapped, again. As wary fans knew all too well, many gifts often turn out to be Pandora's boxes.

For the third time in his short career, Roger was selected to an All-Star Game. The 1990 game was held July 10 at Chicago's Wrigley Field. A rain delay threatened to move the play to the next day, but friendlier skies prevailed and the game commenced. If a delay had been necessary, it would have been almost impossible to reschedule the game. Since the All-Star Game is pegged in the middle of a short break in the season, and with so many schedules and other arrangements that have to be made or broken, it would be highly unlikely that the game would have been postponed to another date. The year would have to go on without the All-Star Game if such a delay was unavoidable. However, the 1990 game did go on as scheduled that day, with the American League winning it, 2 runs to 0. Roger was scheduled to pitch but did not. His teammate, outfielder Ellis Burks, was also not able to participate in the game because of an injury. The only Red Sox team member able to play in the game was Wade Boggs at third base. The MVP for the game went to Julio Franco of the Texas Rangers.

The rest of the season was purely the Rocket's. On July 25 he was the winning pitcher in the Brewers game, 2 to 0, and on the 30th defeated the Chicago White Sox 3 to 0. On August 4, Clemens's 28th birthday, the Detroit Tigers were his victim, losing to the Red Sox 3 to 1. One of Roger's best games of the year was the defeat of the Angels on August 9, 14 runs to 3. The winning never seemed to stop for Roger and the Red Sox, with defeats of the Athletics, the Blue Jays, the Cleveland Indians and a repeat performance of their defeat of the Angels on their return visit. One of Roger's few losses came in the September 4 game, where the Athletics won over the Red Sox 6 to 2. But on September 29, the returning Blue Jays suffered a 7 to 5 loss.

The American League Championship Series, held October 6–10, was a repeat command performance of the Eastern Division's Boston Red Sox and the West's Oakland Athletics. It was a nerve-racking game for the entire Red Sox team, everyone remembering all too well the past and their inability to overpower the Athletics. It would again be a series where Oakland would bounce Boston in a 4-0 sweep. The first game, held October 6 in Fenway Park, had Roger on the mound as starting pitcher. As he always did, he held off Oakland's advance, not allowing them to score for six innings. Boston scored early in the fourth inning. The Athletics came back in the seventh and eighth innings, each time scoring a run, and in the ninth inning they scored an unbelievable 7 runs. The Red Sox lost 9 to 1. Clemens and Larry Andersen were the losing Red Sox pitchers in that game. Wade Boggs scored the only home run in the game. The Red Sox did not fare much better in Game 2, with Oakland winning it 4 runs to 1. Game 3, in the Oakland Coliseum, gave little chance to Boston, and the press was all over the hype that it would again be a four-game sweep even though the series was only half over. Oakland would win again, as predicted, 4 runs to 1. Game 4 was the nail in Boston's coffin, as the press put it. Not only was the press unfair to Boston, they were unfair to Roger, the lighting rod of the Red Sox. Dave Stewart, pitcher for the A's, said that Boston was making a "big mistake" by pitching Clemens on such short rest and being tired. The Rocket was the starting pitcher in Game 4,

Clemens and his University of Texas teammates won the 1983 College World Series. University of Texas

Clemens's career took him to Fenway Park in Boston . . .
Aiden Segal

. . . and the Skydome (now Rogers Centre) in Toronto . . .
Minestrone

. . . "The House That Ruth Built," Yankee Stadium in New York City . . .
Kjetil Ree

. . . and Minute Maid Park in Houston. Trei Brundrett

Clemens followed teammate Andy
Pettitte from New York to Houston
and back again. Googie Man

*Clemens once said that he
would hang out in the team's
dugout at just the right angle in
order to watch Greg Maddux
pitch.* VermillionBird

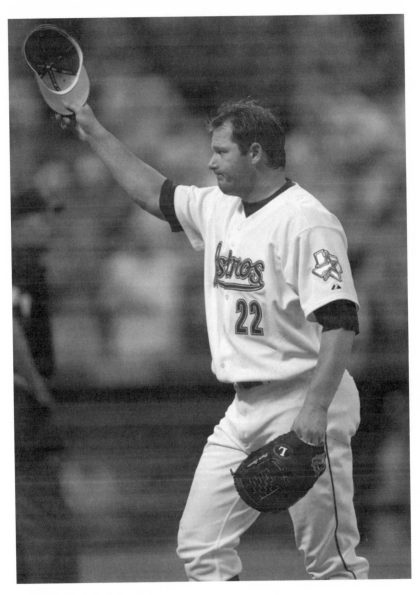

Roger Clemens waves to the crowd as he walks off the mound in Houston for the last time in September 2006. Ronald Martinez, Getty Images

Clemens meets the press after his May 2007 seventh-inning-stretch announcement that he would return to the Yankees. Jim McIsaac, Getty Images

"Did you hear? Clemens is coming back to the Yankees!"
Googie Man

*Past and current manager Joe Torre, shown here with Yogi
Berra, jokingly said of Clemens, "You like him once he's on
your side."* Googie Man

but the negative atmosphere toward Roger, in which he was the object of ridicule for appearing on short rest, led him to argue with home plate umpire Terry Cooney about the strikes and balls. Roger was ejected from the game in the second inning. Oakland would win Game 4, 3 runs to 1. It was a humiliating defeat, again, for the Rocket, and even more humiliation awaited the Red Sox on their return to Boston, when the press proved to be so unfair to the team members that it seemed as if they were drumming up the ill will of the fans. Clemens responded to the press, "I'm too intense, you could hold that against me, because I'm very intense...." This led Oakland's manager Tony La Russa to say that Clemens "... went too far."[1] Although 1990 was one of his best years, the ALCS loss made this year, as with those past, a double-edged sword that seemed to follow Roger throughout his career.

But the Rocket did indeed end up with one of his greatest seasons. As Joe Morgan would always say, "Roger has spun another beauty."[2] Weighing in with the good and the bad, he recorded 21 wins and 6 losses. He led the American League with his 1.93 ERA for the year. In his 31 starts, he attained the 100th win of his career, with his total career wins pegged at 116 at the end of the season, and he looked forward to shortly attaining his 200th win.

The momentum of 1990 began to sputter in the early part of the 1991 season. This was the debut year of the great Mo "Hit Dog" Vaughn, who joined the Boston Red Sox as a major-league batter. Vaughn graduated from Seton Hall University and was a classmate of the all-time great Houston Astros Craig Biggio. Also joining for that season was Matt Young from the Seattle Mariners. Danny "Doctor Death" Darwin, a fellow Texan, signed on as a free agent in December 1990. For a while Darwin would be the highest-paid player in the major leagues. However, Roger Clemens was still the most dominant star of the Red Sox team.

Opening Day would start off great for Roger. He was the starting pitcher against the Toronto Blue Jays, who were defeated 6 runs to 2. Roger's next start was against the Cleveland Indians, and they were also defeated 4 to 0 on April 13. For the first six of his games of the 1991 season, Roger was on a significant roll, and it seemed as if it was going to be another great year for the Rocket and for the Boston Red Sox. He began the season by winning his first six starts and had a spectacular ERA of just .73 for those games!

The team as a whole was again bouncing around the .500 mark and would still be a powerhouse to deal with during the season. The Rocket's roll was broken early in the season when he served a suspension of five games for his ejection from Game 4 of the ALCS in Oakland the previous year. Roger had appealed the suspension and the $10,000 fine, but baseball commissioner Fay Vincent denied the appeal. He served the suspension from April 26 to May 3. But even with a suspension averaged into the equation, he had a run of 30.2 scoreless innings in five starts from April 8 through May 3 and came close to breaking a Red Sox record in doing so. He was even named the American League's pitcher of the month, which seemed to make up for the negative impression left by his suspension. On May 12, the Red Sox celebrated Ted Williams Day to honor the Red Sox great. Before the game on that day they renamed Lansdowne Street adjacent to Fenway Park as Ted Williams Way. Following the celebrations, Roger was on the mound for eight innings, beating down the Chicago White Sox, but his efforts were in vain as the Red Sox would lose the game 4 to 3 in 10 innings. The May 28 game saw Roger defeat the Yankees 6 runs to 2, and one of Roger's best games came on June 8, when he defeated Boston's nemesis, the Oakland Athletics, 8 to 1. The Angels were his next victim, losing to the Red Sox 9 to 4. But on June 19 there was an upsetting loss to the Mariners, 4 to 3, with Clemens getting the tag as the losing pitcher. Making up for it, on July 1 he helped knock out the Brewers 6 to 0, and on July 6 he easily knocked over the Tigers 7 to 4.

The 1991 All-Star Game was played on July 9 at the Skydome in Toronto. It saw Cal Ripken rip out a three-run home run to help the American League win the game 4 runs to 2. Ripken was named the game's MVP. Roger was selected to the game, his fourth so far in his career. He would allow a solo home run to Andre Dawson of the Chicago Cubs in the fourth inning. Wade Boggs and Jeff Reardon joined the Rocket. Roger would also meet Craig Biggio at the game. They would become teammates in a few years as Roger would move to the Houston Astros during the final years of his career.

A July 12 loss to the Twins, 5 to 4, with the Rocket as the losing pitcher, was followed by one of the worst days that season for the Red Sox with a loss to the Twins, 14 to 1, on July 21. Tom Bolton was the losing pitcher. The next day, it was Roger's turn to face the Twins, who again defeated the Red Sox 2 to 1. A few days later Roger would repair his win-to-loss ratio and bring it up to 12 and 7 with a defeat of the Toronto Blue Jays at Fenway Park, 5 to 3, on August 2. One of the best games of the season for the Red Sox occurred on August 21 as they defeated the Cleveland Indians 13 runs to 5. The winning pitcher for the game was the Rocket's teammate, Joe Hesketh. After that win, the Rocket would again be on a straight shot to stardom with a win over the Athletics, 3 to 0, on August 26, and a sweet revenge defeat of the Mariners on August 31 with a 4 to 1 score. The next day would be another best for the team, when it defeated the Mariners again, 13 runs to 2, with Kevin Morton as the winning pitcher. Roger helped continue the winning streak by defeating the Tigers on September 10, 4 to 0, in a game where he retired his first 19 batters until Alan Trammell stopped his advance. The Rocket's next victory was over the Yankees, 5 to 4, on the 15th at Yankee Stadium. A few days later on September 20 the Rocket again defeated the Yankees, this time on home turf at Fenway, 2 to 0. On the following day Joe Hesketh would work his magic at Fenway and defeat the Yankees 12 runs to 1. Hesketh, known as "Fungo," would post a career high of 12 wins during the 1991 season for Boston. For his brilliant work during the season, he would see his earnings increase to over $1 million for the 1992 season.

Roger returned to the mound on September 26 and defeated the Orioles, 2 to 1. His last two starts for the season ended in a loss on October 1 to the Tigers, 8 to 5, and to the Brewers on October 6, 6 to 3. The previous day, another bad loss had come to the team, on October 5, with a 13 to 4 collapse to the Brewers, with Tom Bolton as the losing pitcher.

By season's end the Red Sox were tied for second with the Detroit Tigers in the American League with 84 wins and 78 losses and a .519 average. At first place in the league was the Toronto Blue Jays with 91 wins to 71 losses and an average of .562. The Boston Red Sox were again shut out of the postseason.

In 1991 Roger signed a four-year contract extension worth a reported $21.5 million, averaging out to $5 million per year, plus any extras that might come in for any postseason activities. That made him baseball's highest-paid player. But the year off the field had not been without its downs. In January 1991, in charges that were eventually dismissed in court by a district judge, Roger and his brother Gary Clemens were arrested in a Houston nightclub. Roger and his brother had just been to an area entertainment venue, and afterward they both went into an eatery. Some patrons began to argue with the Rocket's brother, and the police were called in. An officer attempted to arrest Gary for alleged disorderly conduct when Roger tried to deal with the developing situation. Roger ended up being arrested for allegedly placing his arm on the officer and was charged with interfering with a public servant. The charges were eventually dropped. This incident was an obvious misunderstanding by all parties involved. Had Roger Clemens been a relatively unknown citizen, the entire episode would have been corrected with a handshake and gone unnoticed. This, and the major-league suspension Clemens received in November 1990 for arguing with the umpire during the ALCS, caused some negative publicity for Roger. But Roger worked with the situation and with time came out of both incidents with a more positive image. The news media in Boston and in Houston blew the incidents out of proportion for their own ratings and at Roger's expense.

The American League Championship Series for the year was played out between the Toronto Blue Jays and the Minnesota Twins. Even though the Blue Jays were the chosen

> *In January 1991, in charges that were eventually dismissed in court by a district judge, Roger and his brother Gary Clemens were arrested in a Houston nightclub.*

favorite of the press, the Twins defeated them 4 games to 1. In the National League, the Atlanta Braves took on the Pittsburgh Pirates. The fight there went on for all seven games, with the Braves coming out on top, 4 games to 3 over the Pirates. The World Series, which was played October 19–27, had a very excited Atlanta in its first World Series ever, facing the Twins. The Series was unusual in that it used 69 innings in all and in that the home team won each of its home games. In the end, the Twins won it all, 4 games to Atlanta's 3.

For the season, Roger did quite well again. In November, he won his third Cy Young Award. His 2.62 ERA was the best in the American League. He also led the league in strikeouts—for his sixth straight season—at 241, innings pitched at 271, and shutouts at four. His record was 18 wins and 10 losses in 35 starts, a tie for the most starts in his league. In seven of Roger's games he had 10 or more strikeouts.

Shortly after the end of the 1991 season, the Boston Red Sox's management fired skipper Joe Morgan, even though he still had a year left on his contract. Morgan had been extremely popular with the Boston fans, and his replacement, Butch Hobson, would have to work hard at gathering that same amount of loyalty. Hobson was a major-league baseball player for the Boston Red Sox from 1975 to 1980, then played with the California Angels in 1981, and then had a short stay with the Yankees in 1982. He retired and was hired to manage the Boston Red Sox's minor-league team at Pawtucket, and then promoted to the major-league Red Sox as skipper after Morgan was fired. He would remain skipper for three seasons until replaced by Kevin Kennedy in 1996.

In early 1992, the Red Sox signed free agent Cy Young Award–winning Frank Viola to their pitching staff. Known as "Frankie V," he had left the New York Mets after a not-so-good season. His new year with the Red Sox brought an improvement to his game, and he pitched a near perfect game, which was broken in the ninth inning, on September 30 against the Toronto Blue Jays.

In February of that season, the majority owner and president of the Red Sox team, Jean Yawkey, passed away at the age of 83. She had survived her husband, Thomas Yawkey, who had been the owner since the 1930s. He and members of his family saw the Red Sox go through many turbulent years and many close attempts at the World Series. Tom and Jean Yawkey had both become an institution within an institution. After Jean's death, rumors circulated that the team would be up for sale to an outsider, which would eventually occur, but not for another few years. Even after selling the team, the Yawkeys continued to influence the area through the Yawkey Foundation, which focuses on charitable goals throughout the Boston area. To this day, many Red Sox fans call themselves "Yawkeys" to acknowledge their place in the Yawkey Red Sox Nation.

The Red Sox's problems with success didn't disappear with the promotion of Butch Hobson. Shortly after leaving spring training, where they shut down their Winter Haven Training camp for good, the Opening Day game with the Yankees was a disappointing 4 to 3 loss, with their ace, Roger Clemens, as the losing pitcher. Roger was able to make up for that with a win over the Indians on April 12 in a twin-billed doubleheader at Cleveland Stadium. The Rocket appeared in the second game of that bill, helping the Red Sox to win in a shutout, 3 runs to 0. The game on the 17th seemed to put Roger and the team on another roll, with a victory over the Toronto Blue Jays, 1 to 0, with Roger as the winning pitcher. His only other loss during April was to the Brewers, 3 to 2, on April 23. From that point on, he was more successful than his team, which can be attributed mostly, again, to a lack of run support. A pitcher can be the best there is, but when his team doesn't put up some numbers when its turn comes to bat, it many times is a losing combination. Even with all the success and hard work that Roger Clemens had attained, this lack of run support seemed to be a specter that followed his entire career.

Roger blasted off again with a Chicago White Sox defeat on April 28, 6 runs to 3. A week later it was the Royals' turn to face him, and they lost 5 to 0. On May 15, the Angels lost their halos when the Rocket topped them 3 to 0. The Mariners met the same fate on the 20th, 6 runs to 4. Roger traveled to Anaheim Stadium to defeat the Angels again on May 26, 4 to 1, and then on to the Mariners at the Kingdome. A home-field advantage didn't protect the Mariners from the Rocket; they lost to the Red Sox 7 to 1. On June 6 the Indians ventured into Fenway Park, Roger's territory, and were soundly defeated 5 runs to 1. A loss for Roger came on the 11th when the Blue Jays won, 4 to 0, over the Red Sox at the Skydome. A small losing streak in midsummer cut into his power: the June 21 game against the Rangers was a 3 to 2 loss in Arlington, and a July 2 loss to the White Sox, 8 runs to 3, disappointed the Rocket.

The American League again defeated the National League, 13 runs to 6, during the 1992 All-Star Game at Jack Murphy Stadium in San Diego. Wade Boggs and Roger Clemens were the only Red Sox players at the game. It was the Rocket's fifth appearance at the game, and his pitching in the fourth inning ensured the inning would be scoreless for the National League. With the American League win, it was now clear the National League was on a losing streak, which would continue into the next decade. Making matters worse for the National League would be a new rule in 2003 that the winner of the All-Star Game would have home-field advantage in the World Series.

In midseason trades, the Red Sox gave up Tom Bolton in exchange for Billy Hatcher of the Cincinnati Reds. Hatcher is best remembered for his incredible batting during the 1990 World Series. In that series he had seven hits in a row. He's also remembered by baseball fans for being suspended in 1987 for a bat-corking incident, which he claimed was unintentional.

After the All-Star break, Roger Clemens turned a small losing streak around with a victory over the Twins on July 18, where he won the game for his team, 1 to 0. But when the Twins visited him at Fenway, they won 5 to 0 in the first of a doubleheader on July 24. In the game later that evening the Red Sox won, 5 to 4, with Daryl Irvine as the winning pitcher. The next few games provided more notches on Roger's belt with wins against the Rangers on the 29th, 6 to 5, and against the Blue Jays on August 3, 7 runs to 1. The August 8 game against the Yankees at Yankee Stadium saw the Rocket handily defeat them 4 runs to 2. The same was the case with the Indians at Cleveland Stadium; the Rocket pounded them 4 runs to 2 on August 13. On the 18th, the Angels visited Roger at Fenway, but he again swiped their halos in an 8 to 0 Red Sox victory. But on August 23 the Mariners proved too much for the Red Sox, and Clemens suffered a 9 to 3 loss at Fenway.

> *Making matters worse for the National League would be a new rule in 2003 that the winner of the All-Star Game would have home-field advantage in the World Series.*

For the rest of the season Roger would flounder between wins and losses. The August 28 win over the Angels, 7 to 1, at Anaheim Stadium; the September 2 win 5 to 3 at the Kingdome over the Mariners; and the 3 to 0 victory over the Rangers on September 7 were the Rocket's last wins for the season. He lost his last three games to the Tigers, 9 to 5, on September 12; the Brewers, 10 to 4, on the 17th; and the Indians, 4 to 2, on the 22nd.

The Red Sox as a whole also floundered during the remainder of the season. With a mix of wins and losses, they ended up with a record of 73 wins to 89 losses for the 1992 season. It was a nightmare year for Butch Hobson, who feared, as do all skippers during lackluster years, being fired. The Red Sox placed seventh in the American League and were again out of the postseason.

But for 1992, Roger led the league in ERA at 2.41 in his 32 starts. This was the third year in a row the Rocket won the ERA distinction, making him only the fourth player in major-league history to attain that honor. With a win-to-loss record of 18 to 11, he led the American League for the third straight year in a record-tying five shutouts, also. The Cy Young Award for the season went to the American League's Dennis Eckersley of the Oakland Athletics and to the National League's Greg Maddux of the Chicago Cubs. Maddux and Clemens would both become great admirers of each other's style. Clemens once said that he would hang out in the team's dugout at just the right angle in order to watch Maddux pitch. Maddux would return the complement to Clemens, saying, "He's the Rocket. He has an aura about him that I've never experienced."[3]

During 1992, baseball commissioner Fay Vincent was forced to resign his post after a no-confidence vote by the team owners. He was replaced on what was to be a temporary basis by the Milwaukee Brewers president Bud Selig. Selig eventually gained the confidence of the owners and through the years has brought the sport of baseball to a new level.

In 1992 Roger and Debbie Clemens started the Roger Clemens Foundation. Roger has always devoted much of his time and effort to help the needy of the community, especially children and their families. By 1992, his efforts had become so numerous that he decided to facilitate them all through his own foundation. The Roger Clemens Foundation strives to support educational, charitable, scientific, literary, and religious activities for children, especially the underprivileged and at-risk child. Over the years that Roger has been in the major leagues, many institutions have benefited from his and Debbie's efforts, as discussed in chapter 1. Starting with the Jimmy Fund at the Dana-Farber Institute in Boston, he reached out to such others as the Boys and Girls Clubs of America, Cystic Fibrosis Foundation, Make-A-Wish Foundation, Multiple Sclerosis Society, Star of Hope Mission, the Sunshine Kids, Texas Children's Hospital, the Twin Towers Fund, and the Variety Clubs International, as well as others. As each year progressed, there were numerous requests for the Clemenses to attend various functions, such as golf tournaments, galas, and silent auctions, which they most graciously accepted in order to use their impact on society to help those who need help the most. They have helped many more charities as time goes on, and today Roger and Debbie are regarded as true benefactors in their community. Debbie doesn't step back in her role as wife to a baseball great. She has shown that the best luxury one can have is to just be one's own self and to help others in the process.

Also in 1992, Roger infamously played himself in episode 17 of season three of *The Simpsons* titled "Homer at the Bat" in which a hypnotist convinces Clemens that he has been turned into a chicken. He joined other baseball greats, such as Wade Boggs, Ken Griffey Jr., José Canseco, Darryl Strawberry, Ozzie Smith, Steve Sax, Don Mattingly, and Mike Scioscia, who also provided their voices. In the episode, Homer carves a bat from a tree limb that was felled by a storm. He's then struck by lightning while trying to hide in a metal shed from the storm. This gives him unusual powers at bat, which he uses in the local nuclear power plant's baseball game playoffs. The power plant owner, Montgomery Burns, makes a bet with the other nuclear power plant's owner that his team is the best, and to prove it, he buys off several major-league greats, performed by the actual players. As Mr. Burns tells his team, "All right, you ragtag bunch of misfits! You hate me, and I hate you even more. But without my beloved ringers, you're all I've got. So I want you to remember some inspiring words that someone else might have told you over the course of your lives, and go out there and win!" Several unfortunate events cause all of the professional team members to stay out of the game, leaving only Strawberry and the rest of the plant's team to win the game on their own. Roger couldn't play the game because he had been hypnotized into thinking he was a chicken and clucked away on the mound. It was a situation that has since thankfully worn off. In addition to his TV debut, Roger made several appearances on the silver screen, in *Anger Management* in 2003, where he played himself in a cameo; *Cobb*, in 1994, where he played an opposing pitcher; and *Kingpin*, in 1996, where he played the role of Skidmark.[4]

The postseason for 1992 was a near repeat of the 1991 playoffs. In the American League the Toronto Blue Jays took on the Oakland Athletics, and the Blue Jays won 4 games to 2. In the National League the Pittsburgh Pirates again took on the Atlanta Braves and were again defeated by the Braves, 4 games to 3. The Braves moved on to their second World Series to take on the Blue Jays October 17–24. The Blue Jays won it in six games. It was the first World Series ever to be played outside the United States and the first time the fall classic was won by a team based outside the United States; however, the final winning game, Game 6, was held in Atlanta on October 24, 1992.

In November 1992 Drayton McLane Jr. purchased the Houston Astros from team owner John McMullen for a reported $115 million. McLane had worked his way up in his father's grocery and delivery business, eventually controlling the McLane interests and making his fortune. In 2007, the Houston Astros were worth over $400 million. McLane has also been one to work with his city in order to better the conditions of the underprivileged. His Astros in Action Foundation has helped many inner-city children through various charity luncheons and silent auctions. It was Mr. McLane, with help from Clemens's buddy Andy Pettitte, who would later convince Roger to eventually become one of the Houston Astros in the 2004 season, one of the last few seasons of his career.

This is one of the most misunderstood sides of Roger Clemens. When he retired from the Yankees in 2003, he did retire. In many ways, he made it clear that he might, from time to time, come out of retirement for a season, or partial season. It was the media frenzy that made him appear indecisive on this matter.

Chapter 8

ROCKET SCIENCE

From 1992 and through the mid-1990s the seasons for the Red Sox and for the Rocket turned out to be years of more frustration. The fans, the team, the ownership, and Roger were stuck in a conundrum. The 1993 season was to be one of the worst for the Rocket. There were a few causes for this slump. Roger ended up on the disabled list twice during the season. And the team as a whole seemed to be in transition and trying to find itself. Just before spring training the Red Sox acquired Jeff Russell as a free agent along with a few other players through signings and trades. There was not much offensive help from the team to stave off the advances of other teams. Roger could pitch his best, but if his team lacked run support, it would be an uphill battle of one.

For the Rocket, 1993 would be another forgettable season. He ended up with a losing season record of 11 wins and 14 losses, with only 160 strikeouts. This was the first time he attained fewer than 200 strikeouts in a long while, and the year would be his first major-league losing

163

season. His ERA was his worst in his long career at 4.46 in his 29 starts for the team that year.

When Clemens pitched against the Kansas City Royals on Opening Day, April 25, he was the winning pitcher with a score of 3 to 1. In his next wins he defeated the Texas Rangers 10 to 2 and the perennial favorites, the Seattle Mariners, 5 to 2. Actually the first month and a half were looking great for the Red Sox and the Rocket, and the team was either in first or second place in the American League East, keeping the fans and the team ownership happy. The Rocket helped to open the season strong with his 5 wins and 2 losses and an amazing 1.73 ERA for his first eight starts. In May he tossed three 10-plus-strikeout games in a six-game time span. On May 11 the Rocket struck out a season high of 13 for a win against the Baltimore Orioles 4 to 0. The May 19 game was a memorable one, a 10 to 5 win over the Toronto Blue Jays, and on the 29th the Red Sox defeated the Texas Rangers 15 to 1 at Fenway Park. The ALCS and maybe even the elusive World Series, the fall classic, were topics once again in the papers and other media. In 1993, Roger reached the 2,000 strikeout level.

Roger's low ERA was not something he rested easily with; the Rocket never relaxes his guard when he is winning or losing. But by June, things began to unravel. There were consecutive losses to the Kansas City Royals, Chicago White Sox, Cleveland Indians, Baltimore Orioles, New York Yankees, Blue Jays, and the Detroit Tigers. One of the Rocket's worst days came when he was the losing pitcher in the Toronto Blue Jays game, losing 11 to 2 on June 18 at the Skydome. Without mercy, the media began to hype that it was the beginning of the end of the team for the year. But it didn't bother the Rocket or the team as they had repeatedly heard this before, even in their best years. True to form, there was an amazing turnaround for the better in late July, when the Red Sox defeated the Oakland Athletics, the Seattle Mariners, the Los Angeles Angels, and the Athletics again for a short-term rise above the .500 mark. Sadly, during the winning streak, the Rocket was put on the disabled list from June 19 to July 15 because of a sore right elbow and a strained hip muscle. But upon his return on July 16 he destroyed the Seattle Mariners in Fenway Park 5 runs to 3. Next up, he leveled his aim at the Angels, 4 to 1, on July 21. In his first few starts upon his return from injury he allowed just three runs in 21 innings and improved his ERA to a respectable 3.22 after 18 starts, with 9 wins and 6 losses. But by August and into September Roger and the Red Sox were in a spin again, and in the Rocket's last 11 starts he lost eight games and won only two with his ERA now at a bloated 6.82. On September 5 he let slip through his very first grand slam in his major-league career, and the Red Sox lost to the Kansas City Royals, 5 to 2, with Tom Gordon as the winning pitcher.

On September 18, in a highly unusual game, the Yankees beat the Red Sox, in part because of the interference of a fan who ran onto the field during final play. The Red Sox were wining at the end of the ninth when the interference took place. The play was called and was redone, the second time ending favorably for the Yankees; they won it, 4 runs to 3. As the season drew to a close, Roger saw his team place fourth in the division with 80 wins and 82 losses.

There would be no ALCS this year again for Clemens and his team. For Roger, there would not be a Cy Young Award, no MVP, and no glory in losing. The 1993 Cy Young Award went to a young up-and-comer, Greg Maddux of the Atlanta Braves, for the National League, and for the American League the award went to Jack McDowell of the Chicago

White Sox. The MVP for the National League that year went to a fresh new player with the San Francisco Giants, Barry Bonds, for his unusually spectacular performances on the field, and to Frank Thomas of the Chicago White Sox in the American League.

Red Sox skipper Butch Hobson saw the writing on the wall for his second nonwinning season. What went on behind the scenes soon made its way into the media, with the fans consuming the news with an almost morbid glee.

In September 1993, the Rocket's role model and idol, Nolan Ryan, at the age of 46, retired from the game that he had reigned over for almost a quarter of a century. He announced his retirement earlier in the year and planned it for the end of the season. However, on September 22 while pitching a game to the Seattle Mariners, he tore a tendon in his pitching arm. He tried to recover from the pain while on the mound and attempted one more pitch, which he knew would be the last in his major-league career. After the pitch, the Rangers announced that he would be on the disabled list for the remainder of the season and that the September 22 game had indeed been his last. Ryan was a strong Texan even up to the end of his career. A month and a half before, on August 4, was the infamous brawl on the mound between Ryan and Robin Ventura of the Chicago White Sox. Ryan had pitched and hit Ventura. While being hit by a pitch is an almost everyday happening in baseball, Ventura suddenly lost his temper and rushed Nolan Ryan on the mound. That's what is

> *What went on behind the scenes soon made its way into the media, with the fans consuming the news with an almost morbid glee.*

really called a bad decision in baseball. Ryan immediately took hold of Ventura in a headlock, smacking him as if teaching the twenty-years-younger player a lesson in etiquette, Texas style. Ventura was thrown out of the game, but Ryan was able to keep on pitching his Texas Rangers to victory 5 runs to 2. When Nolan Ryan retired, he left a legacy of 324 wins, seven no-hitters, and 5,714 strikeouts, but he had no Cy Young Awards. Sometimes actually winning games means more than what an award can bring.

The 1993 year put what a loss really means into surreal perspective. At the beginning of the season during spring training, three pitchers from the Cleveland Indians went fishing during an off-day. Golf and fishing were the most common activities outside of baseball during that time of the year for players. One of Roger's former teammates, Bob Ojeda, was one of the fishermen, with driver Tim Crews and Steve Olin. While cruising at a high rate of speed, the boat hit a dock, fatally injuring Crews and Olin. Bob Ojeda was badly injured but survived. The two were the first active major-league players to die since an accident that killed Thurman Munson of the New York Yankees. Munson was piloting his private plane when it crashed into some trees just after takeoff in Ohio on August 1, 1979. He died in the crash, but his two passengers survived. No other major-league player would suffer an accidental death until another New York Yankee, pitcher Cory Lidle, died along with his flight instructor in October 2006. Their plane somehow veered off course and crashed into a multistory apartment complex. Miraculously there were no deaths on the ground.

The 1993 All-Star Game took place on July 13 in Baltimore. The only Boston Red Sox player chosen for the game was Scott Cooper, at third base. The American League won over the National League 9 runs to 3. Chosen as MVP for the game was Kirby Puckett of the Minnesota Twins (1960–2006). The much-loved Puckett ended his career, which was entirely with the Minnesota Twins, in 1995, after glaucoma took its toll. He was elected into the Baseball Hall of Fame in his first year of eligibility in 2001. His death from a stroke in 2006 took baseball and the nation by surprise. The Twins retired his number, 34, shortly after his retirement.

With tensions high between owners, players, and fans, there was a drop in interest for the playoff games and the World Series. The players' association threatened to go on strike during the 1993 season and stop any play in the American League and National League, even if the World Series had to be cancelled. Whether this threat was a bluff, as many in the media proposed, or if the association was just positioning for attention was a question that would play out in the 1994 season.

In the 1993 ALCS, the Chicago White Sox were beaten by the Toronto Blue Jays, 4 games to 2, and in the NLCS the Philadelphia Phillies beat the Atlanta Braves, 4 games to 2. The Toronto Blue Jays won the World Series 4 games to 2 over the Phillies, and for the second time in a row, a team based outside the continental United States participated in and won the World Series.

Again in 1993, baseball movies seemed to rule the box office and airwaves. *Rookie of the Year* told the story of a young fan who threw a ball back into the game from the stands and made such an impression he was signed as a rookie by the Chicago Cubs. It starred Gary Busey and Thomas Ian Nicholas. Another movie, *Cooperstown*, which starred Alan Arkin, Ed Begley Jr., Hope Lange, and Jason Orman, followed the life of a baseball player who had always dreamed of a stellar major-league career and was visited by the ghost of a pitcher from his past. His perspective about the game, and life, was changed.

Tensions between players and owners were simmering behind the scenes for several years on issues such as salary caps, free agency, and revenue sharing among the teams. As time went on things began to get even more hostile. A strike was narrowly averted in 1993 when the players decided to go ahead and finish the season. Over the winter break normal business took place, albeit with tension, in the team offices, and player trades, scouting, and other roster changes continued. At year's end the collective bargaining agreement expired, and there was no new agreement between the two sides. The start of the 1994 season seemed to proceed with business as usual, but the media carried almost daily talk from the players and owners about the situation. Making everything even more complicated, team owners had forced baseball commissioner Fay Vincent to resign more than a year previously, eventually appointing Bud Selig as acting commissioner at the time of the negotiations. Possibly, to some extent, an acting commissioner didn't seem to have the same authoritative pull as a fully vested commissioner.

> *Tensions between players and owners were simmering behind the scenes for several years on issues such as salary caps, free agency, and revenue sharing among the teams.*

Between seasons, Wade Boggs announced that he had signed with the New York Yankees, ending many years as a Boston Red Sox player. Although his averages had fallen during the last year of his career with Boston, he decided that the Yankees would offer a fresh start away from a turbulent Boston fan base and media critics who seemed to hound him at every corner for his conduct both on and off the diamond.

The Boston Red Sox again started off the 1994 season with a bang. The season opener on April 4 saw Roger Clemens start and defeat the Detroit Tigers 9 runs to 8 at Fenway Park. The entire opening homestand was a sweep of the Tigers. One of the more spectacular games came on April 12, where the Rocket's team demolished the Kansas City Royals at Royal Stadium 22 to 11. On April 15, the Rocket himself defeated the Chicago White Sox 5 runs to 3 at Fenway for his first win. The April 20 game in Fenway saw the defeat of the Chicago White Sox, 2 to 0. It would be one of Roger's last shutout games until the 1996 season. By the end of April and the start of May, the Rocket and the Red Sox were 20 to 7 in wins, helped by Roger's win over the Angels, 4 to 1, on April 30. Some of his best games were the Sunday, May 22, game at the Metrodome— defeating the Minnesota Twins 9 runs to 2, and bringing the team record up to 27 to 15—and his win over the Mariners on July 24 at Fenway, 8 runs to 2. This was the year the Rocket came closest to pitching a no-hitter; he took the streak through the seventh inning with the Oakland Athletics on July 14 until Ruben Sierra finally popped a single. In any case, the Rocket would win it 2 to 1.

The 1994 All-Star Game took place in Pittsburgh at Three Rivers Stadium on July 21. Again the Rocket was passed over for a spot on his league's team. Scott Cooper of the Red Sox was voted on as the sole representative of the team. Wade Boggs, who had moved to the Yankees, was on the roster as he had been many times during his career. That year's All-Star Game was one to remember. Throughout much of the game the score was close, and it went into extra innings, one of the few times this has happened for the game. Finally, the National League scored a hit and won it 8 runs to the American League's 7. The NL finally broke the AL's winning streak after six years.

Shortly after the All-Star Game, Roger became a father again for the third time. Another boy, Kacy, was born on July 27, 1994. Again, the "K" in his name was in honor of the many strikeouts in Roger's career. After the strike went into effect, Roger went home to be with his wife, Debbie, and their growing family. Among all things in baseball, he set the image of a stable family man beyond any reproach, and that was and still is the main thing his legions of fans adore about the Rocket.

By July 24, Roger's last win for the year, the team was struggling with a record of 47 wins to 50 losses. On August 10, the Red Sox lost to the Twins 17 to 1, resulting in a 54 to 61 record, thus ending the season. The fans, already livid over the infighting about salaries, were ready to walk out on their own, but they wouldn't have to do that. On August 12 the players' association made the call for a strike, and the players walked off the field. They wouldn't return until well past the time when the 1995 season should have been under way.

But for the strike-shortened season, the Rocket went 9 to 7 in his 24 starts for his team, resulting in an ERA of 2.65. He ranked in second place in the American League for his ERA. The batters who faced him had just a .204 batting average, the best for a pitcher in both leagues.

The 1994 season was the year of the Central Division, with a realignment of the teams to divide up the East and West in both the American and National Leagues. Before the realignment there was even talk by some of the teams of creating their own independent league, but little came of this talk. The creation of the Central Division, designed to help facilitate the growing list of expansion teams, especially during the playoffs and championships, was of absolutely no use because of the 1994 strike. It would have to wait one more year to show its value.

By the end of 1994 at least some activity resumed in baseball. Trades, signings, management changes, and other events all took place with business as usual. In early December 1994 the Boston Red Sox obtained José Canseco, who arrived from the Texas Rangers. His career was turbulent, and even after his retirement in 2003 he would end up in the spotlight often. Oddly, the Boston Red Sox fired their skipper Butch Hobson after the 1994 season's early end, and in the middle of October they hired as skipper Kevin Kennedy, who had been Canseco's skipper with the Texas Rangers a few weeks earlier.

Honors for the season were awarded as usual. The Cy Young Award for the National League went to Greg Maddux of the Atlanta Braves and David Cone of the American League. The Rookie of the Year award went to Bob Hamelin of the American League and Raul Mondesi of the National League. For the American League, the Most Valuable Player went to Frank Thomas of the Chicago White Sox.

With no playoffs for the year, the final standings for 1994 were released on the 11th of August. At the top of the heap in the American League East Division were the New York Yankees with 70 wins and 43 losses. In second place were the Baltimore Orioles with 63 wins and 49 losses; next up at third were the Toronto Blue Jays with a 55 to 60 record. The Rocket and his Boston Red Sox were fourth in line with a 54 to 61 record. At the top of the AL Central were the Chicago White Sox, and at the top of the West were the Texas Rangers. The top spots in the National

League division belonged to the Montreal Expos in the East, the Cincinnati Reds in the Central, and the Los Angeles Dodgers in the West. It was especially painful for the Montreal Expos to be so close to the champion- ships and the World Se- ries and to lose the chance. The team had spent years building public support, and the 1994 season seemed to be theirs. After the strike, public attendance at the games plummeted and remained low for years. In 2004, the team announced it would be leaving Montreal for Wash- ington, DC, because of a lack of public support. Few in Montreal noticed.

> At least the public had baseball-themed movies to enjoy during the strike.

At least the public had baseball-themed movies to en- joy during the strike. Hollywood somehow had a sense that this would finally be the year of the strike and made sure that it would be a record year for baseball movies, with the sequel to *Major League*, *Major League II*, with Charlie Sheen, Tom Berenger, and Corbin Bernsen. Another popu- lar movie was *Angels in the Outfield*, starring Matthew McConaughey, Ben Johnson, and Tony Danza. *Little Big League* starred Tim Busfield, Ashley Crow, and Jonathan Silverman. *Cobb* was about the baseball great and starred Tommy Lee Jones and Lolita Davidovich and costarred Roger Clemens. *The Scout* starred Brendan Fraser, Albert Brooks, and Michael Rapaport. On public television, PBS premiered the epic *Baseball: A Film by Ken Burns* and brought in large numbers of viewers. It remains popular in reruns for the educational network. The first PBS station in the world was founded in Houston, Texas, in 1953. From there it expanded to every city in the United States and

Canada, and the programs are seen in syndication throughout the world.

The long strike in baseball finally came to a close officially on April 2, 1995, after 232 days. Both sides agreed
that the new season would be an adjusted one with 144
games rather than the customary 162-game season. In many
cities, when Opening Day finally did arrive, there were pro-
tests by fans, who wielded their anger at major-league
officials and players alike. The fans of the game felt that
they were the ones who were cheated the most by the
stike. They had invested hundreds of millions of tax
dollars to build sports pal-

> *The long strike in baseball finally came to a close officially on April 2, 1995, after 232 days.*

aces for their teams and to better their teams' chances of
winning at least a few championships and maybe even a
World Series every so often. The fans and the public felt
they had been stabbed in the back by the strike and their
loyalty suffered. There was a movement to no longer pub-
licly finance team improvements, which over the years has
shown little or no return. Even when an All-Star Game or
the playoffs arrived in town, the increase in tourist revenues and sales taxes always went to the team coffers
rather than to reward the fans, who now had to pay
higher ticket prices to go to the games. After all, other
industries located in major cities—such as the oil industry
in the South, or even the movie production industry in
California—had to plow their own fields to bring in revenues. They were never financed with public dollars, and
they were succeeding. Why give billions to teams for a talent that basically was hitting a ball with a stick? they asked.

Public officials, who to some extent were able to stay in office because of alleged campaign contributions from the builders of these stadiums and venues, took the side of professional sports.

As a result there were fewer fans in the stands during the season, and ownership desperately tried various advertising attempts to lure them back. There was a noticeable decline in fan attendance during the entire year and in succeeding years. MLB officials worked up more ways to draw in new fans, such as the new "wild card" position in the playoffs, which was used for the first time during the 1995 division playoff season. The division playoffs remained in the best-of-five format. It was also the premier year for the American League Division Series (ALDS), in which the newly established wild card had significant impact.

The Rocket wasn't present at Fenway Park to greet the fans who did return when the season opener took place after the strike. Roger was placed on the disabled list with a strained shoulder. On April 26, 1995, the Red Sox hosted the Minnesota Twins and defeated them 9 runs to 0, with Aaron Sele as the winning pitcher. It was the start of what would turn out to be another great season at Fenway Park for the Boston Red Sox and the fans. There were quite a few dramatic wins for the team by the time Roger returned from the disabled list in June of that year. The team had a spectacular 24 to 12 record. On June 7 the Rocket helped to defeat the Angels at Fenway Park, 5 runs to 1, and to bring up the Red Sox's record to 25 and 12. In that game he pitched five shutout innings with eight strikeouts. But again he was about to journey on one of his temporary downturns, as most players do at times. In his next 11 starts he won only 3 games and lost 4 with a 5.56 ERA. After this short fall, he corrected himself and was on the upswing, bringing his ERA to an enviable 1.95 by winning 5 games and losing 0 for his next few starts from August 7 to September 6. In the September 6 game versus Oakland, he pitched an 8 to 2 win with a season high of 10 strikeouts.

The Saturday, September 16, game saw a bit of history take place. It was the debut of Brian Giles. Giles began his baseball career in the Cleveland organization's minor-league system until he was brought up to the major leagues with the Cleveland Indians. He then went on to the Pittsburgh Pirates and the San Diego Padres. His statistics have remained remarkable throughout his career. Brian recalls of that day: "Roger was the first major-league pitcher that I had ever faced. I had butterflies in my stomach because I was so nervous as a rookie. It was all I could do to concentrate on the ball. To face Roger was actually an honor, and I feel honored to have had him out there, and even today. There's no way I would have preferred another pitcher even though the situation was tougher on me. Look at me now!" Brian actually got a hit off the Rocket and made it to first base. From his very first at-bat, he has kept his on-base percentage one of the highest in major-league records and is one of baseball's underappreciated greats.[1]

In Brian's debut, the Indians won the game 9 runs to 6. Jeff "Soop" Suppan was the winning pitcher. Getting a hit off Roger, that little bit of history in the making, put Giles on the major-league roadmap and gained him a following. In some way the Rocket must have looked at Brian, up at his first chance at-bat, and seen himself as a rookie. Roger didn't take out revenge on Brian's team by hitting a batter with a pitch. To help make ends meet before he was in the minors, Brian pumped concrete for a living in the San Diego area, which must have given him that strong arm and swing. His brother, Marcus Giles, is also a Padre for the 2007 season, on second base.

One of the last Red Sox games of the season was a defeat of the Milwaukee Brewers, 11 to 6, with the Rocket as the winning pitcher. The Red Sox came close to sweeping the Brewers in that four-game series but lost to them in their last game of the season on October 1. The Red Sox finished in first place in the American League East Division, winning 86 games and losing 58 with a resulting average of .597 for the season. The Boston Red Sox faced the Cleveland Indians of the newly established Central Division in the first ever American League Division Series. The division was created during the 1994 strike season to facilitate the growing number of new teams and allow more teams to have a chance at the number one spot. When teams do not have at least a chance at making it to the top because of the increased number of teams, their fan base becomes disenchanted with them and revenues drop. Baseball needed a new division.

On August 13 of that season, baseball great Mickey Mantle died in Dallas, Texas, from liver cancer. He was 63 years old. In his last days he sought to make amends to friends and family for his hard and sometimes difficult life. He made a famous remark to fans, speaking especially to children, when he told them: "This is a role model: don't be like me."[2] Within a few days, he died.

In game one of the ALDS, the Red Sox appeared to be the favorite, although the Indians' track record for the year was a superior 100 wins and 44 losses and a galactic .694 winning average. The Red Sox did score the first few runs, but the Indians countered them and won the game. This was the case for the next two games, and the Indians won the series with their 3 games to the Red Sox's 0. What had been a glorious year of wins, first place in their division, and hopes for the fall classic turned out to be more fuel to burn down what was left between the Red Sox and their fans. The news media only served to fan the flames, making a bad situation worse. As a team the Red Sox would struggle to find themselves for the next few years.

The rest of the ALDS for 1995 had the wild card winner New York Yankees facing the Seattle Mariners for a classic baseball showdown. The Yankees wore black armbands with the number seven in honor of their late teammate, Mickey Mantle. The Yankees sent their rookie ace Andy Pettitte out to the mound to face the Mariners' ace veteran Andy Benes. The Mariners beat the Yankees and went on to the American League Championship Series to face the Cleveland Indians. After a four-decade-long wait, the Cleveland Indians had made it to the World Series.

In that World Series, the Indians faced the National League's Atlanta Braves. The Series would become known as a "pitchers series" because 18 pitchers would be used in the six-game affair. Favored pitchers Tom Glavine, John Smoltz, Mark Wohlers, Alejandro Pena, Greg Maddux, Steve Avery, Greg McMichael, Pedro Borbon, Brad Clontz, and Kent Mercker of the Braves all played, and for the Indians, Charles Nagy, Paul Assenmacher, Julian Tavarez, Jose Mesa, Alan Embree, Ken Hill, Jim Poole, and the great Orel Hershiser were sent to the mound. It would be a game to remember for years when Atlanta won it 4 games to 2. It was Atlanta's first win at the fall classic although they had previous appearances in 1991 and in 1992.

The awards announced at season's end were full of surprises. The Cy Young Award went to the American League's Randy Johnson, and for the National League it went, for the unprecedented fourth time, to Greg Maddux.

The MVP awards were given to the American League's Mo Vaughn and the National League's Barry Larkin. Interestingly enough, because of the previous year's strike, the public took an interest in the Japanese and other Asian leagues. For 1995, the Rookie of the Year for the National League went to Hideo Nomo, just out of the Japan leagues and now with the Los Angeles Dodgers. For the American League the Rookie of the Year went to Marty Cordova of the Minnesota Twins.

> *Behind the scenes at the Boston Red Sox, talks were not going well between the Rocket and the general management and owners of the team.*

Behind the scenes at the Boston Red Sox, talks were not going well between the Rocket and the general management and owners of the team. Things would eventually come to a head during the upcoming 1996 season, when Roger's contract came to a close and negotiations broke down between the two sides.

The 1996 season would be the Rocket's last in Boston. It would turn out to be the second losing season in his career, and he would finish the year with just 10 wins and 13 losses. His ERA floated above the 3.00 mark to a 3.63 ERA in total for all of his 34 starts as pitcher. Without a doubt the major reason for the Rocket's lower averages was the tense negotiating with the Red Sox's front office.

Chapter 9

YANKEE GO HOME

During the previous 1995 season, the Red Sox obtained veteran pitcher Mike Maddux, the older brother of the Cy Young Award-winning Greg Maddux.[1] The Red Sox pitching roster swelled to a record 26 members in 1995 and then settled to 23 members in 1996. This increase depleted the Rocket's and other veteran players' pitching time by a proportionate amount.

The fans might have looked upon the season opener on April Fools' Day 1996 as an omen of what was to come later in the season. The Rocket was the pitcher for that April 1 game against the Texas Rangers at the ballpark in Arlington. It was a game that the Red Sox lost 5 runs to 3, with Roger as the losing pitcher. The entire series with the Rangers was a wipe out. The April 3 game was lost 7 to 2, and the April 4 game was even worse, with an unrecoverable loss of 13 to 2. In addition, the next two games were losses to the Kansas City Royals, leaving the Red Sox with a road record of 0 wins to 5 losses. The team didn't permanently work their way up to the .500 mark until the August 22 game, when the Rocket defeated the Oakland Athletics 2 runs to 0 at Fenway Park. Roger's track record for the year at that point was 7 wins and 11 losses. One of the worst defeats for the Red Sox happened on April 13 when they lost to the Indians, 14 to 2, which was followed by a 10 to 0 loss to the Royals on April 27. A standout game for the year was the May 1 game where the Rocket struck out 13 Detroit Tigers and won the game for the Red Sox, 5 runs to 1. It was Roger's first win of the season. Ironically, during the May 23 game Roger did something he hadn't done in his entire major-league career, he had his first hit in a game where he appeared as both a hitter and a pitcher. He pitched the entire game and defeated the Mariners 11 to 4.

But in all of these defeats there were days of glory for the Rocket and the Red Sox. On July 11 he was the winning pitcher over the Detroit Tigers, 11 to 4, at Tiger Stadium. There was the 6 to 0 smackdown of the Angels on August 17 at Fenway Park, which was Roger's first shutout since April 20, 1994. Of all of the wins in his last year for the Red Sox, the Rocket would be remembered most for the win on September 18 at the Detroit Tigers where he again hit a milestone and struck out 20 batters in a nine-inning game for a 4 to 0 win and brought up the Red Sox win-to-loss record to 78 to 73. The Red Sox swept the three-game series versus the Tigers. It was the second time in his career that Clemens reached the 20-strikeout mark; the first time was 10 years earlier when he struck out 20 batters in a game with the Seattle Mariners on April 29, 1986. Oddly enough, both events were missed by most of the baseball world in that both games had very low attendance. Most people received word of Roger's achievement later on the late evening news.

In the 1996 season, he propelled himself to a 28-inning scoreless winning streak August 1–22, which was the longest streak in the major leagues for that year. This streak included the Rocket's win over the Brewers, 2 runs to 0, on August 11; the victory over the Angels, 6 to 0, on August 17; and the Athletics game where he finally pushed the team up to the magical .500 mark. That August 17 game was also the end of his shutout dry spell. It was the first time since April 1994 that he finished off a team in that manner. In September he was even hotter, with a 9 to 5 victory welted on the Chicago White Sox on September 13 and a 4 to 0 win over the Detroit Tigers. On September 28, Roger struck out 10 Yankees, but the opposition was too strong for the Red Sox, who lost to the pitching abilities of Yankee ace Andy Pettitte. That game was Roger's last bit of pitching in a Red Sox uniform.

During the season Debbie and Roger became parents to their fourth child, a boy named Kody born on May 15. Sticking with tradition, the name began with a strikeout "K" for good luck and in honor of Roger's career strikeouts.

Mo Vaughn was the only member of the Boston Red Sox to be selected, by popular vote, to appear in the 1996 All-Star Game, which took place in Philadelphia, Pennsylvania, at Veterans Stadium on July 9. The National League swept the American League with 6 runs to the AL's 0. It was the first time in years that the score had such a spread. It is also remembered as the first All-Star Game with no walks for either team.

A few days after the All-Star Game, the Summer Olympics took place in Atlanta, Georgia. The boost to the city was said to have helped the Atlanta Braves concentrate on getting themselves to the World Series. The Olympic Games became a center of attention for stadium security around the United States and the world, when on July 27, 1996, a backpack filled with explosives detonated in a pedestrian area of the Olympic Park, killing one and injuring 111. One more bystander died from a heart attack from the shock. The bombing had a profound impact on security personnel in all of the baseball stadiums in both leagues. For the first time, police and security guards made an intense effort to screen all fans coming into the games. In addition, security cameras became commonplace and were posted at strategic areas in the stadiums so that such an event could hopefully be averted. If the worst did happen, it would end up being recorded so that the perpetrators would be apprehended and punished.

When the All-Star break was over, the Rocket was again able to zone in on his game while at the same time work on contract negotiations with team management. It was like working two jobs simultaneously, and the stress began to show in some of his performances.

On September 17, 1996, Hideo Nomo of the Dodgers pitched a no-hitter and an almost perfect game against the Colorado Rockies in a 9 to 0 victory. Nomo came to the United States as a result of the 1994 strike, when management sought out new players either as possible replacements or as new, more cooperative blood. Nomo's achievement opened the eyes of American fans to the Japanese league players for the first time. Soon other players from Japan would venture into the major leagues in America. In terms of audience draw, baseball is even more popular in Japan than it is in the United States.

By the end of the season the Red Sox record was 85 wins to 77 losses, which placed them third in the East Division with a .525 winning average. In first place were the New York Yankees, and the Baltimore Orioles won the wild-card slot. With the Red Sox out of contention for any postseason, the fans walked off in droves, which did little to ease the tensions between the Rocket and the Red Sox's ownership.

In the division series for the year, the Yankees took on the Texas Rangers and won 3 games to 1. The wild-card Orioles took on the Cleveland Indians and also won their series 3 games to 1. In the National League, the Braves won over the Dodgers, 3 games to 0, and similarly the St. Louis Cardinals took over the San Diego Padres, 3 games to 0. In the league championships, the Yankees won the American League and the Braves won the National League, resulting in a classic World Series between the Yankees and Braves. The Yankees would win 4 games to 2.

> *The 1996 season would be yet another year in a dry spell of awards for the Rocket.*

The 1996 season would be yet another year in a dry spell of awards for the Rocket. The Cy Young Award went to John Smoltz of the Braves and to Pat Hentgen of the Toronto Blue Jays, who in the voting just squeezed in over the Yankees' Andy Pettitte. Pettitte had the most wins for the season in the AL at 21. That year the MVP went to Juan Gonzalez of the AL and Ken Caminiti of the NL.

Even though the Rocket's last year with the Red Sox was a losing one for the team and for him personally, with 10 wins and 13 losses, he led the AL with 257 strikeouts and had eight 10-plus strikeout games. The Rocket tied Cy Young, the greatest Red Sox to ever grace baseball, in earning the most wins for the team at 192. Clemens was also tops on the list for starts, at 382; bases on balls, at 856; strikeouts, at 2,590; and first on the list for walks, at 856.

In summing up his career for the Red Sox, the powers that be probably knew what they would be losing but chose to become ostriches with their heads in the sand. To some, talent such as Clemens was believed to come around more often than not, and it wouldn't be difficult for them to find a replacement. The management was most famous for the "twilight" speech at a press conference. Most of the press took the press conference as a slap in the Rocket's face, but a close analysis of the speech reveals that, although not completely positive about Clemens, it was in some underlying way complimentary to him.

In late 1996 contract negotiations that were going on during the season eventually broke down. The Red Sox's management said that Roger's last few seasons, although with some highlights, were average at best. General Manager Dan Duquette told a press conference on December 14, 1996, after Roger had signed as a free agent with the Toronto Blue Jays:

> The Red Sox and our fans were fortunate to see Roger Clemens play in his prime and we had hoped to keep him in Boston during the twilight of his career. We want to let the fans know that we worked extremely hard to sign Roger Clemens. We made him a substantial, competitive offer, by far the most money ever offered to a player in the history of the Red Sox franchise. Unfortunately, we just couldn't get together. We were hoping he could finish his career as a Red Sox and we also wanted him to establish a relationship beyond his playing career. We wanted him to have the status of a Ted Williams, but at the end of the day we couldn't get it done.[2]

The previous day, on December 13, 1996, Roger signed with the Toronto Blue Jays as a free agent in a three-year deal. When he applied to be a free agent a few weeks earlier, it was a sure sign to Boston that Clemens wanted out. To the fans of the Blue Jays, grabbing undoubtedly one of the best pitchers in baseball was a coup. To many of the fans of the Boston Red Sox, it was treason. His betrayal was only alleviated by the fact that he hadn't signed with the New York Yankees, which would have resulted in even more hostilities between the two teams and even toward the Rocket. In the stroke of a pen, the Rocket went from Red to Blue. But the Red Sox nation would not yet have to yell out, "Yankee, go home!"

During spring training the Rocket met many of the opposing pitchers and batters whom he had been up against during his dozen-plus years with the Red Sox organizations. Among them were Carlos Delgado, Alex Gonzales, José Cruz Jr., Benito Santiago, Pat Hentgen, Chris Carpenter, and Woody Williams. Roger had much in common with Woody as he also graduated from a Houston area high school. Woody had attended the University of Houston before making it to the big leagues. The team's skipper for the past eight seasons was Cito Gaston. He was the hitting coach before replacing Jimy Williams as the team's manager in midseason 1989.

The Toronto Blue Jays were a relatively new team in the major leagues, chartered in 1977 in the American League. This was also the same year that the Seattle Mariners were chartered, also in the American League. The Blue Jays had a few years of growing pains, but from the late 1980s into the 1990s the team suddenly blossomed into a contender not only for the championships but also the World Series, as shown in 1992 when they fought off several better-financed teams to make it to the 1992 World Series. The Blue Jays won the Series after Game 6 went 11 innings against the Atlanta Braves. They won the World Series again the following year when up against the Philadelphia Phillies. Eventually they brought in more fans to the Skydome than each of their rivals, such as the Yankees, Red Sox, and Braves. The Skydome, the first stadium in the world with a retractable roof, was the first of the covered ballparks built since the Houston Astrodome opened in 1965.

The 1997 MLB season was the first to have interleague play as part of standard practice. When the concept was first revealed to the media and fans, there was intense interest on one hand and intense apprehension on the other. Many fans wanted to continue playing and beating their league rivals, without interference from the other league. They held on strongly to traditions in baseball, and at first it was hard for them to get used to seeing their teams play cross-league rivals that they had seen play only in the World Series, the ultimate interleague game.

The first of the interleague games was held on June 12, 1997, when the Texas Rangers hosted the San Francisco Giants at the ballpark in Arlington. Eventually all other teams began to include a few interleague games in their schedules. Fans began to take a liking to the games. It was interesting for them to see a team such as the New York Yankees play a regular game against the Atlanta Braves or the Boston Red Sox playing the St. Louis Cardinals. The change brought in revenues from fans who had become jaded with the same old repetitive league action. In addition, Major League Baseball's policy on the matter stated that the wins and losses, along with other statistics, would remain part of each team's records and would be reflected in their standings at season's end. The play at first took place between teams

within divisions, but for the 2002 season play was expanded
to include play between various divisions.

The Rocket put on a great show for the Toronto Blue
Jays as the winning pitcher for their second game of the
season on April 2, 1997. Although they lost their season
opener to the Chicago
White Sox on April 1 with
the White Sox's 6 runs to
their 5, the Blue Jays, with
Roger at the helm, went
on to defeat Chicago in
the April 2 game 6 runs
to 1 at the Skydome. He
was again on one of his
legendary rolls, going for
11 wins and 0 losses dur-
ing his first few games of
the season. On April 29, the Blue Jays suffered a 6 to 5 loss
in a game where Chili Davis marked his 300th home run in
a 10-inning game versus the Kansas City Royals. A few of
Roger's standout wins were the April 9 win, when the Blue
Jays triumphed over the White Sox at Comiskey Park; the
April 30 win over the Kansas City Royals, 1 run to 0, at
Royals Stadium; and the defeat of the Tigers at the Skydome
on May 5 with 3 runs to 1. The Rocket leveled the Minnesota Twins on May 10 in a 6 to 4 game, and he continued to
fill his gas can on the Cleveland Indians with a 5 to 2 win
on May 16.

> *In what would perhaps be his most illustrious game of the season, on May 21 Roger helped defeat the Yankees 4 runs to 1 for his 200th win and became the 94th pitcher in major-league history to reach that mark.*

In what would perhaps be his most illustrious game
of the season, on May 21 Roger helped defeat the Yankees
4 runs to 1 for his 200th win and became the 94th pitcher in
major-league history to reach that mark. He was going strong
with 8 wins and 0 losses to his name so far that season, which

was his best start since his famous 1986 season. The Rocket continued his roll on May 26 by defeating the Texas Rangers 8 to 1 with a home-field advantage at the Skydome. On May 31 he brought in the team's most dramatic game for the season with a 13 to 3 win at the Oakland Athletics. A few days later when the Athletics ventured onto the Blue Jays' field, Oakland was again dealt a loss, 4 runs to 1. The June 6 game saw the Rocket extend his win to 11 straight for the year when he blasted eight scoreless innings, beating Oakland 4 to 1 and striking out eight of his opponents. A few days later on June 11, he had his first loss when the Seattle Mariners and their pitcher Jeff Fassero beat the Blue Jays 5 runs to 1.

On July 12 the Rocket returned to face his former team and fans at Fenway Park. He made Blue Jays history that day with 16 strikeouts in that 3 to 0 lopsided win over the Red Sox. The Boston fans in the bleachers were so irate that they continually hurled insult after insult at Roger when he was on the mound and even when he returned to the dugout after his innings. The rowdy fans also touched off the media to launch verbal barbs at Roger, but at the end of the game, the Rocket was the one in the driver's seat. This type of displeasure aimed at Clemens had become standard in Boston with Red Sox fans, especially as the years advanced and after he became a Yankee.

Still going strong on August 22, he won his 20th victory for the year against the Kansas City Royals. It was his fourth career 20-win season but his first since the 1990 season. The 1997 season with the Blue Jays was the Rocket's best; he had his longest winning streak since going 14 wins to 0 losses in his historic 1986 season. His debut season with the Blue Jays also saw him go for 63 innings without allowing a home run, from the August 7 game with the

Cleveland Indians to the September 12 game with the Seattle Mariners.

Things were also looking up for Roger on other fronts. He was voted onto the All-Star roster for the game that occurred at Cleveland's Jacobs Field on July 8. He joined fellow Blue Jays pitching teammate Pat Hentgen as the only two all-stars from the team that year. In the All-Star Game, the Rocket pitched an entire scoreless inning. In the nine-inning game the American League won it 3 runs to the National League's 1 run. It was the Rocket's sixth All-Star appearance. Sandy Alomar Jr., a catcher for the Indians, was named the game's MVP for his two-run home run. The 1997 game was the first win for the American League in years. It would continue on a winning roll until a tie in 2002 and then win every year thereafter.

As the season neared its close, the Blue Jays sank far below the .500 mark and eventually settled their last homestand with a sweep against the Red Sox. On September 26, the Blue Jays defeated Boston 3 runs to 0; the September 27 game saw the Red Sox lose 12 to 5; and in the last game on September 28, the Red Sox again lost to the Rocket's new team 3 runs to 2. But the Blue Jays would have to settle for fifth place at the end of the year, just under the fourth-place Boston Red Sox. The Blue Jays' record of 76 wins and 86 losses left them with a winning average of just .469 for the season.

With no division playoffs for the team, it seemed as if September 28 was too early to be leaving for home. But already there were changes. Near the close of the season Gaston was fired as skipper for failing to reach performance standards during the season, even though he had steered the team to two World Series during his stay with the Blue Jays. Mel Queen, a hitting coach for the Blue Jays, was hired on as temporary skipper until a new one could be named before the upcoming 1998 season commenced. Just before the new season, that new skipper would be Tim Johnson.

Despite a losing season, the Rocket had good news come his way in November of 1997: he won his fourth American League Cy Young Award. When he received the award, he commented that each of the Cy Young trophies was for each of his sons: "I got one for Koby and Kory. I got one for Kacy, and I needed one for Kody," he said.[3]

For the National League, the award went to Pedro Martinez of the Montreal Expos. The MVP went to Larry Walker of the Colorado Rockies in the National League and Ken Griffey Jr. of the Seattle Mariners in the American League. In the 1997 season Roger had 21 wins with just 7 losses and was able to claim a 2.05 ERA in his 34 starts. Roger won the coveted Triple Crown for the year, the first time since 1945 that a pitcher in the American League had won the honor. The Triple Crown title is earned by a batter or pitcher who leads his league in certain categories. Pitchers must attain the best ERA, the most strikeouts, and the highest number of wins; a batter must have the best batting average and highest number of home runs and number of runs batted in. For the entire season, Roger led the league in wins, he was the ERA champion again, and he led in strikeouts at 292. He also led in innings pitched at 264 and posted 14 games of 10 or more strikeouts. Even though the Rocket had a spectacular season, his achievements were somewhat diminished because he

> *Roger won the coveted Triple Crown for the year, the first time since 1945 that a pitcher in the American League had won the honor.*

lacked the run support of other team members. If they had been more successful hitting, the combination would have gotten them to at least the playoffs.

The World Series for 1997 featured the Cleveland Indians and the underdog Florida Marlins. The Marlins won 4 games to 3. It was also another World Series win that focused attention on the team's abilities and desire to win rather than on their status as a highly financed war machine.

Between seasons, José Canseco, who had been the Rocket's teammate on the Boston Red Sox for two seasons, signed up to join the Blue Jays. Canseco hoped to bring about a revival in his career, and, in some ways, he did for the 1998 season. He was able to appear in 152 games, something he had not done since the early 1990s, and hit almost 50 home runs for the Blue Jays.

The owners back at the Boston Red Sox were by now eating crow at what they had let go after watching Roger's stellar performance in the year following his exit to the Blue Jays. The fans especially were upset about how Roger's departure had been handled, but they comforted themselves that at least he hadn't gone off to the dreaded Yankees, as Babe Ruth had done.

In between the seasons, there were changes in the Blue Jays' management and roster. Other than the addition of Mike Stanley and the reappearance of Canseco as Roger's teammate, the biggest change was the permanent hiring of Tim Johnson as manager. Tim allowed interim manager Mel Queen to stay on board as a pitching coach, but reports of how the two didn't get along were legendary. Even though Johnson was able to work with the team members and at least get them up to within earshot of the wild card that year, he also had alleged rows with a few key players, all of whom left at the end of the season or, as in Roger's case, were traded away.

On April 1, 1998, Roger put on a good show for the season opener by defeating the Minnesota Twins 3 to 2 at the Skydome. Roger had a small scare on April 7 when he had to leave the game with a strained groin. It was the shortest start in his career. But by the April 22 game he was able to take part in a duel between two rival teams but two friendly pitchers. Andy Pettitte of the New York Yankees, who lived in Houston and had also attended San Jacinto Junior College, was by then one of the Rocket's good friends. Pettitte was the winning pitcher in that game against the Blue Jays, winning it 9 to 1. But not all was lost in that game, for Roger reached his 2,900th strikeout. A few days later on April 27, a game between the same rivals resulted in a score of 1 to 0. Pettitte was again the winning pitcher, and the Rocket was the losing pitcher.

On May 17 David Wells of the Yankees pitched a perfect game, the 13th in major-league history. The Blue Jays and the Rocket would struggle through the first seven weeks of the season and found themselves at the .500 mark at the May 21 game, defeating the Tampa Bay Devil Rays 6 to 1. Roger struggled at first, only to even his wins to losses at 6 and 6 with a defeat of the Detroit Tigers, 5 runs to 1, on June 3. From that day forward it was pure Rocket-fueled excellence for the team. The Tigers game was the start of Roger's longest winning streak, which would span more than a year, involve two seasons—from June 3, 1998, to June 6, 1999—and a total of 20 games. The win over the Royals on June 14, 7 runs to 4, set his record to 7 wins and 6 losses. In rapid succession he claimed victories over the Mets, 6 to 3, on June 30 and the Tigers, 7 to 2, on July 12. The Yankees game resulted in a 9 to 6 win for the Rocket on July 17, then the White Sox fell to him on July 22 with a score of 4 to 0, and the Rangers collapsed on July 28 with only 3 runs to the Blue Jays' 8. The Twins were his next victims, with 4 runs to the Blue Jays' 6 on August 2, and the Mariners soon followed, losing 7 to 0 on August 20.

In perhaps the best game of the year, or at least the one that gave Clemens the most attention, the Rocket struck out the 3,000th batter in his career on July 5, 1998, at the Skydome against the Tampa Bay Devil Rays. The player at bat was Randy Winn, and with this strikeout the Rocket became only the 11th pitcher in history to reach the 3,000-strikeout level. The Blue Jays won 2 to 1, but ironically since Roger didn't pitch the required number of innings, he didn't attain the winning pitcher title. That honor went to his teammate Paul Quantrill.

Another standout game for the Rocket came on August 25, where he nearly repeated his 20-strikeout performance. He struck out 18 batters in a nine-inning game with the Kansas City Royals. The resulting score was a healthy 3 to 0 win for the Blue Jays. The Rocket allowed only three hits during the game, and he issued no walks. Roger Clemens became, in that game, the first and only pitcher to get 18 or more strikeouts three times in a career, which included his 20 strikeouts in his historic 1986 and 1996 games.

On August 22 the team lost to the Angels, 5 runs to 1, with winning pitcher Steve Sparks. Sparks was also from the Houston area, was an ace pitcher on the winning collegiate baseball team at Sam Houston State University, and was coached by longtime SHSU head coach and distinguished alumnus John Skeeters.

The Rocket was the only representative of his team at the 1998 All-Star Game on July 7 at Coors Field in Denver. It was Roger's seventh All-Star Game. The American League won it over the National League 13 runs to 8. The game's MVP was Roberto Alomar of the Baltimore Orioles for hitting the only home run in the game. He is the brother of Sandy Alomar Jr., who was the previous year's MVP winner at the All-Star Game. Two days after the All-Star Game, during the break, the owners of the major-league teams voted to elect Bud Selig as the commissioner of baseball. He had been interim commissioner since before the strike in 1994. Selig became the ninth commissioner in the history of the leagues.

Even though the Rocket took off slowly for the season, he ended with a total of 20 wins and won his last 15 games in a row. He had a total of 6 losses during the year, almost all during the first half. With a 2.54 ERA, he was again the ERA champion for the leagues that year. And with his 271 strikeouts, he was also the best in the leagues in that column as well.

At season's end, the Blue Jays had won 88 of their games and lost 74, giving them a respectable average of .543. They expected to at least win the wild card for the year, but the Boston Red Sox won the slot, to the glee of their fans. The Red Sox would again make it to the playoffs, and Roger's new team, the Blue Jays, did not.

After the division and league series, the World Series was played out between the New York Yankees and the San Diego Padres in October. The Yankees won it 4 games to 0. The Yankees had an incredible winning average of .704 and ended the year winning 125 games, including the championship wins and World Series wins, a major-league record.

In November of that year, Roger was awarded his fifth American League Cy Young Award, the most ever by a pitcher in history. Greg Maddux had recently achieved that honor four times, as had Steve Carlton. Clemens was also awarded the Triple Crown again for that year, making it two in a row for him. Because the Triple Crown requires a player to attain the best in all categories (for a pitcher: ERA, strikeouts, and wins), it is not usually achieved each year. Thus it was an exceptional accomplishment for Roger Clemens to achieve the Triple Crown for two consecutive years and he was the fourth pitcher ever to do so. Its rarity accounts for the reason why so few in baseball are familiar with the award.

In other award news for the 1998 season, the MVP awards went to Sammy Sosa in the National League and Juan Gonzalez in the American League. The Rookie of the Year went to Ben Grieve of the American League and a newcomer in the National

He had many successes after he left Boston and showed them just how much they lost in letting him go.

League, Kerry Wood. Kerry Wood's debut year proved to be as promising as the Rocket's. In the fifth start of his career he struck out 20 batters, shutting out the Houston Astros, on May 6, 1998. That game is in the history books of major-league baseball as one of the most memorable games ever played.

The Rocket was content with his achievements during the past two seasons with the Blue Jays. He had many successes after he left Boston and showed the team just how much it lost in letting him go. Roger could have been the kick start to get the Boston Red Sox over the wild card and into the playoffs, or even to the World Series, but he wasn't one to focus on the past. And despite all his success, the trade winds began to blow, and rumors began to circulate about Clemens departing the Blue Jays. Several teams were mentioned in the rumors, and no one but the Rocket knew for certain. During the off-season the baseball world finally learned that the trade rumors were true. On February 18, 1999, the owners of the Toronto Blue Jays traded the Rocket to the New York Yankees for Graeme Lloyd, David Wells, and Homer Bush. When the clamor of the fans dissipated, Roger realized that his childhood dream of being a Yankee had become reality. When he was a child he wore not a Houston Astros outfit or one from the Boston Red Sox or any other team. He wore a New York Yankees uniform. When he was a Red Sox pitcher all those seasons, the Yankees were his nemesis, and now, as a Yankee, he would have to consider how he would react to Boston's scorn. While Boston may have had the first laugh and ended up regretting it when Roger went to the Blue Jays, Boston certainly wasn't laughing now. The Rocket was now its visceral enemy. According to Yankees skipper Joe Torre, the Yankees had always despised Roger Clemens as a Red Sox pitcher. He was an enemy. But now that Roger was part of their team, Torre famously quipped to the *New York Times*, "You like him once he's on your side."[4]

On January 5, 1999, the Rocket's mentor, Nolan Ryan, was elected to the Baseball Hall of Fame, along with George Brett and Robin Yount. All three of them were elected in their first year of eligibility, or five years after their final retirement from the game. Without a doubt, Roger Clemens knew that one day there would be a plaque of him in Cooperstown at the Hall of Fame, possibly alongside the great Nolan Ryan.

The Rocket may have had feelings of apprehension and excitement about his trade. He was excited to work with his new teammates, some of whom he had been friends with for years, such as Andy Pettitte. Roger realized that he was the oldest member of the team, outside of

Darryl Strawberry and Chili Davis. Also on the Yankees' roster were such greats as Mariano Rivera, Jason Grimsley, David Cone, Joe Girardi, Jorge Posada, Derek Jeter, Chuck Knoblauch, Tino Martinez, Alfonso Soriano, Shane Spencer, and Bernie Williams. Bernie Williams was from Puerto Rico and had come up through the Yankees' organization from the minor leagues, as had Jorge Posada, Derek Jeter, and Mariano Rivera, who all played their entire careers with the Yankees' organization. By the time Roger joined the team Bernie had already established a good friendship with a young up-and-comer from his hometown area in Puerto Rico by the name of Carlos Ivan Beltran. Beltran would win the American League Rookie of the Year award for 1999 and go on to fame, especially in the first few years of the next century.

The cover photo for the March 1, 1999, issue of *Sports Illustrated* was of Roger Clemens in a Yankees uniform. The caption exclaimed in bold letters: "The Yankees get Roger Clemens and strike fear through the rest of baseball." That caption hit dead center of the issue. As the Rocket told *Sports Illustrated*, "I definitely met my match with Mr. Steinbrenner. He's someone who wants to win as bad as I do."[5] Brian Cashman, the general manager of the Yankees, said of Roger, "He's not just a pitcher, he's an animal. And he's our animal now."[6]

During spring training, the baseball world lost a legend with the sudden, yet not unexpected, death of Yankees great Joltin' Joe DiMaggio, also known as the "Yankee Clipper." He died on March 8, 1999, in Hollywood, Florida, after a struggle with lung cancer. A few days before his death, a major television network prematurely announced the death of the baseball great at his home in a rolling captioned ticker. DiMaggio was at home; however, he was alive and watching that very program with his family. After his death many speculated that he would be buried in the empty crypt at the mausoleum in Brentwood, California, next to his late wife, Marilyn Monroe, who had died in 1962.[7] Instead, he was buried in the family plot in a cemetery just outside of San Francisco, California.

For the first few months, from spring training and through the season, hitting coach Don Zimmer served as the team's skipper as Joe Torre underwent successful treatment for cancer. Torre started in the major leagues in 1960 as a catcher and first baseman for the Braves, then moved on to the Cardinals, and finally to the Mets. Eventually he went on to manage each of the teams on which he once played. He was hired as the manager of the American League's Yankees after the close of the 1995 season. Torre had never been part of the AL, but as a native New Yorker he quickly gained the confidence of the team, the media, and, most important, the fans by leading the team to the World Series in 1996. The team had not gone that far in 15 years. Although they didn't make it past the playoffs to the fall classic in 1997, they did make it to the World Series from 1998 through 2000. Joe Torre became a New York Yankees icon. He once famously said after winning that first World Series game in 1996, "Maybe the Good Lord was just waiting for me to put on the pinstripes."[8]

Possibly Roger Clemens had the same thought in mind. But Torre wasn't the only recent addition to the Yankees' hierarchy. Early in 1998 the general manager, Bob Watson, retired to serve as one of Major League Baseball's vice presidents, and a young 30-year-old by the name of Brian Cashman took the helm. Cashman had worked his way up through the Yankees' management organization and had gained the confidence of the owners for his promotion to general manager.

The Yankees' 1999 season opened with great anticipation, because a few months earlier, in October, they had won the World Series over the San Diego Padres 4 games to 0. Hopes were high in 1999 for a repeat of that performance. The season opener on April 5 was one of the few missteps of the year, with a loss to the Athletics in Oakland 5 runs to 3. This game was the Rocket's debut start as a Yankee. From that point it was the road to glory for the team and for the Rocket. Roger was the winning pitcher at the game where he first appeared in a Yankees uniform at Yankee stadium

> *He joined the historic ranks of Rube Marquard, Elroy Face, and Carl Hubbell for that honor.*

on April 10, devouring the Detroit Tigers 5 runs to 0. The entire homestand against the Tigers was a sweep for the Yankees, with a 12 to 3 win on April 9 and an 11 to 2 win on April 11. The April 21 game saw Roger win over the Rangers, 4 to 2. During an April 27 game at Texas, Clemens had to leave the mound after two innings because of a hamstring injury and was placed on the 15-day disabled list. On May 18, there was a cheer among team members as Joe Torre returned to manage them following the first round of his cancer treatment. Roger himself was back on the mound as the winning pitcher with a spectacular 10 to 2 defeat of the Chicago White Sox on May 22. A few days later came another glorious win for the Rocket when he cut off the run support of the Boston Red Sox and their rowdy fans at Yankee Stadium on May 27 and allowed the Yankees to win it 4 runs to 1.

A few days later there was Roger's 11 to 1 victory over the Cleveland Indians on June 1. In that game he became one of only a few pitchers in major-league baseball history to win 20 decisions in a row. He joined the historic ranks of Rube Marquard, Elroy Face, and Carl Hubbell for that honor. On June 23 the Rocket was the winning pitcher in a great victory over the Tampa Bay Devil Rays with a total of 12 runs to 4. Another historic event came on June 29 when he threw his first complete game, which was a shut-out, as a Yankee for a 3 to 0 win versus Detroit at Yankee Stadium.

Just before his July 25 start at Yankee Stadium with the visiting Cleveland Indians, his uniform number was changed from 12 to 22. The Yankees' management approved the Rocket's request after his 12-year-old son Koby had asked him to change his number so that his dad's uniform number would match his own Little League uniform number. The number 22 would from that date on become an iconic representation of the man who had done so much for the game. The Yankees would defeat Cleveland 2 runs to 1 in that July 25 game.

On July 31, he was the starting pitcher for his first game at Boston's Fenway Park in a Yankees uniform. The crowd and media were again obnoxious to the team as always, but they were particularly so since their new enemy, the Rocket, was on the mound. The Yankees would lose that game 6 to 5; however, since Roger didn't pitch the required number of innings, he was not given the losing pitcher label. Up to the month of August he had a 13-game winning streak with wins over such adversaries as the Mariners, the Red Sox, the White Sox, and the Indians. But the Oakland Athletes snapped his winning streak on August 10, when the Rocket was the losing pitcher in a 6 to 1 loss. In an August 16 game versus the Minnesota Twins, Roger threw eight shutout innings for a 2 to 0 win over the Twins.

During a game facing the Red Sox on September 12 at Yankee Stadium, Boston got the best of Roger and won the game 4 to 1 with the Rocket as the losing pitcher. It was his first loss to Boston after three previous wins in his career against them since he left the team for the Toronto Blue Jays in 1997.

Derek Jeter, David Cone, Mariano Rivera, and Bernie Williams were the four members of the Yankees on the 1999 All-Star team. The game took place on July 13 at Fenway Park in Boston, and the honorary first pitch was from Ted Williams to Carlton Fisk. The Rocket didn't attend the game. The American League won 4 runs to 1.

On October 2, the Yankees had a 3 to 2 victory over the Tampa Bay Devil Rays. In the game, Bernie Williams had the 100th walk during the season. Known for his walks, he also was to get 202 hits and 116 runs for the year. On October 10 during the National League Division playoffs, the Houston Astros had a dramatic game as they shut down the Houston Astrodome, the eighth wonder of the world, for the last major-league baseball game ever played there. For the next season, their new home would be Enron Field. Later, the Wall Street giant collapsed in scandal, taking down its investors and many pension funds. This led to the highly publicized removal of Enron's name from the Astros' ballpark, which was renamed Minute Maid Park after that company won the naming rights' bidding.

The Yankees under Torre finished the season in first place in 1999 with 98 wins and 64 losses. Their winning average of .605 placed them above the Red Sox, who won the wild card again that year, and above the third-place Blue Jays. In the division series, the Yankees faced the Texas Rangers and won the division 3 games to 0 over the Rangers. In the National League Division Series, the Atlanta

Braves won out over the Houston Astros 3 games to 1. The American League Championship Series had the Yankees stepping over the Red Sox 4 games to 1. During that series, the Rocket again had to face surly crowds in Boston as well as in New York, when Red Sox fans traveled to Yankee Stadium. Some came to the games just to taunt Roger. After Boston was defeated, Torre took his team to the World Series to face the Braves, who had won out over the New York Mets 4 games to 2 in the National League Championship Series.

The 1999 World Series would be the first World Series victory for Roger Clemens. Game 1 took place in Atlanta at Turner Field on October 23, 1999. The game was scoreless for the first four innings until Chipper Jones slammed a home run for the Braves. The only other runs came four innings later in the eighth for the Yankees, who won the game 4 runs to 1. The next day, Game 2 had the Yankees on the warpath and making all their 7 runs within the first five innings. Atlanta finally woke up with 2 in the ninth, but it was all over for them anyway and the Yankees won it 7 runs to 2. Game 3 at Yankee Stadium saw both teams in a life-or-death struggle to win, and the Braves desperately tried to avoid being swept. In the 10-inning game the Yankees would again be victorious with 6 runs to the Braves' total of 5.

When the Rocket walked onto the mound for Game 4, Atlanta decided to roll over and give up. The Yankees were the first to score, in the third inning, with 3 runs. For a while it looked as if Atlanta was never going to score, but they finally had 1 run late in the eighth, matched by the Yankees. But in the ninth it was all over, and the Rocket was the winning pitcher for his first World Series win. Roger Clemens was the oldest starter in the World Series in almost half a century. With players getting younger every year, he realized that he was no longer a rookie. "It was an exciting time for me personally because the number of times I've been to the playoffs, that was the opportunity to obtain the first ring. That was special, that's for sure."[9]

The World Series was not without tragedy. On October 25, the day before Game 3, golfing great Payne Stewart died in a private plane crash. The jet lost cabin pressure shortly after takeoff but continued to fly on autopilot until it crashed in South Dakota. Sadly, before Game 4, Yankees baseman Paul O'Neill was told that his father had died, which cast a pall over the entire team.

After the win, each of the Yankees' team members was paid $326,000 in bonuses for winning the fall classic. During the year, the average player's salary in the major leagues had risen to just under $2 million. The Yankees' front office sent out a press release that stated the average Yankees' player salary was just over $3 million. Many in the media were upset by this revelation and again started to report that organized sports were won by dollars rather than by talent. Some in government circles began to point out that the sports industry indeed had enough money to build and organize its own stadium constructions. Further, it shouldn't be up to the taxpayers to either bail out their teams, which could leave their town whenever they chose, or to pay unusually high ticket prices to see their own teams playing in a publicly owned building.

After the close of the season, the Cy Young Awards went to Pedro Martinez of the American League and Randy Johnson of the National League. The Rookie of the Year award went to the good friend of Bernie Williams, Carlos Beltran, and to Scott Williamson of the National League.

As the year 1999 drew to a close, there was a lot of anxiety about the end of the century and the beginning of the new century. The phenomenon of the Y2K bug, which would allegedly shut down the world's computer systems, was the talk of the days leading up to the next millennium. It was even widely discussed that the new century didn't even begin until the first of January 2001, not the year 2000, as an entire year needed to be completed until a century could end and a new one could begin. Either way, a shutdown never materialized. The world happily went on to the 21st century or at least went on to have one long happy year to end the 20th century.

The 2000 season would indeed prove to be improbable. The first major-league game to be played that season happened when the Chicago Cubs played the New York Mets in the Tokyo Dome in Tokyo, Japan. It was the first regular season major-league baseball game ever to be played outside the United States. The Cubs defeated the Mets, 5 runs to 3. The game brought U.S. attention to Japanese baseball and, in turn, brought U.S. baseball to the Japanese fan. Interest turned out to be mutual, and the groundwork for World League Baseball was laid.

With the exit of Darryl Strawberry and Chili Davis from the 2000 season roster, Roger turned out to be the oldest member on the Yankees' team. Dwight Gooden reappeared as one of Roger's Yankees teammates. The years had flown by as if they had only been days, and it seemed that only yesterday Roger Clemens had been a young rookie with the Red Sox. Now, he was one of the oldest players in the leagues. And he was proud of it.

The season opener wasn't at Yankee Stadium that year. Instead it was at Anaheim Stadium, where the Yankees defeated the Angels in a 3 to 2 victory. Roger's first win was on April 14, and he defeated the Royals in a 7 to 5 game at Yankee Stadium. A few days after that, Roger would have the first of his defeats, 7 to 3, when he was the losing pitcher against the Minnesota Twins on April 24. There was sweet revenge for the Rocket when he defeated the Blue Jays on the last day of April.

The Rocket was blasting off in the new season with an incredible roll of victories. His most famous for the season was his victory over the Baltimore Orioles, 3 to 1, on May 6. It was the 250th career win for the Rocket, and he became the 39th pitcher to reach that milestone in history. At that point the Yankees were 20 to 8 in their wins.

The Chicago White Sox were handed a loss on May 17 in a 9 to 4 win for the Yankees. Roger was the losing pitcher to the same team a few days later at Comiskey Park II in an 8 to 2 loss. Kip Wells was the winning pitcher. In his last game for May he was again the losing pitcher to the Red Sox with a 2 to 0 score. Then there was the 12 to 2 loss to the Mets on June 9, leaving Roger with a win-to-loss ratio of 4 to 6. He turned it around during midseason by defeating the Devil Rays 5 to 2 at Tropicana Field, and on July 8 there was an unusual day/night doubleheader with the Mets. The day game was a win over the Mets, 4 to 2, at Shea Stadium with Dwight Gooden as the winning pitcher. That evening, at Yankee Stadium, the same score resulted again when Roger was on the mound as the winning pitcher and brought up his win record to 6 and 6. In that game, he somehow beaned the Mets' catcher, Mike Piazza, in the helmet. Piazza fell to the ground, and after later examination it

> *The Rocket was blasting off in the new season with an incredible roll of victories.*

was determined that he had a concussion from the incident. Piazza later allegedly said that he had lost respect for the Rocket. The media pointed out that in the past Piazza had quite a few base hits when up against Clemens since interleague play came into existence. In addition Piazza had recently hit a grand slam when Roger was pitching. The press claimed that Clemens frequently hit the players of rival teams or had a way of getting back at their key players (such as in the case of Alex Rodriguez in the 2000 ALCS). A logical analysis of this situation would show that the Rocket ends up hitting the batter with less frequency than is the case with other active pitchers in either league. Clemens is nowhere near the top of the list in frequency of hits.

The first All-Star Game of the new century was played out on July 11 at Turner Field in Atlanta. Derek Jeter, Jorge Posada, Mariano Rivera, and Bernie Williams were the four Yankees selected to play at the game. Jeter filled in for an injured Alex Rodriguez and was voted as the game's MVP, oddly the first time in major-league history that a New York Yankee was voted MVP. Jeter, commenting to the press on his MVP status, said, "In due time when I sit down and get a chance to reflect on it, then you realize how special it is. And I wasn't aware that no Yankee, no other Yankee, had won this award, and it's kind of hard to believe."[10] In the game there was only one home run, by Chipper Jones, and the American League won it over the National League 6 to 3.

In the last half of the season, the Rocket continued to dominate, defeating the Florida Marlins 6 to 2 on July 14, the Tigers 9 to 1 on July 19, and the Orioles 4 to 3 on July 24. On August 13 Roger gave the Angels halos, when they lost the game 4 to 1, and defeated the Mariners on August 28 with a score of 9 to 1.

On September 8, 2000, which was the 100th anniversary of the 1900 storm that destroyed Galveston and Roger's adopted hometown of Houston, he was able to fire up his gas can, defeat the Boston Red Sox 4 to 0, and bring up his win-to-loss record to 12 and 6. His former teammates at the Blue Jays were his next victims in a 3 to 2 loss to the Yankees. On September 23 Clemens had to leave the game after being hit by a ground ball, injuring his hamstring, but he quickly recovered. In the final game of the season the Yankees lost to the Devil Rays 11 to 3.

For the season, the Rocket had 13 wins and 8 losses with a 3.70 ERA in his 32 starts. He was second in the American League in ERA. During the season he reached the 3,500-strikeout level, but in total for the year he had 188 strikeouts, falling under his usual 200 per year. This was in part because of the enlarged roster of pitchers for the Yankees, which again started to eat into the number of times he was able to stay on the mound.

The Yankees easily won first place in their division with their 87 wins and 74 losses. They faced the Oakland Athletics, who they then defeated 3 games to 2 in the division series. In the American League Championship Series, the team faced the Seattle Mariners, and the Yankees won the series 4 games to 2. In Game 4 of the ALCS in Seattle, Clemens pitched the first one-hitter in league playoff history and struck out 15 Mariners. For a while it looked as if Clemens was about to pull off another 20-strikeout game. By beating the Mariners 5 games to 0, the Yankees were back in the fall classic. The resulting World Series for the 2000 season was between the Yankees and their crosstown rivals, the New York Mets. The Mets won their division and league after defeating the Giants 3 games to 1 and then the St. Louis Cardinals, 4 games to 1, respectively.

The 2000 World Series was another fall classic for the history books. With the Yankees playing the Mets in a World Series dubbed the "Subway Series," because of the close proximity of the stadiums, the entire city and nation were drawn into the action. Not for almost half a century, since 1956, had the two teams met head to head in the fall classic. Not only were the fans and the media anticipating an exciting outcome, they were also looking forward to seeing another matchup between the Rocket and Mike Piazza, who had recently recovered from the concussion Clemens allegedly gave him. The press had still not subsided on that issue, and the enmity between the two players was the talk on sports radio airwaves. Previous to this World Series, it was rare for anyone to even bring the two up in the same conversation. For comparison, the other batters whom Roger had hit with a pitch were usually not named in the press, because the incidents were dismissed almost immediately. Why the incident between Piazza and Clemens remained such a focus of media attention is something that the history books will probably have to decide, if the incident is mentioned at all in the decades ahead.

> *The dugouts of both teams emptied onto the field in a massive brawl as the crowd unleashed itself.*

Game 1 of the 2000 World Series took place on October 21 at Yankee Stadium and unfolded in an exciting, but drawn-out, 12-inning game. The game was one of the longest ever in World Series play in terms of the number of innings. The first five innings were scoreless, and it took most of the sixth for the Yankees to bring in 2 runs. In the seventh, the Mets made out with 3 runs, and, with no runs in the eighth and most of the ninth, it appeared as if the Mets were going to claim the first game. But later in the ninth the Yankees brought their man in and scored again in the 12th inning to win it 4 runs to the Mets' 3.

Game 2 the next evening saw Roger Clemens on the mound. Mike Hampton was the counterpart for the Mets. The Yankees immediately claimed 2 runs in the first inning with the Mets scoreless until the ninth inning when they scored 5 runs. Mike Piazza had already made a home run earlier in this game and later came up to bat again, against the Rocket. The anticipation in the air was like a great electrical storm. The Rocket pitched, Piazza hit it, his bat shattered, and the barrel cartwheeled toward the pitcher's mound as Piazza was making it to first base. The electrified crowd watched to see what would happen next. No movie studio could have planned or executed such a play. Roger picked up the broken bat to "get it out of the way" of the game and threw it off the field. He threw it directly into the path of the running Piazza, as if to field the bat instead of the ball to get Piazza out. The dugouts of both teams emptied onto the field in a massive brawl as the crowd unleashed itself. Clemens received bad press again in magazines the world over. The resulting flack from the incident didn't subside for weeks, and the video was replayed countless times on television. In the ninth inning the Mets moved up fast, with 5 runs. But when the game was over, the Rocket had won another for the Yankees with 6 runs to 5. The bat-throwing incident only served to increase the talk about the derision that the two baseball greats now had for each other. While Clemens was ready to dismiss both episodes, Piazza wasn't. In the weeks ahead, Roger would be threatened with suspension, and he eventually had to pay a $50,000 fine.[11]

With all of the excitement generated by Game 2, people tried any method they could to get into Game 3, which took place October 24. In this game the Mets were out for revenge, and they scored the most runs, 4 to the Yankees' 2, to win it. But Game 4 belonged to the Yankees. They were the first to score in each of the first three innings, followed by only a home run by the unscathed Mike Piazza in the third. The rest of the game resulted in nothing on the scoreboard, and the Yankees again won 3 runs to 2. Roger pitched his only appearance in a winning World Series that day. He pitched eight shutout innings with nine strikeouts and only two hits. It was the longest amount of time he had spent on the mound during his four career World Series starts.

Again at Shea Stadium for Game 5, the Yankees ruled the field. Until the sixth inning the Mets were ahead by a run, but in the ninth the Yankees scored a double and won 4 runs to 2. Bernie Williams and Derek Jeter of the Yankees made the only home runs of the game.

After all his World Series appearances, this was the Rocket's second World Series win, and he did it two times in a row. His fans, friends, family, and team all finally understood why the Rocket did this year after year. He routinely says that he's not out there for his own enjoyment, that he does it for the fans. When he returned home to Houston, it was as if Houston's own team had won the World Series. Roger was treated similar to a rock star at various charity events or while at autograph-signing sessions, even though he has always been a low-key family man.

Chapter 10

————— PROMISES MADE AND KEPT —————

The new century saw a rebirth in the career of Roger Clemens. Now pushing 40 years of age in 2001, his continuing success in the game wasn't because of his need to prove a point; it was a result of the Rocket's having stayed in shape. Roger would have still another halcyon year in his career. He would finally reach the $10 million salary mark for the first time in his career and, as a result, was one of the highest-paid pitchers in the leagues.

Clemens would prove his worth in the first season opener of the new century on April 2, when he helped demolish the Kansas City Royals 7 runs to 3 at Yankee Stadium. The crowd went wild with the hopes that it would be yet another World Series year. In that game he struck out five Royals to tie the 3,508 strikeout record set by Walter Johnson as the American League's strikeout king. The next week, on April 8, he would surpass Walter Johnson's record, and the Rocket would become the AL's strikeout leader. That April 8 game versus his old teammates of the Toronto

Blue Jays underscored the mistake of letting the Rocket go to another team. His victory of 16 to 5 sealed that mistake for the ages. Over the course of the rest of the season, Clemens would, in rapid succession and with few losses, defeat the Oakland Athletics 3 runs to 1, beat the Minnesota Twins 2 to 0, lose to the Seattle Mariners 6 to 2, score a great victory over the Cleveland Indians 12 to 5, and do the same thing a week later with home-field advantage, 9 to 4 on June 2. The Baltimore Orioles did not fare much better against the Rocket's skill when they were also defeated 4 to 0. The Montreal Expos were also laid waste by the Yankees' 9 runs to their 3. One of his best games of the season came on June 18, when he annihilated the Detroit Tigers 10 to 1 in their den at Comerica Park. That summer was one of his best, with further defeats of the Tampa Bay Devil Rays, 2 to 1, and also 7 to 5 in a game the next week. When the Orioles received the Rocket on their turf, they were defeated, as they were earlier in the year, 4 runs to 3.

The 2001 All-Star Game saw the Rocket perform in that midsummer classic for the seventh time. There he threw two perfect innings and helped the American League win the midsummer classic 4 runs to 1. Joined by fellow Yankees Andy Pettitte, Jorge Posada, Mariano Rivera, Mike Stanton, Bernie Williams, and Derek Jeter, who hit one of the few home runs of the game, the Rocket and his teammates were powerhouses and the ones to watch. That July 10 game at Seattle's Safeco Field was the final All-Star Game for Cal Ripken Jr., who was on a farewell tour in his good-bye year before retirement. Fans looked upon the game as his final curtain, and everyone got together in appreciation. As a cap to his career, Ripken hit a home run in the game and was voted the game's MVP. Safeco was built after the world famous Kingdome was demolished after only 20 years of service. To avoid losing their home team, Seattle built the new ballpark so that an increasing amount of revenue could be generated for the team. This development would be reflected in a speech by California governor Arnold Schwarzenegger where he roughly stated, "we will tear down thirty-year-old stadiums for new ones when we tear down thirty-year-old schools for new ones." The American League would again win the All-Star Game that year over the National League 4 runs to 1.

The Rocket continued his blast of energy over the Detroit Tigers, defeating them 8 runs to 5 on July 18. The Blue Jays returned for revenge on July 23 but were disappointed to lose to the Yankees again. A few days later on July 28 at their Skydome, they were again defeated by their former team member in another one of the Rocket's best games of the season, 12 runs to 1. The August 15 game with the Devil Rays had the Rocket with a fuel line running under the turf to the pitcher's mound, defeating Tampa Bay 10 to 3. The Angels and the Red Sox were his next victims, where at the Red Sox game the Rocket's record stood at 18 and 1 for the year. The September 2 game two days later saw Roger's Yankees teammate Mike Mussina arrive within one strike of a perfect game over the Red Sox, but the upset came after a hit by pinch-hitter Carl Everett. Roger made the record books again in the September 5 victory over the Blue Jays, when he became the second pitcher in the history of the leagues to win 19 of his first 20 decisions. Sixteen of the Rocket's wins were consecutive, which was the best streak in the Yankees' history and his second best. His previous 20-game winning streak had ended in the 1999 season.

After a weekend game with the visiting Boston Red Sox, Roger was at home in his apartment in New York City early in the morning of September 11, 2001. He was still resting after a very exhausting sweep of the Red Sox that brought the Yankees' win-to-loss ratio to 86 to 57. As everyone else, his morning routine was disturbed by the horror of the news that a jet had crashed into one of the towers of the World Trade Center in downtown Manhattan. On television, another plane hit the other tower, again resulting in a huge plume of fire and smoke. Roger rushed to a better vantage point near his building to see the towers billowing smoke and called home to Houston to say that he was unharmed.

> *After the national shock and confusion had settled somewhat in baseball, the team owners and commissioner Selig met as soon as possible and decided to hold off on games until a later date.*

Other teammates began to call, and some team members were woken up and told that the towers had already collapsed. Other players were jolted awake by phone calls and were presumed to already know about the tragedy going on around the United States. When the callers asked what should be done about the cancelled games, it confused the freshly awakened players.

After the national shock and confusion had settled somewhat in baseball, the team owners and Commissioner Selig met as soon as possible and decided to hold off on games until a later date. In that meeting they had to balance a sense of mourning for the nation and the world yet also realize that getting the nation back to an undisturbed routine would be paramount in showing national unity and strength. At first the hold on games was five days, but then they decided to resume play on September 17.

When the games did resume on that day, each stadium held a memorial service for the heroes who were lost, and the heroes who made the day, on September 11. The long-time broadcaster Jack Buck seemed to sum it up the best. At Busch Stadium in St. Louis, he read aloud to the fans and players a poem with the important passage: "With one voice we say, 'There's no choice. Today, there is only one thing to do.'" It seemed to represent the sentiments of all of baseball on that day.[1]

The Yankees' first game after the attacks was with the Chicago White Sox at Comiskey on September 18, where the Yankees won it 11 to 3. There was a remembrance ceremony also at Comiskey. It was rumored at that time that the Sears Tower in Chicago was also on the list of attacks scheduled for September 11, and with the prompt order that all planes should be removed from the sky, the threat was averted. The Rocket took the mound the following day, on the 19th, and he defeated the White Sox again 6 to 3 for his 20th win of the season. At the age of 39, Clemens became the first pitcher to start a season 20 and 1 in the history of the major leagues. One of his last starts for the 2001 regular season was on September 30. The game with the Baltimore Orioles resulted in a tie of 1 run to 1. His last start for the season was October 5 with the Devil Rays, where the Yankees lost 8 runs to 4 at Tropicana Field. The last Yankees' regular season game of the season was on October 7 against the Tampa Bay Devil Rays, where the Yankees won the game 1 to 0. Roger's teammate Orlando Hernandez was the winning pitcher.

The Yankees' standing for the year was 95 wins, 65 losses, and 1 tie, which resulted in a winning average of .594 and brought them to first place in the American League East. Again, the Yankees were in the race for the World

Series. Roger rose from eighth place in the all-time strikeout list to third when he passed Walter Johnson, Gaylord Perry, Don Sutton, Tom Seaver, and Bert Blyleven with his 3,717 strikeouts. Only Steve Carlton and Nolan Ryan were in front of the Rocket on the list.

The Yankees easily defeated the wild-card champions, the Oakland Athletics, in the division series 3 games to 2. They went on to face the Seattle Mariners in the ALCS. The Mariners put up a weak offense and were also defeated by the Yankees, 4 games to 1. Andy Pettitte was awarded the MVP for the ALCS. With the defeat of the Mariners, the Rocket had made it to pitch in his fourth World Series. The Yankees' opponent, the Arizona Diamondbacks, were seen throughout the press as the easily defeated underdog. Because of the September 11 attacks, the October 27 starting date would be the latest start for a World Series in major-league baseball history. When the Series used all seven of its games, the last game was on November 4, the latest date ever for play in a World Series and also the latest date ever for any exhibition major-league game.

In Game 1 of the World Series, President George W. Bush threw out the ceremonial pitch, the first time a president had done that since Eisenhower had in the 1956 World Series. The Diamondbacks easily took the lead from the Yankees in front of an astounded media. Curt Shilling was the winning pitcher for the Diamondbacks' 9 to 1 win over the Yankees in Game 1. Game 2, also in Phoenix, had the Yankees determined not to let the snakes out of the box as they had in the first game. Arizona's starting pitcher for the game was Randy Johnson, and for the Yankees the pitcher was Andy Pettitte. The Big Unit struck out 11 Yankees in the game, and Matt Williams of the Diamondbacks hit a three-run homer off Andy Pettitte in the ninth inning, giving the underdog Arizona team a 4 to 0 defeat of the Yankees in Game 2.

Stunned fans in New York waited for Game 3 to take place at Yankee Stadium. This time the Rocket would be on the mound and pilot the Yankees to a 2 to 1 victory over the Diamondbacks. Roger struck out nine Arizona players and allowed only three hits in his seven innings on the mound. The Rocket restored hope to New York that a World Series victory would be theirs yet. Game 4, on Halloween, had the Diamondbacks taking a 3 to 1 lead by the eighth inning. The ninth and 10th innings saw the Yankees come alive, along with their hopes, and win the game 4 runs to 3. The Yankees duplicated their win in Game 5 in a 12-inning game. By winning the game 3 runs to 2, they placed the World Series firmly back into Yankees' hands, 3 games to 2.

Game 6, back in Phoenix, put the Diamondbacks in a desperate situation. When a diamondback is in such a situation, dangerous things happen. And it did in Game 6. It was a duel between giants Randy Johnson and Andy Pettitte. It would be the most lopsided World Series game in Yankees' history, with the Diamondbacks winning it 15 runs to the Yankees' spare 2. The games were now tied at 3 for each team, and Game 7 would determine whether a well-financed machine such as the Yankees could defeat what the press had deemed a small-town dream team, the Arizona Diamondbacks.

Game 7 was scoreless until the sixth inning, when the Diamondbacks brought it to 1 to 0. By that time, Torre was frantic and brought out big gun Rivera, who was able to save the Yankees and get some run support onto the scoreboard with 2 runs. But in the ninth Arizona scored 2 and won their first World Series in Game 7, 3 runs to 2.

It was an upset that was hard for the Yankees to swallow. Putting it all into perspective, many of their fellow New Yorkers had lost much more during the year, and it all made the team and the fans closer by the season's close.

Roger had his sixth Cy Young Award on his mantel by the middle of November 2001. He was the third-oldest pitcher to win the award. His counterpart Cy Young winner in the National League was Randy Johnson, the opposing pitcher in the Yankees' failed bid at the World Series. Roger's season had been another great one, one of his best. His 3.51 ERA was very respectable and his win-loss record of 20 to 3 was also one of his best.

For the Rocket, there would never be another year like 2001, and thankfully, in some respects. He had witnessed one of the worst horrors but had also finished off a successful season that most major-leaguers only dream about. The 2002 season was approaching, as was his 40th birthday. Few players in the majors were his age. Rather than seeing that as a disadvantage, he saw himself as an example, as did the oldest player in the leagues, Julio Franco.[2]

As the nation began to recover from the barbaric attacks of September 11, so did baseball. The 2002 season held the promise to heal a nation, but almost at the outset of the new season, trouble began to brew. Players had talked, even before the attacks, of another baseball strike, but they had been subdued by the importance of pulling their own weight in getting the nation back on track. When the new season commenced the healing that had taken place in baseball was replaced by salt rubbed into the old wounds of the 1994 strike. Talk of another work stoppage surfaced and would not go away until well after the middle of the season. Though it appeared as if it all would be worked out "backstage," the fans got wind of it when the press began to expound on the issue, and some were threatening to stay away from the game. On August 30, 2002, there was finally an agreement not to strike, and the players' association agreed to a no-strike clause. According to association head Don Fehr, "All streaks come to an end, and this was one that was overdue to come to an end."[3] Fehr was referring to the last-minute, and surprise, agreement between owners and players that would avert stoppage of the 2002 season. The players chose to play rather than to strike. It was the first time since the 1970 baseball season

> *The players chose to play rather than to strike. It was the first time since the 1970 baseball season that owners and players agreed to a collective bargaining clause without stopping work.*

that owners and players agreed to a collective bargaining clause without stopping work. This agreement remained in effect until the end of the 2006 season, when it was renegotiated and renewed.

The Rocket's 2002 salary was just over $10 million. This was less than fellow Yankees players Mike Mussina, Jason Giambi, Derek Jeter, Bernie Williams, and Raul Mondesi made. Jeter was making almost $15 million annually with incentives. The newly signed collective bargaining agreement increased the minimum salary in the majors from $200,000 to $300,000 annually. In the 1970s when the last agreement expired, the average salary was $51,500 annually. For the 2002 season, the average salary was a rounded $2.38 million. To many people, the high salaries paid to star athletes were no different than the good money paid to others in the entertainment industry. If they earned it, they deserve it, they said. But, the high salaries caused a wave of cynicism in the media and in public opinion. If professional sports could afford these record high salaries for what amounted to hitting a ball with a stick, then it could well afford to build and maintain its own facilities or at least concede something to the fans in terms of ticket prices or other concessions.

Spring training for the 2002 season saw the soon-to-be 40-year-old Rocket remain one of the top aces in the game. After all, today's 40 is the new 30. While younger, he had worked hard to maintain himself, and now very aggressive players began to vie for his place on the mound. Yet, Roger continued to hold them off well. In the season opener the Rocket was the losing pitcher in a 10 to 3 game against the Baltimore Orioles on April 1. A quick turnaround by the Yankees saw the Orioles defeated in the next two games by David Wells and Mike Mussina. Roger's first win decision was on April 7 versus the Devil Rays at Yankee Stadium with a score of 7 to 2. The April 11 game against the Blue Jays resulted in an 11 to 3 loss, with Roger pitching on just three days' rest, replacing an injured Orlando Hernandez. But when the Yankees ventured to the Skydome on April 21, the Rocket was himself again and pitched a 9 to 2 win over the Blue Jays.

The Rocket was on a roll in the first two months of the 2002 season, with wins against the Mariners, 7 to 1; against the Oakland Athletics, 9 to 2; against the Devil Rays, 7 to 2, at Tropicana Field; and against them again when they ventured into the Yankees' home turf on May 14 with a score of 10 to 3. The Twins were his next victims, losing 3 to 0. On May 24, the Red Sox won in an 11-inning game, 9 to 8, in a no-decision for the Rocket. On June 3, he had another no-decision in a 13-strikeout game against the Orioles, which tied his season high and career high as a Yankee for the fourth time.

On June 8, baseball stopped to remember the great broadcaster Jack Buck of the St. Louis Cardinals, who died that day after a long career with the team. He was respected across the baseball and broadcasting world. Just a few months earlier, he had delivered the speech that restarted baseball after the September 11 attacks. It was now time for baseball to return the favor in his honor.

Roger's June 9 game defeated the San Francisco Giants 4 to 2. One of his few losses for the season came against the Mets on June 15, 8 to 0. As with many of his losses, it could be chalked up to a lack of run support from his own team. Roger had to leave the game in his June 20 start in Colorado after only four innings when he was hit by a line drive by the Rockies' Juan Pierre, resulting in a mild forearm injury. There was never any retaliation against Pierre or any of his teammates as a result. After a short stay on the disabled list, Roger's start in Cleveland was also cut short after five innings because of tightness in his hamstring. This injury put him on the 15-day disabled list.

There was more sad news for the baseball family, when on June 22 St. Louis Cardinals pitcher Darryl Kile died suddenly in his sleep at the age of 33 in his hotel room while on the road with the rest of the team to face the Chicago Cubs. Kile did not show up to pregame activities the following morning, and it was unusual for him to be late to anything. A search was undertaken, and he was found in bed in his hotel room, dead from an apparent heart attack. When word got back to Wrigley Field, the fans were told that the game had been cancelled because of "a death in the Cardinals family." Word soon circulated that it was Kile and a somber wave circulated around the stadium, the fans stunned to hear the news. Kile was in the majors for 10 years and had started out with the Houston Astros in 1991. After a brief period with the Colorado Rockies, he moved to the Cardinals in 2000. There he gathered legions of adoring fans and the admiration of all of his teammates, especially that of Matt Morris and of Jim Edmonds. For the Cardinals' family, Kile's death was especially hard since it followed so closely after the death of Jack Buck the previous week. It would leave the Cardinals, and indeed all of baseball, stunned and in a state of mourning for the remainder of the season.

When the Rocket returned to the Yankees' mound, he defeated the Royals on August 7, 6 to 2. The opposing ace Jeff Suppan was the losing pitcher. Suppan was the Rocket's teammate while with the Boston Red Sox for three seasons from 1995 through 1997. Roger was himself again as he won against the Royals a few days later in Kansas City, 10 to 5. Suppan was again the losing pitcher. The Texas Rangers were the next visitors to greet the Rocket, and they lost to him on August 24, 3 runs to 2. The September 3 game saw Roger defeat the Red Sox 4 to 2, and the Detroit Tigers on September 20 were also victims of his pitching, 5 runs to 1. The season left Roger with a record of 13 wins and 6 losses and a 4.35 ERA in 29 starts. It was a year of injury and recovery and a year of decreasing run support for the Rocket. He would not receive the Cy Young Award for 2002; that honor went to the up-and-comer Barry Zito of the Oakland Athletics and to Randy Johnson of the Arizona Diamondbacks. The MVP Awards went to Miguel Tejada and to Barry Bonds for the latter's unusually high number of home runs during the season.

For the season the Yankees had a very good 103 wins and 58 losses, resulting in an average of .640. Finishing first in the AL East, they were matched up against the Anaheim Angels for the division series. In Game 1, the Yankees were rocking back and forth with the Angels with no clear dominance until the eighth inning, when the Angels took the lead with a 5 to 4 score. Bernie Williams then came up to bat and hit a three-run homer to put the Yankees in for the win with 8 runs to 5. In Game 2 things started off great for the Yankees, with Jeter and Soriano popping home runs. The Yankees may have suffered from overconfidence as the Angels soon took the lead from them and won Game 2, 8 to 6. Game 3 was a virtual duplicate of the previous game, when the Angels again came back from a deficit to take the lead and win it 9 runs to the Yankees' 6. Game 4 had the Yankees in panic because they were facing elimination from just the division series. The game was no different than the previous two, except that the Angels took over very early and kept the lead for a 9 to 5 win. The Angels, not the Yankees, were going to the American League Championship Series by winning 3 games to 1 the division series. The Angels would go on and defeat the Minnesota Twins in the ALCS 4 games to 1 and ride the wave of success to defeat the San Francisco Giants in the 2002 World Series 4 games to 3.

The 2002 All-Star Game took place on July 9 at Miller Park in Milwaukee, Wisconsin. The Yankees were represented by six of their most popular players in the game. Jason Giambi, Derek Jeter, Jorge Posada, Mariano Rivera, Alfonso Soriano, and Robin Ventura were all present. It was one of the few All-Star Games that ended in a tie, 7 to 7, in an exhausting 11-inning game. Both teams ran out of pitchers, and the skippers, along with the commissioner, decided to call the game a tie and leave it at that. This result had an unexpected consequence. Selig decided that as an incentive in the future the winner of the All-Star Game receive home-field advantage during the World Series, but it would take effect in 2003's season. It sounded simple enough when explained that the new idea was a carrot for the All-Star teams to go at it with more enthusiasm. But the American League had been winning the All-Star Games for several years and have ended up with home-field advantage for each of the years since that decision. As a result of the unusual end to the 2002 All-Star Game, Commissioner Selig said to a press conference after the game, "Nobody wanted to play more than I did, but I have to balance the concerns and hopes of the fans against the welfare of the players and the game.

> *The 2002 season was the year that Roger turned 40 and became the oldest player on the Yankees' roster.*

And every so often you get caught in a really difficult and sensitive situation. This is why they have a commissioner, because somebody has to make those decisions."[4]

The 2002 season was the year that Roger turned 40 and became the oldest player on the Yankees' roster. He worked each day as if he was about to attain the 300-win mark, which would escape him for the season. The 2003 season appeared much more promising for this.

During the early part of the 2003 season, the Rocket wrestled with the idea that it would probably be his last year in the majors and that he should retire as a New York Yankee. For that season, eight of the players on the Yankees' roster were paid more than Roger Clemens was. Derek Jeter was making almost $16 million per year, followed by Raul Mondesi with $13 million. In reality, money probably didn't have much to do with Clemens's retirement decision.

When he moved over to the Astros the next year, it was for considerably less pay.

The Rocket had much pleasure on opening day, March 31, in defeating his old Toronto Blue Jays 8 to 4 at their Skydome. He would continue on his pilgrimage to the magical 300-win mark by defeating the Devil Rays 10 to 5, the Twins 11 to 4, the Angels 9 to 2, and the Athletics 5 to 2. On May 21, he had his 299th win by defeating the Boston Red Sox 4 to 2. He played in the game on May 22, but because there was a no-decision loss to the Blue Jays, 8 to 3, it would not be his 300th win. That mark would wait a few more weeks as the Rocket went on a slight decline in altitude, losing to the Red Sox 8 to 4 at Yankee Stadium during the last week of May 2003. On June 7, the first time the Yankees held interleague play with the Chicago Cubs of the National League, the Rocket ran out of gas and lost to the Cubs 5 runs to 2.

There was also interleague play with the Houston Astros that week at Yankee Stadium. While the Yankees planned on a complete sweep of the Astros, they had another thing coming to them. The first game on June 10 saw a defeat of the Astros, 5 runs to 3, but in the next day's game the ace pitcher for Houston, Brad Lidge, caught the Yankees off guard and smoked them in an 8 to 0 shutout. This was one of the games that put Lidge on the map of major-league greats. In addition, the Astros set a major-league record when they combined six pitchers in the game, leading to the no-hitter. In addition to Lidge, Pete Munro, Kirk Saarloos, Roy Oswalt, Octavio Dotel, and Billy Wagner were used in the game. Roger Clemens caught up with some of his hometown buddies and made new friends. Little did any of the visiting Astros know that in a few months they would be teammates with one of the greatest pitchers in the leagues.

At Yankee Stadium on June 13, 2003, there was great anticipation in the air for the Rocket, with a sellout crowd. Another interleague game, this time with the St. Louis Cardinals, was widely touted in the press as a duel between two giant teams in major-league baseball. Roger, who was 7 and 4 in wins at the time, was hungry for win number 300. Jason Simontacchi of the Cardinals was a pitcher with great promise at the time of the game, and some were comparing him to the younger Roger Clemens. The Rocket was also going for strikeout number 4,000 in the game. During the first two innings, he struck out six batters. Jim Edmonds hit a home run off Clemens, and soon Hideki Matsui had a hit of his own. The score soon was tied between the two teams. The tension in the evening air was electric. Then the great Edgar Renteria came up to bat and was the Rocket's 4,000th victim. The crowd exploded, especially the Rocket's dozens of friends and family members in attendance. Roger's wife, Debbie, was also in the stands and said to the press: "I was shaking and nervous. He worked real hard for this one. He'll remember it and appreciate it because it took a long time to get it."[5] Clemens's battery mate, Jorge Posada, caught the 4,000th-strikeout ball. He walked up to the Rocket, who was still on the mound, and presented it to him as thousands took pictures, causing the evening to appear as with thousands of sparkling stars. For the Rocket, "it was great. It brought me out of what we were doing when I saw him walking out. It clicked right there why he was walking out. It was nice for him to do that. Then we tried to get back in the flow."[6]

But there was one more thing for the Rocket to do, something he had done for almost a quarter of a century— win. And that he did. The Yankees defeated the Cardinals 5 runs to 2 in that game, bringing up the Yankees' wins to losses to 38 to 28 and making the Rocket only the 21st pitcher in major-league history to reach the magical 300-win mark. No one had seen a pitcher reach this achievement since 1985 when Tom Seaver did it as a Chicago White Sox pitcher. Phil Niekro also won his 300th as a Yankee against Toronto, back in 1985. Roger was the first pitcher to do so again in almost 20 years.

After Clemens started the seventh inning of the game, Yankees' skipper Joe Torre removed him and sent Mark Hammond to the mound, causing the crowd to go wild with booing. Torre stood his ground. Torre later said of the win, "It really set the tone for the night. The fans, right from the first hitter, they were standing on their feet. It was a memorable night."[7] He went on, "I told Roger after the game I used to be popular here before you started doing this stuff! You have to do what you think is the right thing. I'm glad it worked out. I would have booed too if I was sitting in the stands."[8] Roger was to the point after the game ended. Clemens simply said, "Just being able to thank each guy on the field that I hugged on the field it was amazing. I'm glad it's done."[9]

Clemens was not the only one in the majors to reach a milestone in the 2003 season. The Cardinals' skipper, Tony La Russa, reached the 2,000-win mark when the Cardinals defeated the Rockies 10 to 2. La Russa, nearing 60 years of age at the time, recorded a 2,000 to 1,782 win-to-loss record in his quarter century with the White Sox, Athletics, and Cardinals. One of the stars of the St. Louis Cardinals that year was Bo Hart. He debuted on June 19, just after the Rocket's 4,000/300 mark. Hart had been drafted by the Cardinals in 1999 while on Gonzaga's baseball team and had moved up through the Cardinals' minor-league system to serve as second baseman for his debut. He quickly attained

popularity with the fans and started his major-league career on a roll with a spectacular batting average, to the
cheers of supporters in the stands. He is still popular in
the Cardinals' organization.

In the Rocket's next win, number 301, he defeated the
Mets at Yankee Stadium 7 to 1. That event sparked just as
much enthusiasm as the previous win earlier in the month.
The game with the Red Sox on July 5 had him experience
his first loss since win 300, 10 runs to 2. But he was back
on one of his rolls again with wins against the Indians, 10
to 4; the Angels, 8 to 0; the Rangers, 6 to 2; and the Royals,
8 to 7. The game at the Boston Red Sox turned out to be
another milestone for the Rocket. At Fenway Park he recorded his 100th win and then the 306th win of his career.
The Tigers were his next prey and lost 5 to 2. The Rocket
then beat the Orioles 6 to 3, the Devil Rays 6 to 0, and the
Orioles again 6 to 2. The Orioles' homestand at Yankee Stadium was a winning sweep for the Yankees in the last game
of the season on September 28, with a 3 to 1 victory. The
Yankees' winning record was a stunning 101 to 61 trail for
a win-to-loss percentage of .623 for the season. They again
made it to first place in the AL East.

The division playoffs had the Yankees facing the Central Division champs, the Minnesota Twins. The Yankees
would win the series 3 games to 1 and move on to the
American League Championship Series to face the Boston
Red Sox. This would be a glorious series for the Rocket, as
he would face the fans of the Red Sox in Fenway Park yet
again. The Red Sox hung onto the series and their hopes of
going to the World Series. In Game 1 the Yankees fought
hard against the advancing Red Sox but lost the game, 5 to
2, in nine innings at Yankee Stadium. Game 2, also on the
Yankees' home turf, had the Yankees on the offensive almost

from the start. With Andy Pettitte on the mound, they won the game, 6 runs to 2. Game 3 moved to Boston, and with the Rocket on the mound, the crowd cheered against him when Boston scored the first 2 runs. New York came back in the next inning of the nine-inning game and pulled one over on the Red Sox by winning it 4 to 3 for Roger's win. Game 4 was also at Fenway in Boston, and both teams battled back and forth in an effort to gain the upper hand. Boston would prove to be better in home territory and won it over the Yankees 3 runs to 2. Game 5 stayed at Fenway Park, and New York was in the lead early on with David Wells and Mariano Rivera on the mound. The Yankees would win that game also, 4 to 2, and the players moved the game to Yankee Stadium for Game 6. In that game Boston was desperate to avoid elimination and fought hard to defeat the Yankees. The Red Sox saw Jason Varitek hit two home runs, as did Trot Nixon. Boston defeated New York 9 to 6.

Even more, they were angry with the Rocket for the perceived stab in the back that had not yet healed.

Game 7 was played on October 16 at Yankee Stadium. Boston quickly moved onto the board with 3 runs. New York didn't score until the fifth inning. The two teams battled each other for 11 innings. In the end, Boston couldn't hold back New York, and the Yankees were sent to the 2003 World Series by squeezing in Game 7, 6 runs to 5. To Boston, the letdown that they experienced was far greater than the proportional joy at a victory they would have celebrated. They were crushed and angry. They were angry with their rivals, the Yankees, and angry with their own players. Even more, they were angry with the

Rocket for the perceived stab in the back that had not yet healed.

The 2003 World Series would have been the Rocket's swan song. He had been on a retirement parade of sorts during the season, and fans poured out in numbers to bid farewell to him. They would also pour out to the World Series.

This World Series was the 100th of the fall classics. Yankee Stadium hosted the first game of the series against the Florida Marlins, who in the first few innings seemed to run away to victory. The Yankees didn't catch up with them until the sixth inning, but by the ninth inning with no more runs, the Marlins won Game 1, 3 to 2. Andy Pettitte dominated the next game for six innings. His strength, along with run support from his teammates, allowed the Yankees to win the game 6 runs to 1. Three of the runs were from Hideki Matsui, known as "Godzilla," who hit a three-run homer in the first inning and became the first Japanese-born player to ever hit a home run in the World Series. Game 3 was an almost duplicate of Game 2, with the Yankees coming on strong, especially in the sixth inning where Bernie Williams hit a three-run home run and gave the Yankees another win, 6 runs to 1.

Game 4 showcased the Rocket as the Yankees' starter. At the outset, the Marlins scored 3 runs against Roger in the first inning, but he was able to hold them down until he left the field in the seventh. The entire crowd and media gave Clemens a standing ovation in what would have been his final exit off the mound, albeit on the Marlins' home turf, to end his major-league career. Roger did, however, pop a hit as a batter in the fifth inning, but it would be all for nothing when the inning ended with him not making it home. "I didn't really care if the ball hit me or not," Clemens said. "I kind of closed my eyes and hit the dirt and just slid. You never know what can happen."[10] In the 12-inning game, the Marlins came back and scored another run against Yankees pitcher Jeff Weaver, who would take the loss for the Yankees, not Roger, and the Marlins would win it 4 runs to 3.

Game 5, also at Pro Player Stadium, saw Florida coming on strong again from the get-go. In the nine-inning game they would rack up 6 runs to the Yankees' 4. The only home run of the game was by Jason Giambi of the Yankees, but more runs from the Yankees would not match Florida's march to victory. Game 6 moved to Yankee Stadium, but the Marlins came on even stronger. Marlins pitcher Josh Beckett, also from Roger's hometown of Houston, was on the mound to smoke the Yankees, who were not even able to get a player past second base. Beckett pumped out a complete game shutout against the exhausted Yankees in nine innings, giving the Florida Marlins their second World Series title in 11 seasons, 2 runs to the Yankees' 0.

The Yankees were stunned. They had again lost to yet another underdog team by underestimating their opponent's capabilities on the mound and in the box. After the game, Torre stopped to say, "I just went in and thanked my ball club right after the game was over. It took us time to come together, but once we did, they realized how much they cared for each other, how they picked up for each other. Very unselfish. It's a lesson that even though you work hard, it's not always a fact that you are going to win."[11]

Andy Pettitte was philosophical about the loss, saying, "They outplayed us, that's the bottom line. In every aspect of the game. They beat us. You have to stand up and be a man about it. But I just want to get home and get over this sickening feeling right now in my stomach."[12]

According to Torre, he was happy that Clemens had ended his career with the Yankees. He told a press conference: "I'm glad that he had the chance to do it here. When he first came here, people didn't care for him because we traded Boomer (Wells) for him. He was sort of robotic, and I don't think the New York fans cared for him that much, because Boomer had that blue-collar thing. Since then, Roger has won them over with his personality, his pitching and his unselfishness with regards to his teammates."[13]

With the loss of the World Series, and the close of his career, Clemens had nothing else left to do but say his good-byes. There was no ticker-tape parade in downtown New York City for the Yankees that year, but there was a lot of press coverage of the Rocket's every move during the postseason.

In what would have probably been his last press conference of his career, Clemens gave what many would call his swan song. It was to have been his victory speech and his long goodbye. He spoke of his long successful career and of his hopes for the future, but he didn't take it all off the table. He told the fans and the media:

> This entire season was like a long closing act. I had the opportunity to say thank you to a lot of fans around town, living and going about New York City. People knew that I was going to retire, and while some of you out there urged me not to, everyone has thanked me for everything that's happened since I've been here wearing pinstripes. Now, I'd like to thank all of the baseball fans out there. Not only the ones in New York, Boston and Toronto, but in all baseball cities and towns all over the world. . . . I want to thank all of you fans, because it works both ways. You give me the inspiration when I go out to pitch. It's been great support, even when I was a visitor here. People have always

expressed how they enjoyed watching me work, they just couldn't cheer for me because I was wearing another uniform. Once I got traded to the Yankees, the fans were unbelievable, and it's been that way for the full five years. I hope you all know that I've given my all, I haven't taken anything for granted. . . . Boston was a great experience as well. . . . Toronto is more of a hockey town than a baseball town, but the Blue Jays have some great traditions with a couple of World Series championships. . . . New York isn't for everyone, but it's certainly agreed with me. It's the most incredible place to play. If you want to win, this is where you want to be. It was meant to be. My sisters told me stories that when I was young, I would wear a Yankees hat and jacket, and that I was destined to play here. In college, guys called me "Goose" after Goose Gossage. My mom says that everything comes full circle, so I guess that's true. As much as I loved Boston, what happened there was a blessing in disguise. With the Yankees, I've always had that same feeling I had with the Red Sox, that there were so many solid guys around, that if you weren't able to get it done on a particular day, someone else would be there to pick you up. We thrive and feed off one another. People look at the Yankees as a bunch of superstars, but you'd never know it from the way these guys handle and carry themselves. The fans are second to none in New York, which is why Mr. Steinbrenner always tries to put a great product on the field. . . . Being here, I've had an owner that wants to win worse than I do, which, as a player, is all you can ask for. Playing for Mr. Torre, it's been incredible. He's been so much fun to work with, to watch him teach and pass along his experience to the younger players, it's inspiring. What the fans have always done for me, being a power pitcher for twenty years, is to help get me going. . . . I'll miss the noise from the crowd when I get two strikes on a hitter, striking a guy out in a big situation.

That's the bottom line. Fans come out to get away from their work, to relax and cheer you on. That makes it fun for us, because if the crowd wasn't there, we wouldn't be playing. I want to thank each and every one of you for making this whole ride as memorable as it's been. I couldn't have done it without you.[14]

With that, he left New York for Houston and to continue with the rest of his life. By the time he left the New York Yankees he was the active player with the most wins, 310, and he had nearly 4,100 strikeouts under his belt. In his last year, he went for 17 wins with only 9 losses in 33 starts. As a Yankee, he threw 946 strikeouts and was 10th on their list of strikeout leaders.

During the off-season, Clemens worked at the offices of his Roger Clemens Foundation with a new sense of purpose. While retired, he could devote even more time to a hectic schedule of fund-raising appearances. It seemed as if wherever he showed up, the media was there to ask him about his future and if the Houston Astros would be part of that future.

Chapter 11

⎯⎯ HOME: THE BRILLIANT UNENDING ⎯⎯ TWILIGHT

In December 2003, Yankees free-agent pitcher Andy Pettitte signed a multiyear deal with the Houston Astros. His contract with the Yankees was up, and Steinbrenner didn't seem to want to part with the cash to keep him. To Houston Astros fans, this was an exciting development. A few weeks later, Roger Clemens would be talked out of retirement in order to join him. Roger kept his uniform number 22 and Pettitte was allowed to have number 21 as a show of solidarity. The world of baseball had been turned on its end. The Yankees flipped over in their chairs at the news. But while the Rocket had been on his farewell tour the past year, there was talk that he wouldn't stay retired for long. Houston offered him the "hometown advantage"; it is said that players pitch or bat their best when they are in their hometown with family and friends. In addition to other incentives, the Astros agreed that Clemens wouldn't have to travel with the team when not needed on the mound. This would allow him to devote time in an already-demanding schedule to his charitable foundation, which would have been impossible if he were on the road for several months of the season.

Roger, and all of Houston for that matter, was very fond of team owner Drayton McLane. McLane had worked his way up in his dad's business as the owner of a firm that mostly did grocery distribution at the time. In the 1960s the firm was able to win a contract with a small store chain out of Arkansas known as Wal-Mart. As Wal-Mart grew, so did the McLane business. He decided to purchase the Astros in the 1990s and built the team into what it is today with the same innate business know-how that he used to build up his businesses.

The Rocket and Pettitte already knew virtually all the hometown Houston Astros because they all lived not too far from each other during the off-season. All of the Astros spoke highly of Clemens and Pettitte coming on board as friends and as teammates. They all looked forward to a successful season, as did the fans and the team owners.

The Houston Astros' season opener, on April 7, had a sellout crowd to watch the newest members of the team, especially the Rocket. The almost 43,000 fans saw him win his first National League game as pitcher against the San Francisco Giants, 10 runs to 1. It was one of the most spectacular days in the history of Houston. Among the crowd were many University of Texas alumni, family, and friends. It was as if one large party had encompassed Minute Maid Park for the Astros' season opener. The Rocket was here, and he won the game for them.

His next win was against the St. Louis Cardinals on April 13 at Busch Stadium in St. Louis. He smoked them 5 runs to 3. His wins continued throughout April, May, and June, with wins against the Brewers, 6 to 1; the Rockies, 8 to 5; the Reds, 6 to 1; the Pirates, 6 to 2; the Marlins, 6 to 1; the Cubs,

5 to 1; and the Mariners, 1 to 0. The Cubs returned on June 14 to land the Rocket in one of his few losses of the year, 2 to 7. When the Anaheim game rolled around, Roger again suffered another loss, 4 to 6. He would regain his composure and defeat the Pirates 3 to 2 in a game where he became the majors' first 10-game winner of the season and also threw the 4,200th strikeout of his career. Next to lose were the San Diego Padres, 5 to 3, and the Diamondbacks, 6 to 1.

The Rocket appeared in the 2004 All-Star Game, which was held in Houston on July 13, 2004. It was his 10th selection to the game during his career and his first in the National League. Nearing 42 years of age, he was the oldest pitcher ever to start the game. Mike Piazza, as catcher, was his battery mate. The pair had given a new meaning to that term in the past, but both appeared to want the past to be just that. Astros teammates Carlos Beltran and Lance Berkman joined Roger at the game, as did several of Roger's former teammates from the Yankees, including Derek Jeter, Jason Giambi, Tom Gordon, Mariano Rivera, and A-Rod. Roger ended up as the losing pitcher at the game by allowing five hits and 6 runs in one inning. Two of them were home runs. A crowd of 41,886 cheered the Rocket and their favorite players on. For the first time, television viewership reached a new record as over 100 million people around the world watched the game. The American League defeated the National league, again, 9 runs to 4. After the game at a press conference, the All-Star team manager, Jack McKeon, was empathetic about Roger's loss and said, "He's been a warrior, and sometimes it happens to the best of them. He's a premium pitcher and just had a bad first inning. What are you going to do?"[1]

As is almost customary during the All-Star break, there were managerial changes with many teams, and the Houston

Astros were no different. The first half of the year was catastrophic for the team. At the time of the All-Star Game the
team was fighting just to stay even at the .500 mark. The
Astros' upper management, including General Manager
Gerry Hunsicker, decided to sack the team's skipper, manager Jimy Williams, and replace him with Phil Garner.
Known by his nickname of "Scrap Iron," he quickly re-
grouped the team, and by August 2004 they were on a roll
that would help them win the wild card for the pennant race.

In August the Rocket went onto a winning streak to
prove his critics wrong. On August 23 he was the winning
pitcher against the Phillies, 8 to 4, and the Cubs, 7 to 6. The
September 3 game saw the Pirates fall to him, 8 to 6, as did
St. Louis, 7 to 5. Milwaukee was his last victim of the season on September 19, 1 to 0. By then the Astros were well
on their way to winning the wild card for the season. The
Astros' season turned out to be one of their best in years,
going for 92 wins and 70 losses for a winning average of a
respectable .568. Roger's ERA for the year was 2.98 with a
win-loss percentage of .818, and he had struck out 218
opponents during the season. This helped the Astros win
the wild card to face and defeat the highly touted Atlanta
Braves 2 games to 3. For the first time in years, the Astros
were going to the National League Championship Series
to face the St. Louis Cardinals.

Game 1 was played in St. Louis at Busch Stadium. Both
Houston and St. Louis were on the scoreboard with 2 runs
each in the first inning. By the third inning, Houston was
clearly in the lead with 2 more runs. But in the fifth and
sixth innings the Cardinals hammered in 2 runs and 6 runs,
respectively. They allowed Houston to make up for lost
ground with a run in the eighth and 2 runs in the ninth,
but the Astros were still no match for the Cardinals, who

won it 10 runs to 7. Game 2, also at Busch, had Houston on the board in the first inning with 1 run, with the Cardinals not scoring until the fifth with 4 runs. Houston was too slow to catch up with the Cardinals, who tacked on 2 more runs in the ninth to win the game 6 runs to Houston's 4. The series moved to Minute Maid Park in Houston for their first ever series game in that building on October 16. There, the Rocket was waiting on the mound for St. Louis. He would pitch for seven innings, leading his team to a 5 to 2 victory over the Cardinals. Game 4, also at Minute Maid, saw the Astros even out the series. It was a dead-even game up to the

Had the format for the NLCS still been the best of five, the Astros would have been going to the World Series.

seventh inning, when Carlos Beltran shot a home run that the Cardinals couldn't match. Houston won the game 6 to 5. Game 5 was nervously scoreless—with Brandon Backe and Brad Lidge on the mound for the Astros and Jason Isringhausen for the Cardinals—until the ninth inning, when the Astros shot a three-run homer to win the game 3 to 0. Had the format for the NLCS still been the best of five, the Astros would have been going to the World Series.

Game 6 took place in St. Louis and was a fight back and forth between the two teams for 12 long innings. Astros ace pitchers Dan Miceli and Pete Munro took the mound for Houston, and Julian Tavarez and Matt Morris defended the Cardinals. By the ninth inning the score was a tie, and the game ran into extra innings until a walk by Jim Edmonds sent the Cardinals to victory, 6 to 4. Game 7, with the Rocket on the mound, had the Cardinals muted for two innings until Tony Womack scored a run in the third. In the sixth both Albert Pujols and Scott Rolen added three to their score with one more in the ninth to shatter Houston's hope of a World Series, 5 runs to 2.

Returning home to Houston, there was a somber pall on the chartered flight. Nonetheless, Astros fans greeted their gladiators back home just as if they had won the pennant. They instinctively knew that 2005 would most definitely be their year to get to the World Series.

The St. Louis Cardinals went on to face the American League champion, the Boston Red Sox, who were going to the World Series for the first time since Roger Clemens was on their mound in 1986. This would be the year that the Red Sox would finally win the fall classic. Boston had not won the World Series since 1918. Fans across the city went wild. Red Sox memorabilia covered the city. Even the fans who were long gone somehow took part in the festivities when their grandchildren placed Red Sox balloons and other merchandise on the graves of relatives who had hoped for a Series win but who had died before seeing the achievement in their lifetime. The Cardinals lost the World Series to the Red Sox in a humiliating 4 games to 0. Boston had clinched the title and wouldn't let go.

The Rocket had good news in November when he was awarded his seventh Cy Young Award. He was now the oldest pitcher to have won the award, and no other pitcher in history had won so many. He now had one for each of his four sons; his wife, Debbie; himself; and his mom.

When Clemens arrived in Houston as an Astro, he and Debbie dived into their charitable works, such as helping out with the local Habitat for Humanity chapter in the greater Houston area. Through the Roger Clemens Foundation, which he and Debbie had set up in 1992 to help facilitate the flow of donations to various local and international charities, their work grew to help other such organizations as the Houston Food Bank, Strike Out Hunger, Texas Children's Hospital, M.D. Anderson Hospital, Make-A-Wish Foundation, the Arbor House, National Paralysis Fund, Children at Risk, the DePelchin Children's Center, the Montgomery County Youth Services, and so many, many more.[2]

With his un-retirement season now over, the media began to follow Roger almost on a daily basis to badger him about what his plans were for the future. His return to the Astros was first on their agenda. In January 2005 the Astros offered Clemens salary arbitration, and he decided to put off retirement for one more year. After negotiations, the Astros were again able to sign the Rocket to the team by the end of the month. The deal would make him the highest-paid pitcher in major-league history. This increase more than made up for the lower-than-usual 2004 salary. During spring training of that year, fans would line the fences just to see him practice or work out. Roger was gracious enough to talk to the fans and to sign autographs on jerseys or T-shirts.

As it would turn out, the 2005 season would be arguably one of the best of the Rocket's many seasons. Now well into his 40s, he wanted to show that age was no barrier with his strict workout and nutrition routines. He posted the best ERA in the majors with 1.85 for the season and went for 13 and 8 in wins. Kip Wells of the Pirates would accidentally hit him with a pitch, but the incident did not lead to any confrontation. During the upcoming year Clemens would have problems with run support; he would pitch efficiently, but his teammates would not be able to put runs on the board in support of his pitching, which in many cases allowed the opposing team to defeat them.

But the season would be marred by yet another scandal that threatened the sport just as much as the baseball strike did a decade earlier. The steroid issue, which in the past had occasionally surfaced only to subside from discussion, was now not only surfacing but washing ashore like a smelly, beached whale. Making things worse was the publication of several tell-all books and magazine and newspaper articles on the subject. Major-league officials were now forced to do more to confront the issue, much more than the weak and watered-down testing policy that had been in effect since the 2002 season, disguised in a last-minute deal. Tension that was approaching a boiling point finally boiled over in baseball. Its testing standards did not measure up to various other sports and their testing policies, which were much more frequent, stringent, and encompassing. Even if a baseball player was detected using

> *The use of steroids is not a relatively recent phenomenon.*

the juice, the punishment was not a deterrent. A few days of suspension only meant a few more days off in some cases. Baseball was also setting a poor example for high school and college athletes who were more likely to use steroids in order to advance their chances at a pro sports career. Baseball Commissioner Bud Selig was confident that players' use of steroids was not as widespread as the press was making it out to be. Originally it was hoped that a player who had tested positive on a steroid test would have the spotlight pointed at him, would be embarrassed enough, and would serve as an example to others. But even the threat of negative publicity had not stopped some players from using the stuff.

The use of steroids is not a relatively recent phenomenon. The practice took off during the 1980s. Before that time a successful player had to do it the old-fashioned way, through workouts and practice. In the modern era, any successful player with a stellar record is suspected of having used some performance-enhancing drug. The accumulation of public distrust, media pressure, and threats from Congress to step in and clean up baseball finally prompted organized baseball to clean up its own act. Congress finally got into the fray by sending out subpoenas to several prominent players to testify at a House committee hearing on steroid use. The committee didn't believe that baseball had done enough to clean itself up, and now the government was considering moving in to do the job for them. All of the players who testified, including Raphael Palmeiro, Sammy Sosa, Mark McGwire, Curt Schilling, and José Canseco, gave emotional testimony, but some were elusive about whether they had used drugs to enhance their performance. Ironically, shortly after his testimony, Raphael Palmeiro was suspended from baseball after tests showed that he had used steroids, although he had denied using them when he testified before Congress. He never returned to the game. After major-league officials and players decided on a more stringent testing policy, it became a less frequent event for a player to test positive for the drugs. As a result, attention to the issue has decreased with time.

The news media routinely brought up Roger Clemens in the steroid discussion for a variety of reasons. Set forth here, there are probably at least a dozen reasons why Clemens has never used any form of performance-enhancing drug in his career. The first and most important reason is his intense and continuous workout regime. At his level of fitness, there would be no reason to add drugs to a body that is already fit and competitive. The second obvious reason is that his pitching is an art form that cannot extensively or artificially be enhanced, especially with the juice. The third is that there has been no unexplainable or erratic upswing in his abilities. He has always been the ace of aces in pitching. He has had streaks of greatness followed by periods of downturn but no sudden sustained "high," which has been seen in others who were users. The fourth reason is the constant scrutiny by the media. The Rocket is a lightning rod of the press. He has never really been able to even step outside his door without something being written up about it in the press. A fifth reason is his batting. He's never been a Ted Williams, and there has

Drugs would not only bring embarrassment to himself but to his whole family, and his mom would have certainly kept him on the straight and narrow on this issue.

been no sudden, spectacular increase in that ability. Sixth, there are no physical telltale signs—no 'roid rage encounters or sudden physical changes. A seventh reason is that he has been a competitor all of his life, not a cheater. He is confident in his abilities, and he knows that confidence will get an athlete much more than drugs will ever do for him. Eight, he's dedicated to his family. Drugs would not only bring embarrassment to himself but to his whole family, and his mom would have certainly kept him on the straight and narrow on this issue. This leads to the ninth reason, the history of cardiopulmonary health issues in his family. His stepdad passed away because of heart problems, and his mom suffered from a lung condition. He knew full well that performance-enhancing drugs would eventually cause him physical harm and that no mantel full of awards would save him from that fate if he did so. He even discussed the cardiac problems that have been a part of his family when he was again, in 2006, along with Andy Pettitte, falsely accused of using steroids. Ten, he has always said that the fan is the reason he does what he does. To be found guilty of steroid use would be the ultimate dishonor to himself and to his fans. Eleven, his honesty is legendary. He looks each and every fan and member of the media straight in the eye when he speaks to them. He has nothing to hide. And the final of the dozen reasons Clemens has never used steroids is that he is subject to steroid testing and has never tested positive for anything other than hard work. When he was selected to the World Baseball Classic in 2006, the testing there was on the caliber of Olympic testing. The rigorous tests found Roger to be in perfect health for a man in his 40s, with no traces of steroidal or other banned substances.

The previously mentioned reasons should be convincing enough to finally drop the steroid issue regarding Clemens. Unfortunately it will probably come up for discussion again, but Roger has dealt with the issue many times, especially since he is such a lightning rod in major-league baseball. Each time it comes up, the accusations will have less attraction for fans and the media, and eventually the accusations will fade from interest and memory.

On April 5 the Astros began the 2005 season by hosting the St. Louis Cardinals at Minute Maid Park. The Astros' losing score of 3 to 7 was the result of a lack of run support for Astros pitcher Roy Oswalt. This lack of run support led to a disastrous win-to-loss record of 32 to 40 by midseason and threatened the skipperdom of Scrap Iron. Garner would eventually survive the season by taking the

Astros to the brink of winning the wild card, to within half of a game, but the Astros still lost the hope of any postseason play. Roger's first win would be on April 8 over the Cincinnati Reds, 3 runs to 2. He would not have another win decision on the mound until the May 9 win over the Florida Marlins, 2 to 1, after a loss on April 29 to the Chicago Cubs, 3 to 2. A May 14 win over the San Francisco Giants, 4 to 1, was followed by two losses attributed to lack of run support: the Astros lost to the Arizona Diamondbacks on May 19, 1 to 6, and to the Cincinnati Reds 0 to 9 on May 30. Clemens then got back into the groove with several wins: the June 5 defeat of the St. Louis Cardinals, 6 to 4; the June 17 win at the Kansas City Royals, 7 to 0; the 6 to 2 defeat of the Colorado Rockies; and the 9 to 0 smoke of the Cincinnati Reds on their own turf on July 3. The July 22 defeat of the Washington Nationals, 14 to 1, was one of the highlights of the Rocket's season, followed closely by the win over the Philadelphia Phillies, 3 to 2, on July 27.

Clemens was again present at the 2005 All-Star Game at Comerica Park in Detroit, Michigan. Fellow Astros Brad Lidge, Roy Oswalt, and Morgan Ensberg joined him there. Ensberg replaced the Cardinals' Scott Rolen, who bowed out of the game to nurse an ailing right shoulder. Again, the American League would win it, 7 to 5.

During the summer of 2005, Roger's oldest son, Koby, who had started study at the University of Texas in Austin and was on its baseball team, just as his father had been back in the 1980s, was signed to a Houston Astros minor-league contract. Koby had attended Memorial High School in Houston, not Spring Woods Senior High School, as his father had. As his father had, he played two sports in high school, baseball and football, in case one didn't work out. Football ceased to be an option for him when he hurt his back during a game. When Koby went to the University of Texas, he played third base, whereas his father had been the pitcher. In a few months he was drafted by the Houston Astros in the eighth round of the amateur draft, was assigned originally to the Greeneville Astros, and then moved to the Class A Lexington Legends. Koby would attract attention while playing for the Legends, not as the son of a famous pitcher, but by his own efforts at the game. It was the beginning of yet another father and son baseball dynasty.[3]

It was the beginning of yet another father and son baseball dynasty.

Other family dynasties in baseball, to name a few, have been the Alou family of brothers Felipe, Jesús, Matty, and Felipe's son, Moises; Sandy Alomar and sons Roberto and Sandy Jr.; the Cruz family of brothers Hector, José, and Tommy Cruz, and José's son, José Jr.; and the Niekro brothers of Phil and Joe, and Joe's son, Lance. There is Cal Ripken and sons Cal Jr. and Billy; Mel Stottlemyre and sons Todd and Mel Jr.; and the DiMaggio brothers of Joe, Dom, and Vince.

The Rocket continued his advance following the All-Star break. On August 2 there was the win over the Arizona Diamondbacks, 3 to 1, and the 8 to 1 defeat of the San Francisco Giants on August 7. After this winning streak, he seemed to go into a downturn, much of it caused by a lack of run support. The August 18 loss to the Milwaukee Brewers, 2 to 5; the 2 to 0 loss to the San Diego Padres on August 23; and the September 9 loss to the Brewers again seemed to have fans and the media wondering what the problem was. Despite these losses the Astros' win-to-loss average was improving dramatically, almost miraculously, and had them aiming at the wild card or the pennant race again as in the previous 2004 season.

September 2005 brought a continued downturn in the health of the Rocket's mom, Bess Clemens. Roger sometimes took her to Minute Maid Park to sit among his fans, and on one occasion she threw out the first ceremonial pitch on the field after she had risen from her wheelchair. Roger quipped that she did a better job of it than he had. She found strength in baseball. Everyone throughout the leagues hoped that she would pull through, but on September 14, 2005, she passed away early in the morning at her home in Georgetown, Texas. It was a home that Roger had built for her. Her children were at her side at the end. Bess Clemens had worked hard during her life to take care of her children, and in her later years her children returned that honor and took care of her. Once, during a speech after he won his seventh Cy Young Award, Roger said, "I don't want to speak to two empty chairs."[4] His comment referred to the fact that he wanted his mom there when he was inducted into the Baseball Hall of Fame. His stepdad had passed away when he was only nine. In some comforting way, both his parents instinctively knew that their son would make it to that hall, and because of that he wouldn't have to be speaking to two empty chairs.

Roger spoke about his mom to Major League Baseball and the *Boston Globe*: "She's responsible for every bit of my success. She's a strong woman who made me who I am. I think that's all hogwash when I hear that a single parent can't raise kids. My mom kept my butt in line. She taught me to respect other people and apologize when I'm wrong and to stick to my guns when I'm right."[5]

All of baseball was grieving just as much as Roger was, but he gathered up enough strength to pitch that same day in her memory at Minute Maid Park. He said that she would have wanted him to pitch that evening. In that game he would bounce back with a win over the Florida Marlins, 10 to 2. After the funeral near Dayton, Ohio, he pitched in the September 19 game at the Pirates' PNC Park, where the Astros were defeated 7 to 0. As a matter of trivia, with that game under his belt he had pitched in every ballpark in major-league baseball. A win over the Cubs on October 1 was a much-needed win for him, 3 runs to 1, to clinch the pennant race for the Astros. Overall, the season brought 89 wins and 73 losses for a winning average of .549. The entire city of Houston, and the state of Texas, was excited that the Astros had made it to the postseason. Something in the air told them that this postseason would take them all the way to the fall classic, including a World Series win. They were right on the money.

On October 5, the Astros took on the Atlanta Braves in Game 1 of the National League Division Series and won it 10 runs to 5. In Game 2, Roger Clemens was on the mound for the loss to the Braves, 7 to 1. The Braves' Brian McCann had hit a three-run homer off of the Rocket to win it for Atlanta. Roger's well-earned seniority was showing, as McCann was only a few weeks old when Clemens first stepped onto the mound for the Boston Red Sox in 1984. Game 3 at Minute Maid Park, with Roy Oswalt on the mound, was a win for Houston, 7 to 3. The only home run of the game came from Mike Lamb of the Astros. Game 4 would be the longest postseason game ever, with 18 innings. The game was so long that Houston ran out of pitchers and had to call on the Rocket as a relief pitcher from the bullpen for the last three innings of the game. It was only the second time in his career that he pitched relief. Even though Atlanta was in the lead for much of the game, Houston defeated Atlanta 7 to 6 in the almost six-hour game and went on to the National League Championship Series against the St. Louis Cardinals.

The Cardinals were the most popular team in Houston, outside of the Astros, of course, as judged by fan attendance. Game 1 on October 12, 2005, took place in St. Louis, and the Cardinals quickly took the lead over Houston and won the game 5 to 3. In Game 2 the Astros were out for revenge. It was the Astros' turn to take the lead, and they did to win the game 4 to 1. The only run scored by the Cardinals was a home run by Albert Pujols. Game 3 moved to Minute Maid Park in Houston, where the Rocket pitched for six tireless innings. St. Louis was never ahead of Houston and lost to the Astros 4 to 3. Game 4 saw Houston inch its way to its first World Series with a 2 to 1 win over the Cardinals. Game 5 teased them to wait a little longer as St. Louis won 5 to 4. The Astros were in the lead and had hopes of winning it there in Houston, but in the ninth the famous hit by Albert Pujols dashed their chances. Pujols popped the ball into the closed roof of Minute Maid Park; it bounced off and landed on the railroad tracks in left field, allowing a three-run homer to finish the game 5 to 4. The Astros and the city were stunned. They were going to have to return to face the Cardinals in St. Louis, and with the Cardinals' home-field advantage, it would be a daunting task.

On the weary plane ride to the game, there was a little turbulence rocking the plane. The pilot jokingly said on the intercom that it was Pujols' ball finally coming in for a landing. The Astros' players took it in stride and somehow used that as the last laugh of the Cardinals, which it would turn out to be in Game 6. The Astros had their victory celebration at Busch, not Minute Maid, with a stunning 5 to 1 win over the Cardinals. Astros ace Oswalt pitched seven terrific innings, striking fear and smoke into the Cardinals. Jason Lane of the Astros furnished the only home run of the game. After 40 years of missing out on it, the Astros were going to the World Series for the first time ever. The city of Houston and surrounding communities went wild. People not able to watch the finale of the last championship playoff game could easily judge who the winner was when traffic and fireworks began to sound off in the late night October air. The news media was frantic. The win taking the Astros to the fall classic provided an exciting boost to Houston, which had just suffered the effects of Hurricane Rita and its helter-skelter evacuation, and to the thousands of Hurricane Katrina evacuees who had come from New Orleans to seek shelter in Houston.

> *People not able to watch the finale of the last championship playoff game could easily judge who the winner was when traffic and fireworks began to sound off in the late night October air.*

For its first World Series, Houston faced the American League Chicago White Sox, who hadn't been to the game since 1917. Even though there was a lot of media hype about Boston's not winning the classic since 1918, there was hardly any mention about the White Sox and their 88-year drought from World Series or the Black Sox scandal of the same era. Predictions for the World Series favored the Astros because of their arsenal of high-caliber players on the roster and their deep-seated desire to win. The White Sox, though, had a roster of intensely dedicated players, but many were relative unknowns outside the Chicago area or the inner circles of baseball. The Astros had won the season's wild card on the last day of their regular season through sheer luck and perseverance, something that they also used to get themselves through the division series and championship games up to the World Series.

Chicago had home-field advantage in Game 1 because the American League had won the All-Star Game in July. The White Sox skipper, Ozzie Guillen, got his team to the classic through his old mantra "If it ain't broke don't fix it." He was not one to tinker by tweaking changes in a team doing so well during the season and postseason. In Game 1, on October 22 with a capacity crowd of 44,206, the Astros wasted no time in putting the Rocket on the mound as starting pitcher. At the age of 43 he was the oldest pitcher to start a postseason game. The Rocket was reflective about the situation just ahead of the game, saying, "I want to make sure that I put all of my energy, all of my efforts into this game, the respect I have for it, what it's given me back, and I think you can tell by the effort I've put forth, even at home, I've shown that to my home state and city. They're very excited. I just want them to enjoy it as much as they can, everyone—not just my family, not just my teammates, but the entire state."[6]

Jermaine Dye of Chicago slammed the game's first home run during the first inning. Unfortunately after just two innings a hamstring injury forced Clemens from the game. He was replaced by Wandy Rodriguez for the third through fifth innings. Chicago was able to hit run after run against Houston without an answer from the Astros' batters. The White Sox won Game 1, 5 to 3. Game 2 was also in Chicago. Astros ace Andy Pettitte on the mound pitched six strong innings, but in the seventh, Paul Konerko of the White Sox hit a home run, and, with the addition of other runs, Chicago rose into the lead. Scott Podsednik closed Game 2 down, serving a final blow to the Astros with Chicago winning it 7 to 6. Oddly, or as luck would have it, Podsednik, who hadn't had a single home run during the regular season, hit two home runs during the postseason.

Game 3 moved to Houston with the team and fans knowing that victory would certainly be theirs. Because of a slight possibility of rain during the game, the Astros' management arranged for the roof of Minute Maid Park to be closed during that time, but an order from major-league offices overruled the decision. The roof would have to be open, to the dismay of Houston fans. Historically, the team had experienced better luck at home against an enemy with the roof closed rather than open. A closed roof echoed the howls and chants of fervent Astros fans against any opponent. In any case, Houston was in the lead during Game 3 for the first four innings, but in the fifth, Joe Crede of the White Sox helped bring in five runs. Houston answered to match it up to an even 5 to 5 in the eighth-inning nail-biter. The opponents remained locked in a dead-even game for five more tortuous innings until Geoff Blum knocked out a two-run homer for Chicago in the 14th inning, winning it for Chicago 7 to 5. Houston was stunned, and, above all, infuriated that the open roof and the intrusion of major-league powers may have led to their loss. The 14-inning, six-hour game was a record setter for a postseason game, and it was all for nothing as far as Houston was concerned. In the postgame conference room, skipper Phil Garner was quite irate at the performance of his team, saying that it was "absolute rotten hitting. We might have played forty innings and it didn't look like we were going to get a runner across the bag. It's embarrassing to play like this in front of our hometown. I'm really ticked off."[7] One can only imagine the conversations going on within the team's closed clubhouse after the game.

Game 4 was a valiant fight by the Astros to avoid elimination and an equally valiant fight by Chicago to finish it off as soon as possible. The national media seemed to all at once turn against Houston and, on many occasions spouted, "Houston, we have a problem," which was clearly aimed at Astros fans. Astros pitching ace Brandon Backe pitched a spectacular and flawless seven innings, fending off the stalled White Sox. In the eighth inning, Chicago's Jermaine Dye hit a single to drive in Willie Harris, scoring the first run of the game. Harris's remained the only run until the end of the game, and Chicago won the game and the Series 1 to 0. It was a completely unexpected sweep of Houston.

> Fans who funneled out of the stadium near midnight were in no mood to continue the World Series party that had engulfed Houston for the past few weeks.

The champagne party had to happen in the visitor's clubhouse at Minute Maid Park, not the home team's clubhouse. That in itself was an insult to Houston and the Astros. Fans who funneled out of the stadium near midnight were in no mood to continue the World Series party that had engulfed Houston for the past few weeks. Instead, they went home and forgot about it. The next day the hometown media carried the Series as an important event and then the next day relegated it to the history files. After the final tally was figured, the media stated that the economic impact of the World Series wasn't as great as had been hoped for by the city and the county.

The season was over, and another spectacular season for the Rocket had ended along with it. In 2005, in his 32 starts, he completed the season with a 13 to 8 win ratio, and with it a 1.87 ERA, the lowest not only in the National League but in all of baseball. Only Nolan Ryan had done better, with a 1.69 ERA back in 1981. Roger's career wins, at 341, placed him at ninth in major-league history, a mark he had passed during the May 9 game at the Florida Marlins. With 185 batters struck out and 62 walks, he ranked second on the list, only behind, again, Nolan Ryan.

Another banner year was in store for the Rocket, as in 2006 he was selected to be on the roster of the World Baseball Classic. It was the first truly internationally organized competition in the sport. In addition to Clemens, the roster included other Houston Astros, such as Brad "Lights Out" Lidge and Dan Wheeler. Three also made it to the reserves, including Andy Pettitte, Morgan Ensberg, and Lance Berkman. Roger was the oldest of all the players, both for the United States and internationally. This was something to be proud of. Virtually all of the players selected to be on Team USA were either current or former teammates of the Rocket's, such as Al Leiter and Derek Jeter, or had played against him in league or interleague play. The team showed up to World Baseball Training Camp on March 2, and the games were held March 3–20. (This is one of the reasons that the Rocket missed out on much of the training camp for the Astros that year.) International teams were divided up into pools, and the United States was placed in Pool B along with Canada, Mexico, and South Africa. The winners of each pool would face each other in the finals. The first games were held on March 3, with Pool A playing in Tokyo,

Japan. Japan was the clear winner of nations that included Korea, Chinese Taipei, and China. Mexico was the winner in Pool B. In Pool C, which included Puerto Rico, Panama, Cuba, and the Netherlands, the winner was Cuba. Pool D included the Dominican Republic, Italy, Venezuela, and Australia. The Dominican Republic won Pool D. In the finals of the 2006 World Baseball Classic, Japan won over Cuba 10 to 6. It was referred to as the World's World Series of Baseball, and fans across the globe were united in one sport.

Roger Clemens pitched in the fifth inning of the Thursday, March 16, game against Mexico. He threw 73 pitches in total and struck out four of the Mexico team players, without hitting one of them in the head. The United States would lose the game to Mexico, and because of baseball regulations, Roger was unfortunately given the title of losing pitcher for the game.

The Rocket was excited to have played on baseball's international stage. He said in a statement to the media: "I felt great tonight. My body responded well. I am very thankful for the opportunity to participate in this event. It made all the work I did in the past six weeks worthwhile. I got to know a number of different players from different teams that, if not for this event, I wouldn't have had that opportunity. They got to see the competitive side of my nature. For me, right now it's good-bye."[8]

The World Baseball Classic brought together a world that was torn by war and discontent with each other. For a few days, distrust from nation to nation was set aside, and a great pastime, once solely American, was now on the world's stage. Japan, the eventual winner, had many followers of baseball from early on. When Joe DiMaggio visited the country while on the way to a troop review in South Korea in the 1950s, he was mobbed by jubilant crowds in Japan who wanted to get a closer look at him. Today, the Japanese Leagues are almost as well known around the world as the American and National Leagues of the United States.

When the classic was first announced, Commissioner Bud Selig told a press conference:

> The World Baseball Classic is an unprecedented and historic international event. For the first time ever, baseball's best players will compete for their home countries in a global tournament. Major League Baseball and the Major League Baseball Players Association have joined together to establish this event. It is sanctioned by the International Baseball Federation, and will be conducted jointly by Major League Baseball and the Players Association in cooperation with Nippon Professional Baseball and the Korea Baseball Organization, their respective Players Associations and the other national baseball federations. This tournament which will take place next March will increase worldwide exposure for our great game and promote the game's grassroot development, not only in countries where the game already is popular, but in nations where the game is less known. The World Baseball Classic will ultimately produce new fans and more players. All of us in Major League Baseball are very excited about this event. All 30 clubs are supportive of this effort, and we expect our players who are chosen by their respective national baseball federations to play with great eagerness and excitement. This is great for our game, and all of us recognize and understand how important it is for the growth of our sport. While we still have many open issues to resolve, we're making very steady progress.[9]

The players' association director, Don Fehr, added to Selig's comments words that also resounded with what the players were thinking:

> It's been a long time since players began to talk about international competitions of this type. It's taken a while for us to get here. Having said that, I think that everybody on the players' side is satisfied that this new partnership with Major League Baseball and the federations Nippon Baseball and Korean Baseball that will be able to put on an event which will be truly remarkable and will be exciting not only for the fans who watch it but for the players who play it, and for those of us involved in the administration of the sport. New ventures like this always take a little longer than you would hope to get off the ground, and there are always a few more wrinkles than you would like. But when they get to a stage where you can see the end result, even if it's still coming into focus, it's a very gratifying thing, and we really look forward to the events. It's going to be wonderful and in the years to come, I hope and expect that all of us will be able to look around as will all of you and remember that we were here when it all began.[10]

For Japan to win the first crown in a truly international competition of baseball was something fans around the world celebrated. The games were a resounding success. Commissioner Bud Selig told a press conference after the games, "Anything you do for the first time is not going to be perfect. But by any stretch of the imagination, this tournament exceeded my expectations in a myriad of ways. Absolutely."[11] The games will not be played annually, but the next ones are scheduled for 2009. By then, even more countries are expected to join the world in playing the games.

Again, during the holiday season and before the new season started up, the media followed the Rocket, asking him if he intended to re-sign with the Astros when talks could resume in May 2006. Even though he considered himself retired, it was the worst-kept secret in the world what his plans were for the upcoming 2006 season. Since Clemens was not a part of spring training for the Astros, or any team for that matter, the press threw around stories about the Rocket going back to his first team, the Boston Red Sox. Other stories had him going back to the New York Yankees. The Texas Rangers were also a team under close watch.

The May 1 opening date for contract negotiations came and went, without any public announcements from either side. Almost the entire month of May slipped by and still nothing. On the morning of May 31, the Astros arranged a late morning press conference at Minute Maid Park. The meeting unfolded with what everyone had expected, the signing of the Rocket for another year with the Astros. Red Sox fans had actually warmed up to the idea of the Rocket returning to their fold, as did the Yankees. There had been talk of the Texas Rangers courting Clemens for a while, but for now it was Houston's turn to shine again as the press conference revealed the signing.

Houston's record so far for the year had been a smack even .500 to the end of May. The signing of Roger Clemens signaled the hope that they could rise above that mark and make it though the pennant race. The Rocket would first have three minor-league starts in order to "get himself back into shape." Then, if it all worked out right, he would start with the Astros on June 22, which happened to be Texas Longhorns Night and celebrated Clemens's alma mater. The original contract was with the Astros' organization but within their minor-league system. When Roger successfully completed those three starts, the Astros' major-league team "purchased" the contract from their minor-league affiliate, and the Rocket officially became a Houston Astro again on June 22.

His start date finally arrived, and he would pitch to a capacity crowd at Minute Maid Park in downtown Houston. The Astros' opponent, the Minnesota Twins, won the game 4 runs to 2. The game was all Rocket, classic like the old days, but he lacked the run support of his teammates. According to Clemens, "I think overall it was positive. My body felt better than expected and I hope and expect to get stronger each time I get out there. My arm feels great, I was really excited about how my legs felt in my warm up session. I expect to get stronger every time now, and that's what I'm looking forward to."[12] He was looking forward to another reasonably successful year with the Astros. On June 27 he had his second start with the Astros, this time against the Detroit Tigers in an interleague game. The Astros also lost this one 4 runs to 0, and Roger's win-loss record as of that date was 2 games lost to no games won. The Rocket would have to wait until the next month before he would be able to chalk up his first win against the Chicago Cubs, 7 to 2, on July 3. "It was a good win," Clemens said. "The guys hit the ball, and I was glad to see it."[13]

The 2006 All-Star Game went on without the Rocket on July 11 in Pittsburgh. Roy Oswalt was the sole Astro to represent the team in a game in which the American League again won, 3 runs to 2. The National League manager was the skipper of the Houston Astros, Phil "Scrap Iron" Garner.

Still running on the high from their win over the Cubs, the Astros set out to defeat the St. Louis Cardinals on July

8 at Minute Maid Park. Roger again pitched a great game but lost the game to the Cards 6 to 7. Another loss happened on July 14 on a visit to the Florida Marlins, where they would lose 3 to 1. The Rocket's win-to-loss record was now an abysmal 1 to 4. The media lost no time in knocking the Astros and, to some extent, the Rocket. They were already dismissing the Astros' season without their consent. On a visit to the Chicago Cubs on July 18, they made up for a lack of run support in previous games and gave the Rocket his second win of the season, 4 to 2. Within a week, he was dealt another loss, to the Cincinnati Reds, an embarrassing 8 runs to 1 on July 25.

On July 21 Mike Piazza of the San Diego Padres reached his 2,000th career hit in the major leagues, proving that even after nearly 15 seasons he was still a major player in the sport. Piazza debuted on September 1, 1992, with the Los Angeles Dodgers. Although he wouldn't face Roger Clemens for some time, he would by the 1993 season make a name for himself with his hitting abilities. He quickly earned a reputation for himself in the majors. In 1993 he was voted Rookie of the Year and eventually appeared in an amazing 12 All-Star Games. He also garnered 10 Silver Slugger Awards in a row for his abilities as a hitter. On May 5, 2004, he succeeded Carlton Fisk for the most home runs by a catcher, which for Piazza would eventually surpass the 400 mark. One of the most moving, emotional events of his career was when he hit the home run at Shea in the first game after the September 11, 2001, terrorist attacks. In the 2006 World Baseball Classic he represented Italy, from which he traces much of his ancestry.

When the Padres visited the Astros on August 11, 2006, I was able to meet up with many of the team members, including former Astro Doug Brocail. Doug talked a lot about his career with the Astros and with the Padres. He still remains friends with almost all of the "old guard"Astros and frequently goes hunting with them near his home in Texas. Brocail, who has high respect for the Rocket, said that there are many chances for youth to make it into the majors, and that "to be honest, after all of the hard work it really comes to the luck of the draw in terms of actually getting in.There are some with twice the talent who didn't make it." Doug says that he spent seven seasons in the minor leagues before being called up to the majors, and even then, it took what he called a "fire sale to put me onto the rotation." He actually didn't believe it when he made it in as a pitcher for the San Diego Padres back at the end of the 1992 season. After a few seasons with the Astros, then Detroit, and Texas, he's back with the Padres. He helped them get into the 2006 postseason by appearing in 25 games for his team.

Woody Williams, also an ace pitcher for the Padres, summed it all up when he said that Roger Clemens "can't be compared to anyone in baseball. He's very well respected around the leagues." Woody, who hails from the Houston area, attended Alvin Community College, as did Nolan Ryan. There, he rapidly advanced on its baseball team and transferred to the University of Houston, where he was eventually drafted into the majors. After that interview, Khalil Greene reminded me that his tuna and oatmeal diet is actually part of a nutrition plan, and that it was not part of any type of superstition for good luck during a game.

Trevor Hoffman, the Padres' pitching ace, brought all of his sons—Brody, Quinn, and Wyatt—along with him. All were dressed in youth-sized Padres uniforms.The kids were able to work out at batting practice with their dad and the rest of the team. It made quite an impression on the fans who watched the practice of the future major-leaguers.

Trevor's brother Glenn is a coach with the Dodgers after a long major-league career.

I also had a chance to meet up with Padres' catcher Mike Piazza. For Piazza, questions almost always begin to circle around his run-ins with the Rocket. But in this instance, I planned to ask a question that had never been asked before. My question for Piazza was, if he thought Clemens had caused the concussion and thrown the bat on purpose, would he forgive Clemens? An answer to this would have absolutely settled the situation once and for all. I don't know if Piazza was tipped ahead of time—there is probably no way to know for sure—but as I approached Piazza in the dugout for a few questions, he carefully avoided the situation and left the dugout. I should note that he did not turn his back on me and apparently had no ill intention. He may have needed to return to the field in a hurry. It's been said that there is no crying in baseball, but one thing is for sure: there had better be forgiveness in baseball, or else why even play the game? I assume that Piazza is a good guy, and if he did think Clemens did it on purpose, he would forgive him—he possibly already has forgiven him in his own mind—and now the situation is finally over for him. This doesn't mean that the Rocket did it on purpose, but he would be forgiven if he had.

> *It's been said that there is no crying in baseball, but one thing is for sure: there had better be forgiveness in baseball, or else why even play the game?*

One day after the Rocket turned 44, the Arizona Diamondbacks were no match for the Astros with Clemens on the mound. It was a win for the Rocket, 9 to 3. In that game

Craig Biggio whopped in the 2,900th hit of his career, and Clemens garnered his 344th win. It was the epitome of run support, with smiles all around. The returning Cubs on August 15 made up for their previous loss back in July by defeating the Astros 8 runs to 6 in an 18-inning game. Roger pitched for six great innings, but it still was no match for the Cubs on a vengeance visit. When the Rocket went up for bat in that game, he was accidentally hit by a pitch from Juan Mateo. At the August 20 game with the Milwaukee Brewers, the Rocket was able to bring up his wins by defeating them 3 to 1. The August 25 game was also a win for the Rocket against the Pittsburgh Pirates, 5 to 1. By the time the August 30 game with the Milwaukee Brewers arrived, the press was putting the Rocket back into full-throttle mode, and he won the game by a 1 to 0 decision.

On September 4, Labor Day, Roger pitched for four innings until he realized that something was going wrong. It was a hamstring injury again, and he was taken off the mound. The Phillies won the game 3 to 2. After the game, it was announced that Clemens was listed as day to day. He returned on September 15 for a 3 to 4 loss against the Philadelphia Phillies. He allowed a grand slam in the first inning by Pat Burrell. Again it should be noted that Clemens did not take out revenge against Burrell in any game for the grand slam.

The Wednesday, September 20, game with the Reds was marked by the press as Clemens's final home game, although earlier, Astros skipper Phil Garner hadn't said anything certain. In any case, the Astros won the game 7 runs to 2, and the Rocket left the mound to a buzz of fan appreciation. It was so intense that Clemens had to be called back from the clubhouse a few minutes later in order to respond to the encore of the sellout crowd, which he did, waving his hat in appreciation of the fans. "I thought that was it," Clemens said. "I got back downstairs and Phil [Garner] asked me to go out and do the warm up before he could pull me out of there to tip my cap to the fans. That's what it's been about for me since I've been home . . . winning and making it enjoyable for the fans here at home."[14]

To the management at the Astros, and for all of major-league baseball for that matter, this is what baseball is all about: appreciating the fans. Garner added to Roger's comments: "We decided to let him have that moment there. I thought it was really fantastic the way the fans responded and the way Rocket responded there, too."[15] Garner and the entire team, including some of the visiting team, stood and applauded also.

A few days later, for the Sunday game against the Cardinals, Roger Clemens stepped up to the plate again, with only three days' rest, because he was needed in the very close race between the Astros and the Cardinals. The Rocket was going to have another try at having a final good-bye. This time, it was personal. The Cardinals had been an Astros arch nemesis for years. Before the game, Roger said, "I have the opportunity to go to the mound again here at home and try to beat a team that's headed towards the playoffs . . . the season's not over yet,"[16] he added. In that game, the Cards lost to the Rocket's fine art of pitching, 7 runs to 3, in an Astros sweep of the Cardinals and their plans in the pennant race. The Astros were able to continue their efforts in the chase for the wild card for the 2006 season because of the Rocket's reappearance. Again, when he left the mound at the top of the sixth, he tipped his hat to his fans who were, according to him, his reason for being there. Clemens brought out the best in the Astros even with his late-season start. He reminisced about the season and said in the press conference: "I wish we could take these last four crowds we had with us on the road. It was a lot of fun playing in front of these fans these last four days. It was extremely loud and very encouraging."[17]

The next week's games were nothing short of an abbreviated miracle. The Astros defeated the Philadelphia Phillies 5 to 4 on September 26 in a late-season makeup game of a rainout from earlier in the year. They swept through the Pittsburgh Pirates in a 7 to 4 victory on September 27, a 7 to 6 victory on the 28th, and a 3 to 0 victory on the 29th. As the St. Louis Cardinals struggled to stay in the run for the pennant, so did the Astros, and they desperately needed to win all of their games in order to assure Houston a place in the 2006 postseason. The September 29 game against the Atlanta Braves at Turner Field was a pivotal junction in that fight, and the Astros brought out their Rocket to make it happen. The Rocket's last home pitching day was supposed to have been the September 24 game against St. Louis, and, previous to that game, his last day was supposed to have been the 20th. Despite a strong showing of the Rocket's red glare, the Astros lost the game to the Braves 4 runs to 1. Roger, also in a reflective mood, spoke of the setback for the Astros. "That's just how things go. When all those circumstances start happening, you really have to buckle down. That inning could have gotten really ugly. But [seeing] Lance's reaction, and I'm always geared up when I think I get the guy . . . I was pumped up and then didn't get the call. That's just the way it is. You just buckle down from there."[18]

> *The next week's games were nothing short of an abbreviated miracle.*

Garner also reflected on the year and the Rocket when he spoke to the press about the game: "It was a stinker. The Rocket did a super job. We needed to score some runs and we didn't get that done tonight. This has slowed us down a bit, but we've been playing mighty good and we still have some momentum. We have to take that to heart tonight."[19]

For the season, Clemens had only 7 wins to match up to his 6 losses. It was the lowest number of wins for the Rocket in all his years in the major leagues. The next day, the Astros defeated the Braves 5 runs to 4 with the pitching finesse of Andy Pettitte. The Astros needed a win to stay alive for at least the wild card regardless of how the Cardinals did in their last games. On October 1, things came crashing down for the Astros and their season with a loss to the Braves, 3 to 1, and with St. Louis losing their game against the Milwaukee Brewers 5 to 3. The loss nailed shut the entire season for Clemens and the Astros. Back in Houston, after a brief period of fan disappointment, the city simply turned its attention to the fresh season of the NFL and the Houston Texans, and began to look forward to the new season of the NBA Rockets. Soon after the Astros' loss, another team in the city was able to make it to their postseason. The Houston Dynamos fought their way up in the ranks of the relatively new sports attraction for the city, major-league soccer, and had the media spotlight's glare focused on their efforts at winning the championships.

The 162-game season showed that there was life left in a team that had sometimes been abandoned by the media but not by the fans. It showed that when backed up against a wall, a team can go far to accomplish its goals. Unfortunately the goal was just a win or two too far away for the Astros to make it that year. The previous few years were miraculous for the Astros, especially with Clemens and

Pettitte aboard. Each year the Astros seemed to die in midseason, only to come back to life and take it to the postseason and, in the case of 2005, all the way to the World Series for the first and only time. In 2006, their 82 wins and 80 losses resulted in a better than average .506 win-to-loss ratio. They did slightly better at home, winning 44 and losing 37, than their road games, where they were a dismal 38 to 43.

The Astros, like baseball, symbolized the best in us all. As Craig Biggio told me, just as many ball players have said, "Baseball is a game of failure." And it is. In order to succeed, you have to win over and above your failures.

Immediately after the season's end, when the players returned to Minute Maid Park to clean out their lockers and to prepare to leave for their homes scattered across the country, the media again began to ask the Rocket what to expect from him for next season. From day one, back in 2004, he wanted everyone to understand that he indeed was retired and had only returned to play on an as needed basis.

On the Astros' last day, almost as if to strike a dagger into an already injured animal, the press began to hound both Clemens and Pettitte about a report that they had taken steroids. This time it was based on a story from the *Los Angeles Times* that carried allegations from former major-leaguer Jason Grimsley, who was their teammate when they played for the New York Yankees. First reports squarely took potshots at the two greats. Immediately, something about the scandal seemed suspect, especially to the fans. Clemens had repeatedly been tested, and it seemed as if once again he was becoming a lightning rod for media scandal. To the fans, it seemed as if Pettitte was being treated as some sort of scapegoat or sacrificial lamb in the downfall of another major-leaguer. Within a few days, the *Los Angeles Times* did an abrupt about-face and said that it was an error to have printed the story that included steroid allegations against the two Astros greats. Jason Grimsley cleared the air about the situation and made a statement through his attorney saying that Clemens and Pettitte "would never in a million years" take illegal performance-enhancing drugs.[20] Regardless of Grimsley's retraction, the story caused much consternation and grief for the Rocket, Pettitte, and their fans. What seemed to be the salve for them was their spotless reputation in baseball and in the community and all of the support they received during the difficulties in dealing with the issue.

The postseason contained an interesting mix of teams that were bent on getting to the fall classic. The National League Division Series was played out between the St. Louis Cardinals and the San Diego Padres. The Padres could never really surface above the Cardinals, and the Cardinals won the 2006 National League Division 3 games to 1. The wild-card Los Angeles Dodgers couldn't seem to get past the New York Mets in their division series, losing 3 to 0. The Mets would take on the Cardinals in the 2006 NLCS.

The American League Division Series had the wild-card and unfavored Detroit Tigers taking on the New York Yankees. The Tigers pulled off a series of upsets, knocking off the mighty Yankees 3 games to 1. The Oakland Athletics took on the Minnesota Twins, making short work of them and wasting no time in sending the Twins back home, 3 games to 0. The Athletics had made it to the ALDS to take on the Detroit Tigers.

Tragedy struck baseball once again on Wednesday, October 11, 2006, after the Yankees' lost the division series to Detroit. Yankees team members cleaned out their lockers and packed up for home. Cory Lidle, who had been with the team since August of that season, made plans to fly his plane home to California but first decided to take his flight instructor on a sight-seeing tour of Manhattan. They had just circled the Statue of Liberty and were headed toward the skyline when the plane suddenly veered and crashed into the middle of a 52-story apartment building. The crash instantly killed the Yankees' pitcher and his instructor. The part of the building that was struck immediately burst into flames, and parts of the wreckage and building fell to the street. Miraculously only a few on the ground were injured, mostly 14 firefighters and police who rushed in to aid the residents. Immediately there were rumors of terrorism before the background of the crash became known. Area buildings were evacuated, including the entire building that was struck. NORAD sent fighter jets into the skies above New York and all major cities in the United States. After the flight pattern was traced, authorities determined the plane to be Lidle's and that he, in fact, was on board the plane. It wasn't known immediately if the 34-year-old was piloting the craft.

Mayor Michael Bloomberg of New York City praised the work of rescue workers and the swift actions of the police, firefighters, and emergency workers on the scene, stating, "Everything we planned to handle an emergency like this was carried out to the book exactly the way we had wanted."[21] Yankees General Manager Brian Cashman was choked with tears at a press conference, where he said, "It's a sad day, we're very saddened by this news today. It's a shock and . . . there's not much to say."[22]

That evening's ALCS game of the Oakland Athletics and Detroit Tigers carried a tribute to Lidle with a moment of silence. Since the late pitcher had been on seven teams in his short nine-year career, he had become friends with many players on the teams that were now competing for the title. It was a somber moment reminiscent of the death of Thurmon Munson, back on August 2, 1979. He was another New York Yankees team member who had died in a plane crash, leaving major-league baseball and the nation in shock.

The Tigers would eventually overtake the Athletics in a four-game sweep and become the 2006 American League Champions. In the National League, the Cardinals and the New York Mets provided the most excitement in their play-off series. It took all seven games, including two rainouts, for the Cardinals to defeat the Mets 4 games to 3 to become the 2006 National League Champions. Game 7 was the most pivotal and the most emotional of all of the postseason games. The box was tied for most of the game until the end of the ninth inning, when Yadier Molina popped a two-run homer for St. Louis, clinching the title for his team. The celebration in the clubhouse afterward

They devoured every opportunity they had come up against and made it to the top.

was the crescendo of the entire major-league season. Even a usually introspective Jim Edmonds was overcome with emotion. The Cardinals had been an underdog in their chances at a postseason. Their record for the year was not spectacular, even when compared to previous years. But everyone missed one thing about the Cards: they were hungry. They were hungry for the postseason and the pennant. They devoured every opportunity they had come up against and made it to the top.

The Cardinals took on the Tigers in the World Series. As a result of the numerous delays in several games in the

National League playoffs, the Tigers were able to catch up on some much-needed rest, and practice, for their first appearance at the Series in over two decades. The two teams had not faced each other in a World Series since 1968, when the Tigers won over the Cardinals 4 games to 3. In the 2006 World Series, the Tigers ended up as the underdog again, losing the fall classic to the Cardinals 4 games to 1. It was the first time in years that the National League won a World Series. Jimmy Edmonds was overheard telling everyone, "We shocked the World!" referring to the fact that they were so far behind, yet were able to advance to the top in the end.

In November 2006, the Cy Young Award went to Brandon Webb of the Arizona Diamondbacks for the National League, and Johan Santanta of the Minnesota Twins won his second for the American League.

This season would be remembered by the Astros and their fans as the season that was "almost." In the past few seasons they had performed in mediocre fashion up to and during the middle of the season, yet they had managed to pull a fast one and make it at least into the postseason and, as in the case of the 2005 season, to their first World Series ever. The 2006 season was almost a repeat performance of their 2005 triumph, but the miracle that was, almost, is a miracle that will hopefully be waiting for them in future seasons.

As the 2007 season began, it did so with a few changes to the roster. Andy Pettitte had signed with the New York Yankees in December 2006, the team he had left back in 2003 to come to the Astros. Some feared this as a hint as to what the Rocket intended to do, still unsigned as of the beginning of the season. Woody Williams, a native of the Houston area, had always dreamed of being an Astro. In November 2006 he signed a two-year deal as a starting pitcher for the team. He told the press something that he had said many times, "I've been an Astros fan ever since I can remember, and even though I played on different teams, that didn't change."[23] Craig Biggio put off retirement and expressed high hopes for the 2007 season, where he hoped to attain the 3,000-hit level, and did so. Biggio is looked upon as an anchor for the team, upon whom the fans cling to in good seasons and bad. Also for 2007, outside of the Astros, Japan's Daisuke Matsuzaka was taking major-league baseball by storm. Signed as a rookie pitcher for the Boston Red Sox, the media began to follow him much as they had followed Roger Clemens almost a quarter-century previously, covering not only his professional qualifications but also his childhood and family matters. Tom Glavine began to zero in on 300 wins, possibly one of the last of the great pitchers to attain this milestone.

On April 29, 2007, sadness again enveloped baseball. Josh Hancock, a pitcher for the St. Louis Cardinals, died when he accidentally drove his SUV into the back of a parked tow truck. All of baseball mourned in a show of unity.

The 2007 season for the Astros saw young talent make its way up the rotation to fulfill the goals of the team in the absence of Clemens. In a way, it's like one big circle of life. As the Rocket once told *Houston Intown Magazine*, "Being able to close out my career in my hometown is a real blessing. But I couldn't have done it without my team."[24] With or without the Rocket, one thing is for certain. Whatever happens to the Astros in the future, there will never be another season exactly like the ones with Roger Clemens.

His choice to move back to the New York Yankees brought joy to Yankees fans during the seventh inning stretch of the May 6, 2007, game, during which the Yankees defeated Roger's old-time nemesis, the Seattle Mariners, 5 to 0.

Clemens appeared at the microphone stating, "Well, they came and got me out of Texas, and I can tell you it's a privilege to be back. I'll be talking to y'all soon!"[25] The Yankees players in the dugout went wild, as did the fans. To fans watching on television in Houston, there was a stunned sense of loss, but one for which they had been prepared. Many asked why the Yankees didn't learn the first time, alluding to the Yankees' 2003 loss of Clemens to retirement and then the Astros. But by 2007 most realized that baseball was a two-way street for these free agents and a busy one at that.

Mel Stottlemyre recalled in *Pride and Pinstripes* that when Clemens first arrived as a Yankee back in the late 1990s some of the team members were upset about the situation. Clemens had a reputation of hitting them with his pitches while at bat. There were other misgivings, but ones that were quickly put aside once Roger started on their mound. Derek Jeter reportedly put on a full catcher's cage when he first went up to bat opposite Clemens during that first Yankees batting practice. Jeter did it as a fun-loving chide to Clemens, and it helped to bond the team in those early days.

Clemens started up his 2007 season in the Yankees minor leagues, going through rehabilitation assignments in order to fine tune his mid-40s body for a new team. Later in the summer, he moved up to the Yankees mound, again to the sounds of many a returning fan.

Somewhere in all the media attention about Barry Bonds and his home run number 755, the Rocket was focused on attaining his 350th career win, which he grabbed in early July 2007. The ovations of the fans were more like the ones geared for a well-seasoned veteran, such as a DiMaggio, or a Ruth, or a Ryan. Now Clemens takes his place in history.

And Cooperstown must wait still yet another year.

NOTES

Chapter 1

1. Alex Griffin, "It Takes Teamwork to Win On and Off the Field," *Houston Intown Magazine*, May 2005, 25.

2. José Canseco, *Juiced* (New York: Regan Books, 2005), 91.

3. Beverly Denver, "Creating a Balanced Life," *Houston Woman Magazine*, July 2006, 8.

4. Ben Widdicombe and Suzanne Rozdeba, "Catching up on Charity," *New York Daily News*, August 20, 2003, http://www.nydailynews.com/news/gossip/story/110468p-99811c.html.

5. Denver, "Creating a Balanced Life," 7.

6. Eric Schmitt, "Clemens Wows the Gulf Troops (and Vice Versa)," *New York Times*, December 22, 2002, http://www.rogerclemensonline.com/nytimes.htm.

7. Ibid.

8. Ibid.

9. Denver, "Creating a Balanced Life," 8.

10. Memorial Hermann, "Roger Clemens Partners With Memorial Hermann to Advance Sports Medicine & Human Performance Program," news release, June 20, 2006, http://www.memorialhermann.org/newsroom/062006.htm.

11. Alyson Footer, "Notes: Biggio Hosts Party for Kids— Thursday Marks 14th Annual Sunshine Kids Party," August 11, 2005, http://houston.astros.mlb.com/NASApp/mlb/news/article.jsp?ymd20050811&content_id=1166903&vkey=news_hou&fext=.jsp&c_id=hou.

12. U.S. Department of Commerce, "Highlights From Remarks of Commerce Secretary Don Evans: Houston World Affairs Council," news release, April 2, 2003, http://www.commerce.gov/opa/press/Secretary_Evans/2003_Releases/April/02_houston_highlights.htm.

13. Habitat for Humanity, "Habitat for Humanity Fact Sheet," http://www.habitat.org/how/factsheet.aspx.

14. Denver, "Creating a Balanced Life," 8.

15. Ibid.

Chapter 2

1. Major League Baseball, news release, November 1, 2003.

2. In addition to early media coverage during his beginning major-league baseball years concerning his upbringing and childhood, much is also covered in Roger Clemens and Peter Gammons, *Rocket Man: The Roger Clemens Story* (New York: Penguin Books, 1988).

3. Statement made to author at Milo Hamilton's book

signing, Houston, Texas, June 17, 2006.

4. Roger Clemens, address to a Woodlands, Texas, youth rally, Cynthia Woods Pavilion, May 9, 2006.

5. Tom Verducci, "Rocket Science," SI.com, September 10, 2001, http://sportsillusrtated.cnn.com/flash-back/clemens_science/.

6. "Clemens Wins One for His Late Mother," *USA Today*, September 14, 2005, http://www.usatoday.com/sports/baseball/games/2005-09-14-marlins-astros_x.htm?csp=36. Also, www.chron.com/archives; John P. Lopez, "Son Applies Mom's Life Lessons . . .," *Houston Chronicle*, September, 15, 2005.

7. Maureen Backman, "Clemens Sends Off Troops," www.nyyfans.com, March 19, 2003, http://www.nyyfans.com/article/7777/.

8. The H. W. Wilson Company, biography of Roger Clemens, *Current Biography*, August 2003, http://www.hwwilson.com/currentbio/cover_bios/cover_bio_8_03.htm.

9. David Barren, "Houston Sports Heroes," *Houston Chronicle*, June 4, 2006, http://www.chron.com/cda/archives/archive.mp1?id=2006_4128705.

9. H. W. Wilson, biography of Roger Clemens.

Chapter 3

1. Tom Nugent, "Rocket Fuel: What Makes Roger Clemens Run?" *The Alcalde*, September–October 2003, http://utopia.utexas.edu/articles/alcalde/clemens.html?sec=texas&sub=Texans.

2. Nolan Ryan Foundation, telephone conversation with the author, February 19, 2007.

3. Widely attributed to Tom Seaver.

4. Nugent, "Rocket Fuel."

5. Ibid.

6. Jon Robinson, "Roger Clemens Interview," Sports.IGN.com, January 26, 2006, http://sports.ign.com/articles/683/68374p1.html.

7. Eileen McClelland, "Sporting a New Pastime: Denim and (Baseball) Diamond," *Houston Chronicle*, January 23, 2005, http://www.debbieclemens.com/news/chron12305.htm.

8. Ibid.

9. Ibid.

10. Allen Iverson, 2002 NBA playoffs press conference, May 8, 2002.

11. Players' comments are from personal interviews conducted by the author from 2004 through 2006: Carlos Beltran, Houston, Texas, August 4, 2004; Kyle Farnsworth, Houston, Texas, August 21, 2004; Steve Finley, Houston, Texas, July 28, 2004; Tom Glavine, e-mail interview, August 26, 2004; Khalil Greene, Houston, Texas, July 18, 2004, and August 11, 2006; Barry Larkin, Houston, Texas, September 8, 2004; Greg Maddux, Houston, Texas, July 19, 2006; Phil Nevin, Houston, Texas, July 19, 2006; Andy Pettitte, Houston, Texas, August 4, 2004; and John Smoltz, Houston, Texas, August 4, 2004.

12. Henry Schulman, "Astros Truly Were Better Than Record," *San Francisco Chronicle*, October 21, 2005, http://sfgate.com/cgi-bin/article.cgi?file=/c/a/2005/10/21/spg25fc1vu1.dtl.

Chapter 4

1. Josh Lewin, *You Never Forget Your First . . .*

(Washington, DC: Potomac Books, Inc., 2005), 58.

2. Milo Hamilton, *Making Airwaves: 60 Years at Milo's Microphone* (Champaign, IL: Sports Publishing, 2006), 1.

3. Ibid., 146.

4. Official Site of the Boston Red Sox, "Fenway Facts," http://boston.redsox.mlb.com/bos/ballpark/facts.jsp.

5. Answers.com, "Ralph Houk," http://www.answers.com/topic/ralph-houk.

6. http://www.dummyhoy.com/destination_cooperstown/index.html.

7. McClelland, "Sporting a New Pastime."

8. Domestic problems occur with no more frequency in baseball players' families than in the rest of society.

9. Major League Baseball, Roger Clemens retirement speech, 2003, news release, www.mlb.com, November 1, 2003, Mark Feinsand, reporter.

Chapter 5

1. National Baseball Hall of Fame, Tom Seaver record, http://www.baseballhalloffame.org/hofers_and_honorees/hofer_bios/Seaver_Tom.htm.

2. National Baseball Hall of Fame, Cy Young record, http://www.baseballhalloffame.org/hofers%5Fand%5Fhonorees/hofer%5Fbios/young%5Fcy.htm.

Chapter 6

1. The use of some methodology in naming children is not unusual. Another Houston area sports celebrity, George Foreman, named all five of his sons with the same name—George.

2. *ABC News*, October 17, 1989.

Chapter 7

1. Alan Truex, "On Limited Rest . . . ," *Houston Chronicle*, October 10, 1990, www.chron.com/cda/archives/archive.mpl?id=1990_735328 / 735325 / and 735321.
2. Commonly attributed to Joe Morgan.
3. Joel Auerbach, "US Presswire," www.usatoday.com/sports/baseball/nl/cubs/2006-06-27-maddux-forgotten-star_x.htm.
4. The Internet Movie Database, www.imdb.com.

Chapter 8

1. Author interview with Brian Giles, Minute Maid Park, Houston, Texas, July 18, 2004, and August 11, 2006.
2. Press conference, Baylor University Medical Center, Dallas, Texas, June 8, 1995.

Chapter 9

1. Mike Maddux is now a pitching coach with the Milwaukee Brewers. Interview with author, September 18, 2004.
2. Michael Silverman, "End of an Era . . . Brass Tried to Keep Ace," *Boston Herald*, December 14, 1996.
3. Associated Press, "Clemens Wins a Record Fifth Cy Young Award," and Joseph Duarte, "And One for Dad: Clemens Expected to Capture Fifth Cy Young Award," *Houston Chronicle*, November 16, 1998.
4. Buster Olney, *New York Times*, February 27, 1999.
5. Gerry Callahan with David Sabino, "Booster Rocket: The Already Formidable Yankees May Have Locked in Another World Series Berth by Landing Roger Clemens," *Sports Illustrated*, March 1, 1999,

http://sportsillustrated.cnn.com/flashback/
clemens_booster/.

6. Ibid.

7. The crypt next to Monroe's is now owned by
publisher Hugh Hefner.

8. Joe Torre, *Chasing the Dream: My Lifelong Journey to the World Series—An Autobiography* (New
York: Bantam, 1998).

9. Tony DeMarco, "Smoltz-Clemens a Classic Playoff
Matchup: Two Potential Hall of Famers Also Met in
1999 World Series," October 6, 2005, http://
www.msnbc.msn.com/id/9603547.

10. Baseball Almanac, "2000 All-Star Game," http://
www.baseball-almanac.com/asgbox/
yr2000as.shtml.

11. Murray Chass, "Baseball: Subway Series—Yankees'
Clemens Is Fined $50,000," *New York Times*, Octo-
ber 25, 2000, http://select.nytimes.com/gst/
abstract.html?res=F50916F839550C768EDDA90994
D8404482&n=Top%2fReference%2fTimes%20
Topics%2fPeople%2fP%2fPiazza%2c%20Mike.

Chapter 10

1. Rick Weinberg, "98: Jack Buck's Tribute to America,"
ESPN Counts Down the Most Memorable Moments
of the Last 25 Years, 2001, http://
sports.espn.go.com/espn/espn25/
story?page=moments/98.

2. Julio Franco, interview with the author, Minute
Maid Park, Houston, Texas, August 4, 2004.

3. Associated Press, "Strike Averted: Negotiators Avoid
Work Stoppage with Last-Minute Deal," August 30,
2002, http://sportsillustrated.cnn.com/baseball/

news/2002/08/30/labor_friday/.

4. "Abrupt and Disappointing Ending to All-Star Game," *Stanford Daily*, July 11, 2002, http:// daily.stanford.edu/article/2002/7/11/ abruptanddisappointingendingtoallstargame and Associated Press, "Selig Vows Changes to All-Star Game," July 10, 2002, http:// sportsillustrated.cnn.com/baseball/2002/allstar/ news/2002/07/10/selig_react_ap/.

5. "300 & 4,000? Roger That! The Rocket Collects 300th Win and 4,000th Strikeout," MLB.com's Baseball's Best, June 13, 2003, http://mlb.mlb.com/ NASApp/mlb/mlb/baseballs_best/ mlb_bb_gamepage.jsp?story _page=bb_03reg_061303_slnnya.

6. Ibid.

7. Mark Feinsand, "300 wins, 4,000 Ks? Roger That! Clemens Picks Up Two Milestones," MLB.com, June 13, 2003, http://mlb.mlb.com/NASApp/mlb/nyy/ news/ nyy_gameday_recap.jsp?ymd=20030613&content_id= 373510&vkey=recap&fext=.jsp&c_id=nya.

8. Ibid.

9. Ibid.

10. Barry M. Bloom, "Final Liftoff for the Rocket: After Rough First, Clemens Finishes Strong in Last Start," MLB.com, October 23, 2003, http://mlb.mlb.com/ NASApp/mlb/nyy/news/nyy_news.jsp?ymd=200310 23&content_id=590669&vkey=news_nyy&fext= .jsp&c_id=nya.

11. Doug Miller, "Yankees Put Loss in Perspective: Somber Players Credit Marlins, Look ahead to Future," MLB.com, October 26, 2003, http://

mlb.mlb.com/NASApp/mlb/nyy/news/
nyy_news.jsp?ymd=20031026&content_id=594063&vkey=
news_nyy&fext=.jsp&c_id=nya.

12. Ibid.
13. Bloom, "Final Liftoff."
14. Major League Baseball, www.mlb.com, November 1, 2003, news release, Mark Feinsand.

Chapter 11

1. Postgame press conference, MLB, Minute Maid Park, Houston, Texas, July 14, 2004.
2. Major League Baseball Houston Astros, news release.
3. There have been many baseball families in the leagues.
4. Stephen Hawkins, "Clemens Takes Mound After Mom, 75, Dies," *Daily Texan*, September 15, 2005.
5. Globe Staff, "Obituaries: Bess Clemens, 75, Mother of All-Star Pitcher," *Boston Globe*, September 15, 2005, http://www.boston.com/news/globe/obituaries/articles/2005/09/15/bess_clemens_75_mother_of_all_star_pitcher/.
6. Mike Bauman, "Only Fitting to Have Rocket Start Game 1: Baseball's Biggest Stage the Right Place for Future Hall of Famer," MLB.com, October 21, 2005, http://mlb.mlb.com/NASApp/mlb/news/article_perspectives.jsp?ymd=20051021&content_id=1256619&vkey=perspectives&fext=.jsp.
7. Tom Verducci, "Not *My* Fault: After Blowing Game 3, Garner Jumps Ship on Astros," SI.com, October 26, 2005, http://sportsillustrated.cnn.com/2005/writers/tom_verducci/10/26/astros.game3/index.html.

8. Jim Street, "Clemens 'Thankful' for Classic Chance: Veteran's Future Plans Not Known after USA's Exit," MLB.com, March 17, 2006, http://ww2.worldbaseballclassic.com/2006/news/article.jsp?ymd=20060317&content_id=1353139&vkey=wbc_news&fext=.jsp&sid=wbc.

9. World Baseball Classic MLB press conference, MLB Headquarters, July 17, 2005.

10. Ibid.

11. Ibid.

12. Jim Molony, "Clemens Lays Strong Foundation for '06: Rocket Finds Areas to Improve on After First Outing," MLB.com, June 23, 2006, http://houston.astros.mlb.com/NASApp/mlb/news/article_perspectives.jsp?ymd=20060623&content_id=1519112&vkey=perspectives&fext=.jsp.

13. Kevin Yanik, "Clemens Picks up First Win: Berkman Homers From Both Sides of the Plate," MLB.com, July 4, 2006, http://www.mlb.com/NASApp/mlb/news/gameday_recap.jsp?ymd=20060703&content_id=1537633&vkey=recap&fext=.jsp&c_id=hou.

14. Kevin Yanik, "Clemens Right at Home in Win: Rocket Tosses Six Shutout Innings in Final Houston Start," MLB.com, September 20, 2006, http://houston.astros.mlb.com/NASApp/mlb/news/gameday_recap.jsp?ymd=20060920&content_id=1672806&vkey=recap&fext=.jsp&c_id=hou.

15. Ibid.

16. Brian McTaggart, "Burke to Have Surgery," *Houston Chronicle*, September 24, 2006, 7.

17. Kevin Yanik, "Astros Finish Sweep of Sliding Cards:

Win Trims Division Deficit to 3 1/2 Games With Seven Remaining," MLB.com, September 25, 2006, http://houston.astros.mlb.com/NASApp/mlb/news/gameday_recap.jsp?ymd=20060924&content_id=1681164&vkey=recap&fext=.jsp&c_id=hou.

18. Alyson Footer, "Clemens Strong, But Astros Fall," MLB.com, September 29, 2006, http://houston.astros.mlb.com/NASApp/mlb/news/gameday_recap.jsp?ymd=20060929&content_id=1689720&vkey=recap&fext=.jsp&c_id=hou.

19. Ibid.

20. "Prosecutor, Grimsley's Attorney: Report Inaccurate," ESPN.com, October 3, 2006, http://sports.espn.go.com/mlb/news/story?id=2610878.

21. Mayoral press conference, City Hall, New York City, October 11, 2006.

22. MLB press conference, Yankee Stadium, New York City, October 11, 2006.

23. José de Jesús Ortiz, "No Place Like Home," *Houston Chronicle*, February 18, 2007.

24. Alex Griffin, "It Takes Teamwork to Win on and off the Field," 26.

25. Clemens addresses crowds at Yankee Stadium, May 6, 2007, author in attendance. See also, Tyler Kepner, "Clemens Returns, and So Does Hope for Yankees," New York Times, May 7, 2007, http://www.nytimes.com//2007/05/07/sports/baseball/07clemens.html.

SOURCES

Twenty-five years have gone by in the career of Roger Clemens, and even the sharpest of memories fade. Various reference sources were needed to double-check, remind, or to verify the facts. These facts are of scores, dates, events, place names, historical figures, names of players and officials, positions, rosters, schedules, records, awards, and so on. The following sources were consulted:

Newspapers:
The Houston Chronicle, 1962–2006, microfilm and archives
The Houston Post, 1962–95, microfilm

Internet:
http://www.answers.com
http://www.baseball-almanac.com
http://www.baseballlibrary.com
http://www.baseballreference.com
http://www.carlton32.com
http://www.debbieclemens.com

http://www.memorialhermann.org
http://www.nolanryanfoundation.org
http://www.retrosheet.org
http://www.rogerclemensonline.com
http://tomterrificseaver.com
http://www.wikipedia.org

Major League Baseball websites:

http://arizona.diamondbacks.mlb.com
http://atlanta.braves.mlb.com
http://baltimore.orioles.mlb.com
http://boston.redsox.mlb.com
http://chicago.whitesox.mlb.com
http://cincinnati.reds.mlb.com
http://cleveland.indians.mlb.com
http://colorado.rockies.mlb.com
http://detroit.tigers.mlb.com
http://florida.marlins.mlb.com
http://houston.astros.mlb.com
http://losangeles.angels.mlb.com
http://losangeles.dodgers.mlb.com
http://milwaukee.brewers.mlb.com
http://minnesota.twins.mlb.com
http://mlb.mlb.com
http://newyork.mets.mlb.com
http://newyork.yankees.mlb.com
http://oakland.athletics.mlb.com
http://philadelphia.phillies.mlb.com
http://pittsburgh.pirates.mlb.com
http://sandiego.padres.mlb.com
http://sanfrancisco.giants.mlb.com
http://seattle.mariners.mlb.com
http://stlouis.cardinals.mlb.com

http://tampabay.devilrays.mlb.com
http://texas.rangers.mlb.com
http://toronto.bluejays.mlb.com
http://washington.nationals.mlb.com

Other, Miscellaneous:
http://www.gonzaga.edu
http://www.rice.edu
http://www.sanjac.edu
http://www.shsu.edu
http://www.texasexes.org
http://www.utexas.edu
http://www.hwwilson.com
MLB Astros Media Relations Game Day information
    handouts

Selected Bibliography:

Clemens, Roger, and Peter Gammons. *Rocket Man: The Roger Clemens Story*. New York: Penguin, 1987.

Hamilton, Milo, and Dan Schlossberg and Bob Ibach. *Making Airwaves: 60+ Years at Milo's Microphone*. New York: Sports Publishing, 2006.

Ortiz, José de Jesús. *Houston Astros: Armed and Dangerous*. New York: Sports Publishing, 2006.

Stottlemyre, Mel, and John Harper. *Pride and Pinstripes: The Yankees, Mets, and Surviving Life's Challenges*. New York: Harper Entertainment, 2007.

Torre, Joe. *Chasing the Dream: My Lifelong Journey to the World Series*. New York: Bantam, 1998.

INDEX

ABOUT THE AUTHOR

Joseph C. Janczak has been writing about sports and entertainment since the 1990s. While at the general accounting office of Harris County, Texas, he was responsible for accounting and allocating the revenues from the Harris County Sports Authority. It was here that he was able to establish contacts in the sports and entertainment areas. Starting with the Houston Livestock Show and Rodeo he established a bond with entertainers and their management and conducted personal one-on-one interviews with such stars as Brad Paisley, the Judds, Kenny Chesney, Charley Pride, Rascal Flatts, and more. In the 2004–06 Major League Baseball seasons he was able to secure the confidence of the Houston Astros and MLB management to interview a number of baseball players for this book and other projects.

Janczak was born and grew up in Houston and has watched Clemens, who also lived in Houston, rise to the top in baseball. He now lives in Spring, Texas.